Guys and Guns Amok

Domestic Terrorism and School Shootings from the Oklahoma City Bombing to the Virginia Tech Massacre

Douglas Kellner

Paradigm Publishers

Boulder • London

green press
INITIATIVE

Paradigm Publishers is committed to preserving ancient forests and natural resources. We elected to print *Guys And Guns Amok* on 50% post consumer recycled paper, processed chlorine free. As a result, for this printing, we have saved:

8 Trees (40' tall and 6-8" diameter)
3,555 Gallons of Wastewater
1,430 Kilowatt Hours of Electricity
392 Pounds of Solid Waste
770 Pounds of Greenhouse Gases

Paradigm Publishers made this paper choice because our printer, Thomson-Shore, Inc., is a member of Green Press Initiative, a nonprofit program dedicated to supporting authors, publishers, and suppliers in their efforts to reduce their use of fiber obtained from endangered forests.

For more information, visit www.greenpressinitiative.org

Copyright © 2008 Paradigm Publishers

Published in the United States by Paradigm Publishers, 3360 Mitchell Lane Suite E, Boulder, CO 80301 USA.

Paradigm Publishers is the trade name of Birkenkamp & Company, LLC, Dean Birkenkamp, President and Publisher.

Library of Congress Cataloging-in-Publication Data

Kellner, Douglas, 1943–
    Guys and guns amok : domestic terrorism and school shootings from the Oklahoma City bombing to the Virginia Tech massacre / Douglas Kellner.
        p. cm. — (The radical imagination series)
    Includes bibliographical references and index.
    ISBN 978-1-59451-492-0 (hardcover) — ISBN 978-1-59451-493-7 (pbk.)
    1. Violence—United States.   2. Youth and violence.   3. Violence in men—United States.
4. School shootings—United States.   5. Domestic terrorism—United States.   6. Gun control—United States.   I. Title.
    HN90.V5K45 2008
    305.38'96920973—dc22

                                                                                2007045369

Printed and bound in the United States of America on acid-free paper that meets the standards of the American National Standard for Permanence of Paper for Printed Library Materials.

Designed and Typeset by Straight Creek Bookmakers.

11 10 09 08 07   1 2 3 4 5

Contents

Acknowledgments   *vii*

Introduction: Media Spectacle and the "Virginia Tech Massacre"   **1**
    The Time of the Spectacle   3
    Guy Debord's "Society of the Spectacle"
       and Its Limitations   7
    Reading the Spectacle with Critical Social Theory and
       Cultural Studies   9
    Societal Violence and Guys and Guns Amok   14
    The Epidemic of School Shootings   19
    Media Culture, Militarism, and Violent Masculinity   26
    In This Book   28

Chapter 1   Deconstructing the Spectacle:
        Race, Guns, and the Culture Wars   **33**
    The Shootings and the Politics of Race   33
    A Convocation and Cho's Multimedia Dossier   38
    Guns and Political Scapegoating   43
    School and Workplace Security:
       The Debate Begins   50
    Mourning, Copycats, and Ideological Manipulation   53

Chapter 2   The Situation of Contemporary Youth   **61**
    From Boomers to Busters   63
    Post-Boomers and Contemporary Youth   69
    Youth Alienation, Violence, and the War against Youth   74
    The Struggle against the War on Youth   76
    Perils of Youth   83

**Chapter 3   Constructing Male Identities and the Spectacle
of Terror**   **89**

White Male Identity Politics   90

Militia, Right-Wing Extremism,
and Terrorist Bombings   95

Home-Grown Terrorism: Timothy McVeigh
and the Oklahoma City Bombing   100

Harvest of Rage   107

The Unabomber and the Politics of Terror   113

Middle-Class White Male Columbine
High School Shootings   118

The Columbine Media Spectacle and Its Exploitation   119

Shooting at Columbine with Michael Moore:
Guns, U.S. History, and Violence in America   126

Seung-Hui Cho in the Borderlands between
the Korean and the American   131

Chapter 4   What Is to Be Done?   **139**

Aftermath   142

Gun Laws, School and Workplace Safety,
and Mental Health Care: The Delicate Balance   146

Beyond the Culture of Male Violence and Rage   154

New Literacies, Democratization,
and the Reconstruction of Education   159

Politics, Prisons, and the Abolition
Democracy Project   164

Horrors of the Prison-Industrial-Military Complex   165

The Time of Abolitions   167

Notes   *172*

References   *201*

Index   *208*

Acknowledgments

I want to thank Paradigm Publishers, especially Jennifer Knerr, for encouraging me to pursue the project, for providing a wealth of useful suggestions for revision, and for working to get it through an accelerated production schedule. Melanie Stafford and Dianne Ewing once again helped me get through the rigors of the copyediting and production process. I also want to thank series editors Henry Giroux and Stanley Aronowitz for supporting the project and Henry for providing help with the research. In addition, for useful comments on earlier drafts and ideas and research material, I would like to thank Christine Kelly, Heather Collette-VanDeraa, Richard Kahn, Rhonda Hammer, Ben Frymer, and Jackson Katz, who helped me navigate literature on violence and masculinity. Finally, I would especially like to thank my longtime friend Carl Boggs for making many useful comments on the final draft, discussing the project in detail, and having done much important work upon which I drew in writing the book.

Douglas Kellner
Los Angeles

Introduction

Media Spectacle and the "Virginia Tech Massacre"

THE MAINSTREAM CORPORATE MEDIA today process events, news, and information in the form of media spectacle. In an arena of intense competition with 24/7 cable TV networks, talk radio, Internet sites and blogs, and emergent digital media and cultural forms such as Facebook, MySpace, and YouTube, the corporate media are driven to construct tabloid spectacles in an attempt to attract maximum audiences for as much time as possible.

The 1990s saw the emergence and proliferation of cable news networks, talk radio, and the Internet. Major media spectacles of the era included the O. J. Simpson murder trial, the Clinton sex scandals and threatened impeachment, and the life and death of Princess Diana. The era also saw an intensification of celebrity news and scandals (see Kellner 2003a), which continue and intensify to the present day with Britney Spears, Tom Cruise, Paris Hilton, Lindsay Lohan, and other "hot" celebrities under 24-hour surveillance for scandals or tabloid entertainment stories.

The new millennium opened with the contested presidential election between Al Gore and George W. Bush and a 36-day battle for the White House that culminated in a five-to-four Supreme Court decision for Bush that blocked the counting of votes in Florida and generated one of the most momentous political crimes in history, events that I describe in my book *Grand Theft 2000* (Kellner 2001). This spectacle was soon followed by the 9/11 terror attacks on New York and Washington, the deadliest attack on U.S. soil in its history, and perhaps the most extensive global media spectacle ever, inaugurating an era of "Terror War" (Kellner 2003b).[1]

Following the model of his father's 1991 war with Iraq, the second Bush's Iraq war was also orchestrated as a media spectacle, although after declaring victory in May 2003, events flipped out of control and the spectacle in Iraq has often been a negative and highly contested one, leading to a collapse of Bush's approval ratings and the unraveling of his administration (Kellner 2005).

The Bush-Cheney years have been a series of spectacles from 9/11 and Iraq to the abject failure of the Bush administration during Hurricane Katrina.[2] Scandals involving criminal trials of high officials like Dick Cheney's chief of staff, I. Lewis "Scooter" Libby, major Republican congressmembers now in jail like Randy "Duke" Cunningham and Bob Ney, felony charges against Republican House Majority Leader Tom DeLay that forced him to leave politics, and financial scandals involving lobbyist and Republican fund-raiser Jack Abramoff, as well as sex scandals ranging from Mark Foley's shameful episode with White House pages to Larry Craig's bust for soliciting sex in an airport men's room. Another major scandal erupted in Spring 2007 that engulfed attorney general and Bush loyalist Alberto Gonzales. The spectacle of "Gonzogate" involved one of the most systematically political attempts to establish partisan control of the justice system in U.S. history, whereby numerous undeniably competent U.S. attorneys, the highest tier of the nation's federal prosecutors, were fired for failing to carry out politically motivated prosecutions of Democrats, while prosecutors who complied with the administration's blatantly political schemes retained their posts.

In addition to sensationalizing major political undertakings, the media produce spectacles out of events and controversies of social and everyday life, often providing forums through which major political issues and social struggles are negotiated and debated. In April 2007, revelations that three Duke University lacrosse players accused of gang rape were innocent raised issues of a rogue prosecutor and prosecutorial media. During the same week, racist and sexist comments by radio and television personality Don Imus, who called the Rutgers University women's basketball team "some nappy-headed hos," generated a media firestorm and debate over appropriate language in regard to race and gender, the limits of free speech, and corporate media responsibility. The resultant media spectacle and focus on the event and issues led to the end of Imus's long broadcasting career.

The shooting rampage at Virginia Tech on April 16, 2007, generated a media spectacle with local, national, and even global media following every twist of a shooting that was represented in the media as producing the highest death toll of any gun-related mass murder in recent U.S. history.[3] Such a claim was irresponsible and false and is setting the stage for someone to try to break the record. Yet the event has also spawned debates over gun laws and control, school safety, mental health care, and what causes male teenagers and young students to kill their classmates and teachers, themes that I will engage in this book.

There was also a racial dimension to the Virginia Tech shooting, as the assassin was revealed to be Korean American Seung-Hui Cho (see Chapter 1).[4] But most of the school shootings and domestic terrorism that I will discuss involve white, male, middle-class perpetrators that will lead me throughout to interrogate the social construction of masculinity; the hidden and overt dimensions to gender, race, and class in major spectacles of terror; and the ways that the media construct our view of contemporary events and history.

The Time of the Spectacle

> When the real world changes into simple images, simple images become real beings and effective motivations of a hypnotic behavior. The spectacle as a tendency *to make one see the world* by means of various specialized mediations (it can no longer be grasped directly), naturally finds vision to be the privileged human sense which the sense of touch was for other epochs.
> —*Guy Debord*, The Society of the Spectacle *(1970: 18)*

My notion of media spectacle builds on French theorist Guy Debord's conception of the society of spectacle, but differs significantly from Debord's concept.[5] For Debord, spectacle "unifies and explains a great diversity of apparent phenomena" (Debord 1970: 10). Debord's conception, first developed in the 1960s, continues to circulate through the Internet and other academic and subcultural sites today. It describes a media and consumer society organized around the production and consumption of images, commodities, and staged events.

For Debord, "spectacle" constituted the overarching concept to describe the media and consumer society, including the packaging, promotion, and display of commodities and the production and effects of all media. Using the term "media spectacle," I am largely focusing on various forms of technologically constructed media events that are produced and disseminated through the so-called mass media, ranging from radio and television to the Internet and the latest wireless gadgets. Every medium, from music to television, from news to advertising, has multiple forms of spectacle, involving such things in the realm of music as the classical music spectacle, the opera spectacle, the rock spectacle, and, over the last decades, the hip-hop spectacle. The forms and circulation of the spectacle evolve over time and multiply with new technological developments.

The notion of media spectacle also builds upon Dayan and Katz's notion of a "media event" (1992), which referred to how political systems exploited televised live, ceremonial, and preplanned events, such as the funeral of President Kennedy, a royal wedding, or the Olympic Games, to celebrate and reproduce the social system. Interestingly, Katz and Liebes (2007) have recently revised the original Dayan and Katz analysis to distinguish between "media events," "the ceremonial Contests, Conquests and Coronations that punctuated television's first 50 years," and disruptive events "such as Disaster, Terror and War."[6] My own view is that the Bush-Cheney administration has orchestrated events in its "war on terror" to strengthen its regime, but that its media spectacle of the Iraq war got out of control and became a highly disruptive event (see Kellner 2005).[7] In fact, war itself has arguably become an orchestrated media spectacle since the 1991 Gulf War (see Kellner 1992 and 2005).

As we proceed into this new millennium, the media are becoming more technologically dazzling and are playing an ever-escalating role in everyday life and cyberculture with new sites like Wikipedia, Facebook, MySpace, and YouTube, as well as a proliferation of complex computer games, which include role playing and virtual immersion in alternative worlds. Thus, in addition to the spectacles that celebrate and reproduce the existing society described by Debord and by Dayan and Katz as media events, today there is a new domain of the *interactive spectacle,* which provides an illusion of interaction and creativity but may well ensnare one ever deeper in the tentacles of the existing society and technology (see Best and Kellner 2001).

Under the influence of a multimedia-image culture, seductive commodity and entertainment spectacles fascinate the denizens of the media and consumer society and involve them in an ever-expanding world of multimedia, information, and consumption, which deeply influences thought and action. *Commodity spectacles* like Nike and McDonald's became global forces and symbols of U.S. culture, as earlier Coca-Cola and Disney were American brands with global impact. From the 1980s through the present, computers have become major global commodity spectacles and U.S. brands like Microsoft, Apple, Intel, and more recently Yahoo and Google became global symbols of a new era of techno- and digital capitalism.

Experience and everyday life are thus shaped and mediated for Debord by the spectacles of media culture and the consumer society. For Debord, the spectacle is a tool of pacification and depoliticization; it is a "permanent opium war" (1967: 44) that stupefies social subjects and distracts them from the most urgent task of real life—recovering the full range of their human powers through creative practice. Debord's concept of the spectacle is integrally connected to the concept of separation and passivity, for in submissively consuming spectacles, one is estranged from actively producing one's life. Capitalist society separates workers from the products of their labor, art from life, and consumption from human needs and self-directing activity, as individuals inertly observe the spectacles of social life from within the privacy of their homes (Debord 1967: 25–26). The Situationist project, by contrast, involved an overcoming of all forms of separation, in which individuals would directly produce their own lives and modes of self-activity and collective practice.

The correlative to the spectacle for Debord is thus the spectator, the reactive viewer and consumer of a social system predicated on submission, conformity, and the willing insertion into a system of marketable difference and lifestyles. The concept of the spectacle therefore involves a distinction between passivity and activity, and consumption and production, condemning the passive and scripted consumption of spectacle as an alienation from human potentiality for creativity and imagination. The spectacular society spreads its wares mainly through the cultural mechanisms of leisure and consumption, services and entertainment, ruled by the dictates of advertising and a commercialized media culture.

This structural shift to a society of the spectacle involves a commodification of previously noncolonized sectors of social life and the extension of bureaucratic control to the realms of leisure, desire, and everyday life. Parallel to the Frankfurt School conception of a "totally administered," or "one-dimensional," society (Marcuse 1964), Debord states that "The spectacle is the moment when the consumption has attained the *total occupation* of social life" (1970: 42). Here exploitation is raised to a psychological level; basic physical privation is augmented by "enriched privation" of pseudoneeds; alienation is generalized, made comfortable, and alienated consumption becomes "a duty supplementary to alienated production" (ibid.).

On my account, there are many levels and categories of spectacle (Kellner 2003a). Media spectacles are recurrent phenomena of media culture that dramatize its controversies and struggles, as well as its modes of conflict resolution. They include media extravaganzas like the Oscars and Emmys, or sports events like the Super Bowl or World Cup, which celebrate basic values of competition and winning. Politics is increasingly mediated by media spectacle. Political conflicts, campaigns, and those attention-grabbing occurrences that we call "news" have all been subjected to the logic of spectacle and tabloidization in the era of media sensationalism, political scandal and contestation, seemingly unending cultural wars, and the new phenomenon of Terror War.

Media spectacle involves those media events and rituals of consumption, entertainment, and competition like political campaigns or athletic contests that embody contemporary society's basic values and serve to enculturate individuals into its way of life. Yet the spectacle, as my allusion to the *political spectacle* attests, may also embody key societal conflicts, and I see the spectacle as a contested terrain. Since the 1960s, culture wars have been raging between left and right, liberals and conservatives, and a diversity of groups over U.S. politics, race, class, gender, sexuality, war, and other key issues. Both sides exploit the spectacle, as during the Vietnam War when the war itself was contested by the spectacle of the antiwar movement, or the 1990s Clinton sex and impeachment spectacle whereby conservatives attempted to use the spectacle to destroy the Clinton presidency, while his defenders used the spectacle of the right trying to take out an elected president to successfully defend him.

Spectacles of terror, like the 9/11 attacks on the Twin Towers and Pentagon, differ significantly from spectacles that celebrate or reproduce the existing society as in Guy Debord's "society of the spectacle" or the "media events" analyzed by Dayan and Katz (1992), which describe how political systems exploited televised live, ceremonial, and preplanned events. Spectacles of terror are highly disruptive events carried out by oppositional groups or individuals aimed at politics or war by other means. Like the media and consumer spectacles described by Debord, spectacles of terror reduce individuals to passive objects, manipulated by existing institutions and figures. However, the spectacles of terror produce fear that terrorists hope will demoralize the objects of their attacks, but that is often manipulated by conservatives, like the Bush-Cheney administration, to push through right-wing agendas, cut back on civil liberties, and militarize the society.

Spectacles of terror should also be distinguished from *spectacles of horror,* natural disasters such as the Asian Tsunami or Hurricane Katrina, which became major spectacles of the day in 2005. Other spectacles of horror include fires or dramatic failures of the system or infrastructure such as the Minnesota bridge collapse and the Utah mine tragedy, both spectacles of the day in August 2007.

Megaspectacles define a situation whereby certain spectacles become defining events of their era. These include commodity spectacles, such as the McDonald's or Nike spectacle, or Michael Jordan and the NBA basketball spectacle, which define an era of consumption, or entertainment spectacles such as Elvis Presley, rock and roll, or hip-hop, which help define cultural epochs. Megaspectacles also include sociopolitical dramas that characterize a certain period, involving such things as the 1991 Gulf War, the O. J. Simpson trials, the Clinton sex and impeachment scandals, or the Terror War that is defining the current era.

Megaspectacles are defined both quantitatively and qualitatively. The major media spectacles of the era dominate news, journalism, and Internet buzz, and are highlighted and framed as the key events of the age—as were, for instance, Princess Diana's wedding, death, and funeral, the extremely close 2000 election and 36-day battle for the White House, and the September 11 terror attacks and their violent aftermath. As I write in 2007, the spectacles of Iraq and the ongoing Terror War dominate our era and encapsulate basic conflicts and political dynamics, although these megaspectacles can be overshadowed temporarily by the spectacle of the day, like the interlude of the "Virginia Tech massacre" or the Southern California fires in October 2007, which temporarily dominated the news.

Guy Debord's "Society of the Spectacle" and Its Limitations

In using the concept of spectacle, I am obviously indebted to Guy Debord's *Society of the Spectacle* and the ideas of the Situationist International. Acknowledging the debt, I also note that there are three major differences between my engagement of the concept of the spectacle and Debord's model. First, while Debord develops a rather totalizing and monolithic concept of the society of the spectacle, I engage specific media spectacles, like the Clinton sex scandals and impeachment spectacle, the stolen election of 2000, the 9/11 terrorist attacks and Terror War spectacles, and subsequent Bush administration Iraq War and 2004 election spectacles (Kellner 2001, 2003a, 2003b, and 2005), as well as the spectacles of terror analyzed in this book.

Thus, while Debord presents a rather generalized and abstract notion of spectacle, I engage specific examples of media spectacle and how they are produced, constructed, and circulated, and how they function in the present era. In addition, I am reading the production, text, and effects of various media spectacles from a standpoint within contemporary U.S. society in order to help illuminate and theorize its sociopolitical dynamics and culture and, more broadly, globalization and global culture. Debord, by contrast, was analyzing a specific stage of capitalist society, that of the media and consumer society organized around spectacle. Moreover, Debord exhibits a French radical intellectual and neo-Marxian perspective, while I engage specific class, race, gender, and other political problematics and deploy a multiperspectivist model, using Frankfurt

School critical theory, British cultural studies, French postmodern theory, and many other critical perspectives.

Second, my approach to these specific spectacles is interpretive and inter-rogatory. That is, in a series of books over the last decade, I try to interrogate what major media spectacles tell us concerning contemporary U.S. and global society. In *Media Spectacle* (2003), I interrogate what McDonald's tells us about consumption and the consumer society, or globalization and its resistance; what the Michael Jordan and Nike spectacle reveals concerning the sports spectacle and the intersection of sports, entertainment, advertising, and com-modification in contemporary societies; and what the O. J. Simpson trials tell us about race, class, celebrity, the media, sports, gender, the police, and the legal system during the mid-1990s. The last event raised as well how to explain the obsessive focus on this event for months on end and what this megaspectacle tells us about media culture, politics, and society in the contemporary United States (see Kellner 2003a).

In my studies of media spectacle, I deploy cultural studies as *diagnostic critique,* reading and interpreting various spectacles to see what they tell us about the present age, using media spectacles to illuminate contemporary social developments, trends, and struggles.[8] The "popular" often puts on display major emotions, ideas, experiences, and conflicts of the era, as well as indicating what corporations are marketing. Critical cultural studies can help decipher dominant trends, social and political conflicts, and fears and aspirations of the period and thus contribute to developing critical theories of the contemporary era.

Third, I analyze the contradictions and reversals of the spectacle, whereas Debord has an overpowering and hegemonic notion of the society of the spec-tacle. Although he and his comrades in the Situationist International sketched out various models of opposition and struggle, and in fact inspired in part the rather spectacular May 1968 events in France, whereby students and workers rebelled and almost overthrew the existing government (see Feenberg and Freedman 2001), Debord's notion of "the society of the spectacle" is mono-lithic and all-embracing. By contrast, I see the spectacle as contested and have a notion of the reversal of the spectacle. For an example of contradictions and contestation of the commodity spectacle, take McDonald's. When I began my studies of media spectacle in the 1990s, McDonald's was a figure for a triumphant global capitalism. McDonald's was constantly expanding in the United States and throughout the world, its profits were high, and it was taken as a paradigm of a successful American and then global capitalism. George Ritzer's book *The McDonaldization of Society* (1993, 1996) used McDonald's as a model to analyze contemporary production and consumption, while books like *Golden Arches East* (Watson 1997) valorized McDonald's as bringing modernity itself to vast sectors of the world, like Russia and China. McDonald's was praised for its efficient production methods, its cleanliness and orderliness, and its bringing food value and fast, convenient food to the masses.

Suddenly, however, McDonald's became the poster corporation for protest in the anti–corporate globalization movement. Some British Greenpeace activists had produced a pamphlet attacking McDonald's unhealthy food, its repressive labor practices, and its negative environmental impact and called for protests and boycotts. McDonald's countered with a lawsuit against them, and an anti-McDonald's campaign created a website, McSpotlight, that became one of the most accessed websites in history (see http://www.mcspotlight.org). Global and local protests emerged, and whenever there was an anti–corporate globalization demonstration somewhere, a McDonald's was trashed. Suddenly, McDonald's expansion was halted, profits were down almost everywhere for the first time, and new McDonald's restaurants were blocked by local struggles. Moreover, in the United States and elsewhere, lawsuits were brought for false advertising and promoting addictive substances and junk food, and bad publicity and falling profits ensued that continue to haunt McDonald's through the present (Kellner 2003a).[9]

I therefore see the spectacle as a *contested terrain* in which different forces use the spectacle to push their interests. Against Debord's more monolithic and overpowering totalitarian spectacle, I see the spectacle as highly contested, subject to reversal and flip-flops, and thus extremely ambiguous and contradictory. For instance, the media spectacle of the U.S./UK invasion of Iraq was used by the Bush administration to promote its war policy and the so-called Bush doctrine of preemptive war. While the spectacle went through several stages from the opening triumphant "shock and awe" bombing of Iraq through Bush's May 2003 "Mission Accomplished" spectacle, later horrific events in Iraq caused a reversal of the spectacle, and it is now hotly and bitterly contested (Kellner 2005).

Reading the Spectacle with Critical Social Theory and Cultural Studies

Since the establishment of the Centre for Contemporary Cultural Studies in Birmingham, England, in the 1960s, as well as in subsequent versions of cultural studies throughout the world, there has been a long-standing tradition of taking on the big issues of the era. The Birmingham School critically analyzed the assaults against working-class culture by American mass media and consumer culture. In this conjuncture, British cultural studies stressed the need for media literacy and critique, learning to read newspapers, TV news, advertisements, TV shows and the like—just as one learns to read books (see Kellner 1995). The project helped generate a media literacy movement, expanded the concept of literacy, and introduced a new, powerful dimension of pedagogy into cultural studies, one that I'll build upon in the conclusion to this book.

Later, in the 1980s, British cultural studies took on the rise of Thatcherism and the emergence of a new right-wing conservative hegemony in Britain, by explaining how it was produced by British culture, media, politics, and various economic factors (see Hall and Jacques 1983). Larry Grossberg (1992), Stanley Aronowitz (1993), I (Kellner and Ryan 1988; Kellner 1990, 1992, and 1995), and others engaged in similar work within the United States during the Reagan era of the 1980s, applying cultural studies to analyze the big issues of the time.

Indeed, one of my major focuses of the past two decades has been the use of cultural studies and critical social theory to interrogate the big events of the day. These projects include *The Persian Gulf TV War* (1992); *Grand Theft 2000: Media Spectacle and a Stolen Election* (2001); *From 9/11 to Terror War* (2003) on the September 11 terrorist attacks and their exploitation by the Bush administration to push through right-wing militarism, interventionism, unilateralism, and a hard-right domestic agenda, including the Patriot Act; and *Media Spectacle and the Crisis of Democracy* (2005), which demonstrated how the Bush administration consistently manipulated media spectacle during its first term and in the highly contested and controversial 2004 election and Iraq War. In my books *Media Culture* (1995) and *Media Spectacle* (2003), I use cultural studies to critically interrogate major phenomena of the day—such as Reagan and Rambo, Madonna and pop feminism, rap and hip-hop, cyberpunk and the Internet, McDonald's and globalization, Michael Jordan and the Nike spectacle, and other defining cultural phenomena of the era.

Cultural studies is an interdisciplinary, transdisciplinary, and counterdisciplinary approach that can be used to address a wide range of cultural phenomena from advertising to political narratives (see Kellner 1995 and 2003a). A multiperspectival and interdisciplinary enterprise, it draws on a number of disciplines to engage production and political economy of culture, critical engagement with texts, and audience research into effects. As a transdisciplinary enterprise, it has its own integrity as defined by the practices, methods, and work developing in its ever-expanding tradition. And it is counterdisciplinary by refusing assimilation into standard academic disciplines, being open to a variety of methods and theoretical positions and assuming a critical-oppositional stance to the current organization of the university, media, and society.

Cultural studies reads texts in their sociohistorical context and thus needs a critical theory of society to help situate, interpret, and trace the effects of certain texts, artifacts, or events. Critical theory is also historical theory, contextualizing its object in its historical matrix, and so I felt the need to ground my studies of "guys and guns amok" in the contemporary moment in the context of the history of guns in the United States and controversies over guns and their regulation. In 2000 Michael A. Bellesiles published *Arming America: The Origins of a National Gun Culture* with the prestigious Alfred A. Knopf publishers. It was garnished with an impressive array of laudatory reviews and won the Bancroft Award as the best historical study of the year. The book, however, was highly controversial and provoked a firestorm of critique. Right-wing gun advocates and their academic minions ferociously attacked Bellesiles's scholarship, and it turns out he made mistakes—among other things, in his sample and interpretation of probate records that resulted in his underestimating the number of guns privately held in colonial America. With the ensuing scandal and fierce attacks, Bellesiles was stripped of the Bancroft prize and eventually lost his job at Emory University.[10]

Bellesiles's history describes the origins of a national gun culture and the ways that the gun became central to American life and concepts of masculinity. He seems to have underestimated the extent of early colonial gun culture and gun culture after the Revolution, but he convincingly depicts the explosion of gun culture at the time of the Civil War, with the mass production of guns and the manufacture and marketing of guns in the post–Civil War period. He also convincingly reproduces the debates over guns at the time of the Constitutional Convention when Federalists fought for a centralized federal government with a controlled standing army, while anti-Federalists supported state militias (Bellesiles 2000: 208ff.). As Bellesiles argued: "The Constitutional Convention hammered out a document full of compromise and barely obtained concessions. On one point at least there was no disagreement: Congress should arm the militia" (2000: 213). Bellesiles sets out the debates whether the militia should remain under the direct control of the states or federal government, whether or not to have a standing army, and what gun rights should be included. The result was the Second Amendment to the Bill of Rights which held: "A well-regulated Militia, being necessary to the security of a free State, the right of the People to keep and bear Arms, shall not be infringed" (2000: 217).

The context of the Second Amendment suggests an original intent to bestow the right to bear arms within the confines of a militia, itself to be regulated by the federal government (i.e., as in the phrase "*well-regulated* Militia" in the Second Amendment, italics mine). Some have argued that until the last few decades, the Second Amendment was largely read as supporting gun rights within militias, but not in terms of individual rights to bear firearms.[11] But recently, the Second Amendment has been interpreted by law professors, the courts, and the public to provide gun ownership rights to citizens, though controversies over the meaning of the Second Amendment continue until this day, as Note 11 indicates.

Clinton E. Cramer's 2006 *Armed America: The Story of How and Why Guns Became as American as Apple Pie* presents itself as a rejoinder to Bellesiles's account. Critics had already savaged Bellesiles's use of probate material to argue that he misinterpreted data and had incomplete samples that made gun ownership appear artificially low. Cramer attempted to establish the conventional view that America was awash with guns from the colonial period to the present. He also contested Bellesiles's account of foreign travelers to the United States in the early decades of the nineteenth century as having failed to provide published descriptions of guns and violence in the United States. To counter these claims, in chapter after chapter in the third section of his book, Cramer goes through the same and other accounts that show, quite to the contrary, that foreign visitors often remarked on American guns and violence as distinctive features of the country (2000: 194–236).

Perhaps against his will, Cramer confirmed to me that gun ownership and violence in U.S. history is a much more serious problem than most historians and liberals would recognize. Bellesiles seemed to want to posit a Golden Age after the American Revolution when guns were not such an important part of American life. His narrative of American life from the postrevolutionary period to the 1840s stresses civilizing developments in American towns such as schools, libraries, bookstores, and cultural institutions—claiming that white-on-white violence was rare in these days of the Republic and that gun violence was at a minimum (2000: 315ff., 366ff.). Cramer and other critics contest this claim, and probably U.S. life had both the features of Bellesiles's more idealized account and of more conventional accounts of the roughness and violence of frontier life.

I fear that Bellesiles and his impressive array of supportive reviewers wanted to believe that gun culture was not so deeply entrenched in American history and that an earlier period could be pointed to as an ideal to emulate, whereas the problem of guns and violence may be more deeply rooted and intractable than liberals want to acknowledge. Both Bellesiles and Cramer emphasize the violence of the Indian wars that continued into the nineteenth century, the ferocity of the Civil War, and the eventual triumph of gun culture. Both Bellesiles and Cramer also point out how the federal government from the beginning regulated gun ownership and use, preventing at different times gun ownership by blacks, indentured servants, Indians, and other stigmatized groups. Together the books present a national history of gun culture that has bequeathed serious problems to the present age.

In this book, I am not going back to earlier episodes of U.S. history, but the rise of a gun culture plays a background role in the episodes that I will discuss and emerges as a problem that U.S. society has to recognize and engage. In the next chapter, I analyze the construction of the media spectacle of the Virginia Tech shooting and how old and new media together helped produce the event. I examine how the text of the "Virginia Tech massacre" was interpreted and deployed by different groups, and thus how diverse voices, interests, and groups intervened to use the spectacle to promote their agendas. I also discuss the audience reception of the spectacle and how it played out in the months following within U.S. culture, society, and politics. I thus deploy cultural studies to interrogate the politics of representation of the event and critical social theory to contextualize and interpret it and to pursue its aftermath.

I am using the term *Virginia Tech massacre* because this was the phrase that the major broadcasting networks used from the beginning and continued to use through at least the opening days of the spectacle. The initial title for this book, *Guns Amok,* emerged as I was outlining a table of contents. As it turns out, there were many Google references that connected "guns" and "amok." Almost thirty films popped up with "Amok" in their titles, including a Chuck Jones Daffy Duck film, *Duck Amuck,* which I recalled when thinking about the title, as well as a *Star Trek* episode "Amok Time" that I remember well. There are books and journals with "Amok" in their titles, including Stefan Zweig's novel *Amok* (1922) and Glenn Greenwald's 2006 book *How Would a Patriot Act? Defending American Values from a President Run Amok.* Hence, there are enough cultural references to make the title resonant and viable.

To be sure, the problem with the Virginia Tech massacre is not guns running amok, but people with guns killing other people. Thus, the editorial board at Paradigm Publishers suggested the current title, *Guys and Guns Amok.* This seemed appropriate, as I wanted to argue that both an out-of-control gun culture and problematic constructions of masculinity were behind the killing and violence that I am engaging in this book. Moreover, the word "amok" has anthropological grounding. As Steven Pinker writes in *How the Mind Works* (1997: 364):

But running amok is not unique to America, to Western nations, or even to modern societies. Amok is a Malay word for the homicidal sprees occasionally undertaken by lonely Indochinese men who have suffered a loss of love, a loss of money, or a loss of face. The syndrome has been described in a culture even more remote from the West: Stone Age foragers of Papua New Guinea.

The amok man is patently out of his mind, an automaton oblivious to his surroundings and unreachable by appeals or threats. But his rampage is preceded by lengthy brooding over failure and is carefully planned as a means of deliverance from an unbearable situation. The amok state is chillingly cognitive. It is triggered not by a stimulus, not by a tumor, not by a random spurt of brain chemicals, but by an idea. The idea is so standard that the following summary of the amok mindset, composed in 1968 by a psychiatrist who had interviewed seven hospitalized amok men in Papua New Guinea, is an apt description of the thoughts of mass murders continents and decades away: "I am not an important or 'big man.' I possess only my personal sense of dignity. My life has been reduced to nothing by an intolerable insult. Therefore, I have nothing to lose except my life, which is nothing, so I trade my life for yours, as your life is favoured. The exchange is in my favour, so I shall not only kill you, but I shall kill many of you, and at the same time rehabilitate myself in the eyes of the group of which I am member, even though I might be killed in the process."[12]

Running amok, however, takes place in specific societal contexts, and in the following chapters I will situate my analyses within the context of violence and guys and guns amok in contemporary U.S. society and culture.

Societal Violence and Guys and Guns Amok

I am so full of rage that I feel I could snap at any moment. I think about it every day. Blowing the school up or just taking the easy way out, and walk into a pep assembly with guns. In either case, people that are breathing will stop breathing. That is how I will repay all you mother fuckers for all you put me through.
—Kip Kinkel, school shooter, writing in his journal
(cited in Lieberman 2006: 10)

In this book, I examine acts of societal violence that embody a crisis of masculinity and male rage, an out-of-control gun culture, and media that project normative images of violent masculinity and make celebrities out of murderers. By a "crisis of masculinity,"[13] I mean a dominant societal connection between masculinity and being a tough guy, assuming what Jackson Katz describes as a "tough guise," a mask or façade of violent assertiveness, covering over vulnerabilities. The crisis erupts in outbreaks of violence and societal murder, as men act out rage, which takes extremely violent forms such as political assassinations, serial and mass murders, and school and workplace shootings—all exhibiting guys and guns amok. As a backdrop to the school shootings and acts of domestic terrorism that I examine, I also call attention to an escalation of war and militarism in the United States from the long nightmare of Vietnam through the military interventions of the Bush-Cheney administration in Afghanistan and Iraq, as well as escalating societal violence in the media and society at large.

The media made celebrities out of serial killers starting in the 1970s, although there is a long tradition of celebrity murderers in the United States. In the 1960s, a new mode of celebrity shooters began appearing, including political assassins (Lee Harvey Oswald, Sirhan Sirhan, Arthur Bremer, etc.), school shooters (Charles Whitman at the University of Texas in 1966), and serial killers. With the rise of cable television in the 1970s and an increasingly tabloidized journalistic culture, serial killers became focuses of media spectacle, and later books and movies, including the Zodiac killer, the Charles Manson family, Son of Sam, Henry Lee Lucas, and Ted Bundy. This celebrity culture of murderers, highly publicized by the media, may have influenced later mass murderers, serial killers, school shooters, and domestic terrorists.

San Francisco's Zodiac killer went on a rampage from 1968 to 1978, killing young men and women and sending threatening notes and coded messages to police and the media. The subject of two recent movies and best-selling books, the Zodiac killer was never caught, but in David Fincher's 2007 movie *Zodiac* and the best-selling books upon which it was based, it was clear that the killer had a proficiency with and fetish for guns that empowered him and that he created a spectacle in the media, using the media to make himself a celebrity and object of media obsession.[14]

Son of Sam, Ted Bundy, Henry Lee Lucas, and other serial murderers were captured, generating books, movies, TV specials, and a cultural obsession with mass murderers and criminal monsters, leading to academic and popular studies of the phenomenon. Trying to understand societal violence and murder, Richard Rhodes's *Why They Kill* (1999) presents the life and theories of sociologist-criminologist Lonnie Athens, who interviewed scores of killers serving long prison terms and then used sociological theory to construct a general theory of how and why hard-core murderers develop and kill. Athens's research suggests that murderers emerge from a culture of violence, become "violentized" and desensitized to the pain that their violent acts inflict, and construct violent self-images and identities. Such killers go through stages of brutalization, in which they are coached into violence within their families, peer groups, or other communities, become belligerent and aggressive, engage in violent action that helps construct their self-image, and then enter a stage of virulent violence, taking them outside of social bonds and restraints.

In a penetrating chapter very important for the issues of this book, Rhodes discusses the relevance of Athens's theories for explaining violence in war and how soldiers are socialized to kill enemies in warfare. Rhodes indicates how Athens's concept of "dramatic self-change" helps explain the process that goes on in basic training to make men and women soldiers (1999: 287ff.). Citing military expert Gwynne Dyer, who argues that basic training "is essentially a conversion process in an almost religious sense" (1999: 288), Rhodes discusses how soldiers are socialized into becoming members of a community in which acceptance and survival requires killing enemies in battle.

But Rhodes notes that one of the surprising findings of studies of military socialization was army officer and researcher S. L. A. Marshall's finding that during World War II many U.S. servicemen did not want to use their guns. Marshall wrote: "We found that on an average not more than 15 percent of the men had actually fired at the enemy positions or personnel with rifles, carbines, grenades, bazookas, BARS [Browning automatic rifles] or machine guns during the course of an entire engagement. Even allowing for the dead and wounded, and assuming that in their numbers there would be the same proportion of active firers as among the living, the figure did not rise above 20 to 30 percent of the total for any action. The best showing that could be made by the most spirited and aggressive companies was that one man in four had made at least some use of his firepower" (quoted in Rhodes 1999: 291).

Although Marshall's findings were contested, Rhodes notes that other researchers and military experts found confirming data in further studies, such as military expert Dave Grossman,[15] who noted that a 1986 study by the British Defense Operational Analysis Establishment's field studies division reviewed "historical studies of more than one hundred nineteenth- and twentieth-century battles" (Grossman, quoted in Rhodes 1999: 292).

Rhodes then recreated these battles in test trials, substituting lasers for weapons, to see if Marshall's revelations applied to earlier armies in earlier time, and that Grossman asserted: "The researchers' conclusions openly supported the main factor' that kept the actual historical killing rates significantly below the laser trial levels" (Grossman, quoted in Rhodes 1998: 292).

A second surprising discovery that Marshall found was that "fear of killing, rather than fear of being killed, was the most common cause of battle fatigue in the individual and that fear of failure ran a strong second" (1999: 293). These studies indicate that there is nothing "natural" about using guns and killing people and that military training must break down many individuals' natural disinclination to engage in violence. Rhodes notes how Marshall's findings led to transformations of U.S. military training: "It began teaching men to fire their weapons at pop-up targets under simulated battlefield conditions, a form of operant conditioning. More significantly, it began emphasizing killing rather than simply duty and courage—that is, it introduced explicit violent coaching into combat training" (294).

Evidently, this training worked and follow-up investigations during the Korean War and Vietnam indicated that the violent coaching produced higher firing rates, though there has been debate about killing rates. Rhodes notes that "Marshall's investigations imply that killing in combat requires violentization" (1999: 294), and worries about the effect of this training on veterans returning home, noting adjustment problems and combat trauma suffered by Vietnam veterans (297ff.). Indeed, one wonders how volunteering in an army engaging in long-term intense military action in Afghanistan and Iraq is brutalizing young Americans and increasing the possibilities of both long-term trauma and explosions of violent rage—an issue I'll take up in the conclusion of this book.

Rhodes goes into detail concerning Jonathan Shay's book *Achilles in Vietnam* (1995), which discusses the psychological damage done to soldiers who fought in the Vietnam War, their sense of betrayal, and the posttraumatic stress disorder that plagued them after the war. According to Shay, more than 40 percent of the Vietnam vets "reported engaging in violent acts three times or more in the previous year. We're talking about 300,000 men here. The percentage of combat veterans who reported averaging more than one violent act a month was almost five times higher than among the sample of civilian counterparts" (Shay, quoted in Rhodes 1999: 298). Their military experience, according to Shay, precipitated in many soldiers what he called "the berserk state," in which they ran amok and committed acts of violence (299ff.). "Men go berserk, Shay writes, when they become enraged, develop a 'manic obsession with revenge' and lose all restraint" (300).

Once again, we see male rage exploding in violent acts that Shay and Rhodes illustrate with U.S. soldiers going berserk in Vietnam in places like My Lai, where they slaughtered civilians (300ff.), and then when "they came home, betrayed, malefic veterans such as these carried their violence with them" (308). Athens and Rhodes were concerned with how to counter these problems, and I examine their useful "Strategies of Prevention and Control" (313ff.) in Chapter 4.

Although Athens's sociological studies of violence, as presented by Rhodes, provide many important insights into social factors that help produce societal violence, there is a cognitivist and sociological bias in Athens's studies that downplays genetic and mental health problems and unconscious male rage and aggression. Reacting against overly psychiatric explanations of violence, and the use of psychiatry to lessen penalties for hard-core murderers, Athens wants to stress the importance of taking responsibility and seeing the social conditions, subject to modification, that help produce killers. This is admirable and provides important dimensions to understanding and grappling with problems of societal violence, but it fails to adequately address the mental health dimension that also needs to be addressed. It also underplays the role of the media, dominant societal images of masculinity, and the pernicious role of gun culture in serial, mass, and hard-core murderers and the need for gun culture and violent masculinity to be addressed.

Another tradition of social scientists and activists has explored the connections between crime, violence, and masculinity. In *Masculinities and Crime* (1993) and other writings, James Messerschmidt examines the link between masculine socialization and the overwhelming prevalence of male perpetration of crime—including violent crime. Emphasizing the social construction of gender, class, race, and crime, Messerschmidt stresses how these factors are interrelated: that men learn violent behavior as a means both of "doing masculinity" and of asserting dominance over women and other men, behavior that socially reproduces structures of capitalism and patriarchy.

Messerschmidt and R. W. Connell (2005) critically interrogate the concept of *hegemonic masculinity,* whereby dominant models of an aggressive—and sometimes violent—masculinity are constructed that reinforce gendered hierarchies among men and reinforce men's power over women. Hegemonic masculinity is a dominant form of masculinity in a culture at a specific period, although it is shifting and contested over time. Hegemonic masculinities in the contemporary era in the United States are associated with military heroism, corporate power, sports achievement, action-adventure movie stars, and being tough, aggressive, and macho, ideals reproduced in corporate, political, military, sports, and gun culture as well as Hollywood films, video games, men's magazines, and other forms of media culture, and sites like the frat house, locker room, boardroom, male-dominated workplaces, bars, and hangouts where men aggregate.

In *The Macho Paradox* (2006), Jackson Katz explores how conceptions of violent hypermasculinity helps produce violence against women. Calling upon men to question such behavior and to seek alternative masculinities, Katz challenges men to confront violence against women and to struggle against it. All of the above-mentioned scholars share a critical relation to dominant conceptions of hegemonic hyper- and violent masculinities, and all search for alternative modes of masculinity, a project that I share. My work here will show that the school shooters and domestic terrorists examined in the following pages all exhibit male rage,[16] attempt to resolve a crisis of masculinity through violent behavior, demonstrate a fetish for guns or weapons, and represent, in general, a situation of guys and guns amok.

The Epidemic of School Shootings

During the late 1990s, there was a minor epidemic of school shootings, with adolescents joining serial killers and adult mass murderers in spectacles of terror that made for sensationalist presentations on rapidly growing cable news networks like CNN. The phenomenon gave rise to academic and government studies and several books on school shooters, of which I will make use in this book. In a prescient book that appeared soon after the Columbine shootings, Stephanie Urso Spina assembled studies in her edited collection *Smoke and Mirrors* (2000) that engaged "the hidden context of violence in schools and society." In a wide-ranging introduction, "Violence in Schools: Expanding the Dialogue," Spina explores how schools and students are caught up in a wider web of societal violence. Opening with a panorama of facts on violence in the United States, Spina indicates how schools are often scapegoated for the problems of violence in society. Spina argues that while schools are indeed sites of violence, they are caught up in a nexus of societal violence and themselves impose symbolic and sometimes physical violence on students.

Carrying out a critique of contemporary schooling in the United States, an issue generally lacking in liberal and conservative discussions of school shootings, Spina discusses the role of socioeconomic factors in producing school and societal violence, as well as the role of politics and policy factors; the imbrication of issues of gender, race, and class; and how guns, police, and prisons factor into the problems. This broad and comprehensive framework provides a useful context in which to see the problems of school shootings and societal violence. In her conclusion, "When the Smoke Clears: Revisualizing

Responses to Violence in Schools," Spina makes a wealth of useful suggestions, some of which I engage in Chapter 4 of this book.

An article in the collection by Jessie Klein and Lynn S. Chancer (2000), "Masculinity Matters: The Omission of Gender from High-Profile School Violence Cases," is especially important to the problematic of this book. The authors studied five high-profile school shootings in the late 1990s and explain how standard accounts of the Columbine and other shootings either blamed the NRA and failure to enact reasonable gun control in the United States,[17] or blamed such factors as media violence and lax parenting, or interpreted the episodes as random and inexplicable. The authors note that the issue of masculinity is ignored in the shootings, insist that it matters, and advance an important distinction between hegemonic and subordinate masculinities, whereby a dominant tough, macho, and hypermasculinist conception of masculinity marginalizes and scorns subordinate masculinities. Klein and Chancer note that in all of the five cases studied, school shooters complained about being harassed and bullied by jocks, preppies, and the more dominant alpha-male types and saw their actions as fighting back and asserting themselves, obviously in a pathological form of ultramasculine violence, itself a parody of the dominant masculinity that lays bare its destructive forces. The authors suggest the need for alternative masculinities, as well as strategies for diminishing harassment and bullying in the schools, issues that I will take up in the course of this book.

One of the most widely discussed and influential studies of school shootings, *Rampage* (Newman et al. 2004), emerged after the House of Representatives in 1999 "added a provision to the 'Missing, Runaway, and Exploited Children's Act' requiring the U.S. Department of Education to study rampage shootings in schools" (2004: ix). A Harvard University professor at the Kennedy School of Government, Kathleen Newman, received a call asking her to supervise research into the explosion of shootings at schools in small towns and rural communities supposed to be immune from this sort of violence.

Newman assembled a group of researchers who in the summer of 2000 moved to Kentucky and Arkansas, residing in two communities that had recently undergone deadly school shootings. The researchers stayed about three years in each community, interviewed survivors, school officials, and others, wrote up studies, and produced the multiauthored book *Rampage* in 2004. An opening chapter, "Explosions," describes the shootings, beginning with a description of a December 1, 1997, shooting at Heath High School on the outskirts of West Paducah, Kentucky. The authors describe how fourteen-year-old freshman Michael Carneal arrived at school that day accompanied by his popular older sister Kelly, bringing in a bundle of weapons that he had stolen the previous day and began firing at random on students.

The day before Michael had snuck into the garage of a friend, Jered Parker, found a key to the family's gun case, "and stuffed a 30-30 rifle and four .22 rifles into his duffel bag, along with the earplugs and boxes of ammunition" (2004: 5). Observing his weapons cache alone in his room that night provided great satisfaction: "I was feeling proud, strong, good and more respected. I had accomplished something. I'm not the kind of kid who accomplishes anything. This is the only adventure I've ever had." Michael took his weapons to show off to two friends and later told prosecutors: "More guns is better. You have more power. You look better if you have a lot of guns. A kid would say one gun is good, but that Michael had a lot of guns" (2004: 6).

The other shooting described in the first chapter of *Rampage* took place at Westside Middle School near Jonesboro, Arkansas, on the afternoon of March 24, 1998. Eleven-year-old Andrew Golden pulled the alarm bell at the school and, as students marched out, he and thirteen-year-old Mitchell Johnson started firing at their classmates. In a five-minute shooting spree, before they were surrounded by police and surrendered, Mitchell fired five shots from a semiautomatic rifle, killing at least one and wounding at least three, while "Andrew, the more skilled marksman, fired twenty-five shots, killing three people and wounding at least two others" (2004: 12). The two young boys had also stolen the weapons, attempting, first, to break into Andrew's father's gun collection. They could not open the locked safe in which they were stored, but found three handguns in the house that they took. They then broke into Andrew's grandparents' house, where they found a wall full of rifles and easily secured four more handguns and three rifles.

Chapter 2 on "The Shooters" describes the troubled childhoods of the seemingly average young students who had become notorious shooters. Fourteen-year-old Michael Carneal appeared to have a normal family life, although he suffered comparisons with his popular and successful older sister. During the year before the shooting, Michael's grades declined and his psyche began to unravel, disintegration evidenced in disturbing writings anticipating Seung-Hui Cho's troubled and revealing texts. Desperate to fit in, Michael was bullied by older students and accused of being gay in a student newspaper gossip column. The report "precipitated an avalanche of bullying, teasing, and humiliation that followed Michael for the rest of middle school. Michael was unable to escape and unwilling to fight back or enlist the help of adults. Instead, he buried his rage, expressing himself only on paper in an essay he wrote for an eighth-grade teacher" (2004: 27).

To find a peer group that would accept him, Michael emulated outsider behavior to attract the attention of a high school "goth" group to which he wished to belong. There were later indications that he may have carried out the shootings to attract the attention of this group, and there were suspicions that some in the group may have encouraged him and led him to believe that they would participate in the spectacle.

Of the two young shooters in Arkansas, Mitchell Johnson appeared to be friendly and polite to teachers and adults, but those who knew him described him as "angry, belligerent, boasting, and bullying" (2004: 35). What wasn't known was that his father, whom his mother divorced, had badly bullied his young son, and when the boy was sent to his grandparents when he was eight, he was raped repeatedly by a neighbor boy. While the mother remarried and the family appeared happy, obviously Mitchell carried deep scars and acted out tough-guy scripts, seeking attention and validation from fellow students, who tended to mock his pretensions to be a gang member and macho dude.

Apparently many thought that eleven-year-old Andrew Golden may have been the ringleader, as he came from a family of gun enthusiasts and was a skilled marksman (2004: 39ff.). While Golden appeared to be normal and get along with family and friends, some were afraid to play with him because of explosive outbursts of temper, his bragging about killing cats, and his getting in trouble at school. Yet others believed that Andrew was trying to impress Mitchell and that the older boy was dominant, or at least co-conspirator of the murder spectacle.

Rampage develops a comprehensive framework for investigating school shootings, distinguishing "rampage school shootings" from "inner-city violence (52ff.); comparing adult and youth murderers (57ff.); and examining "popular explanations for school shootings," including mental illness, family problems, bullying, peer support, a culture of violence, and gun availability. Discounting the "he just snapped" brand of explanation because the shootings they investigated were clearly the result of careful planning, the writers of *Rampage* argue that no one theory works for the variety of cases, but rather that a combination of factors contributes to the shootings that need to be taken into account.

In its analysis of the locales of the shootings, *Rampage* sketches out changes in U.S. society that make small towns and rural communities susceptible to the kind of extreme violence and mass murders usually associated with urban and underclass areas (77ff.). After in-depth sociological analysis of the community, the shooting, and the young killer(s), Newman and her colleagues develop their own theory of five "necessary but not sufficient conditions" for rampage school shooting. These include: 1) the shooter's self-perception as marginal and alienated; 2) psychosocial problems that magnify the impact of this sense of marginality (229); and 3) the availability of "cultural scripts" that map out ways to carry out the attack and that suggest solutions to the shooter's problems. Newman et al. stress that the media culture helps provide cultural scripts that promote a violent masculinity:

> When we see films featuring macho heroes or villains who shoot their way to greater notoriety, we are looking at the traces of a cultural script that links manhood and public respect with violence. The script provides an image of what the shooters want to become and a template for action that links the method to the goal. Of course, this is not the only available image of masculinity in our culture, but it is one that attracts the attention of boys who have suffered ridicule from their peers for being insufficiently strong or socially capable. These blueprints for the masculine self may help explain why rampage school shooters direct their anger and hopelessness outward, rather than inward. (230)

A fourth factor identified by the authors of *Rampage* involves the institutional failure of school monitoring and mental health systems to identify troubled teens before their problems become extreme, while a fifth factor involves the availability of guns. I agree with the authors of *Rampage* that a multicausal and factor analysis of school shooters and societal violence is necessary, that no one factor should serve as privileged explanatory lens, and that different factors will be operative in different cases. But as the quote on the "cultural script" of violent masculinity indicates, certainly male rage and a concept of violent hypermasculinity are key features in school and many other shootings, and the use of guns to assert masculinity is a particularly problematic and dangerous fact of the contemporary era.

Other examples in *Rampage* of the importance of male rage and images of violent masculinity are found throughout the book, as when the authors write:

> The shooters appear to be working from widely available cultural scripts that glorify violent masculinity.... The shooting solves two problems at once: it provides them the "exit" they are seeking and it overturns the social hierarchy, establishing once and for all that they are, in Luke Woodham's words, "gutsy and daring," not "weak and slow-witted." The problem is they didn't just fail at popularity—they failed at the very specific task of "manhood," or at least they felt that way. The solutions to this failure are popularized in the media in violent song lyrics, movies, and video games. But the overall script of violent masculinity is omnipresent. "Men" handle their own problems. They don't talk;

they act. They fight back. And above all, "men" must never let others push them around. Once a potential shooter has shared his violent fantasies with peers, this script virtually assures that there's no turning back. (269)

The *Rampage* authors cite Jackson Katz, who writes: "The issue is not just violence in the media but the construction of violent masculinity as a cultural norm" (153).[18] This distinction is important, and although I will cite media influences on perpetrators of domestic terrorism and school shootings, I do not want to demonize or scapegoat the media. Rather, the problem is a societal model of violent masculinity and out-of-control gun culture—that is, guys and guns amok—and the media are just part of the mix that creates problematic conceptions of hypermasculinity and contributes to societal violence.

Other books help provide context for my analyses of school shootings. In *The Shooting Game* (2006), journalist Joseph Lieberman (not the senator with the same name) sets out to tell the story of fifteen-year-old Kip Kinkel's rampage at Thurston High, in Springfield, Oregon, in 1998, when he first murdered his parents and then drove to his high school and indiscriminately killed classmates before being wrestled down by other students.[19] Lieberman provides in-depth analysis of the family history and problems of a young middle-class son of an apparently normal but troubled family, who carried out one of the most highly publicized shootings of the day. Arrested on May 20, 1998, for carrying a stolen gun to school, Kinkel was released into the custody of his father. When his parents threatened to take his gun collection away, Kinkel went berserk, planned and carried through their murders the next day, and then attacked his high school, armed with rifles, guns, and knives.

Lieberman makes the useful point that despite the tremendous publicity school shootings receive in the media, incidents of shooting are relatively rare. He notes that the "National School Safety Center's *Report on School Associated Violent Deaths* detailed only 245 shooting deaths in or around schools during the ten-year period from 1992 to 2002" (2006: 299). While this number is unacceptable, "the number pales in comparison with shooting deaths in other nonschool locations" (ibid.). In particular, more "children are killed at home than in any other location. In 2000, there were sixteen school-associated violent deaths. By comparison, approximately sixteen children die at the hands of their parents or guardian every three days in America. From all sources, including family violence, around sixteen youths die from gunfire each two days, mostly at the hands of adults" (ibid.).[20]

Although the book is subtitled "The Making of School Shooters," Lieberman never really comes up with a general model of school shooters, the source of the problem, or how to deal with the issue, but the book is rich with journalistic detail not only of the Kinkel case but also of multiple school shootings in the United States and other countries over the past decades. While Lieberman details Kinkel's obsession with guns and—with his parents' knowledge—amassing a frightening arsenal, parts of which were used in his rampage, Lieberman does not really acknowledge the problem of guns amok until he notes near the end of the book that "although we urgently need to consider how young people so easily obtain high-powered weapons, the arguments and emotions attached to gun control legislation will no doubt prevent this subject from being rationally discussed for a long time to come" (2006: 312). Lieberman recognizes that guns were a religion not only for Kip Kinkel but also for millions of other Americans, suggesting that criticism of people's religions may be highly dangerous. Lieberman cites the example of Timothy McVeigh, who was led to his murderous terrorist attack on the Oklahoma City federal building in part because of his paranoid obsession that the federal government was going to start taking guns away from people, an incident and more general problem that I will engage in this book.

Further, while Lieberman is aware that school shootings are a gender issue (231ff.), with 97 percent of mass killings and serial shootings done by males (232), and acknowledges that guns are a part of male socialization, he does not recognize the issue of masculinity as part of the problem. He does not see that school and many other types of shootings are grounded in a crisis of masculinity. Nor does he perceive the need to reconstruct masculinity and offer new ideals for men as part of the solution to endemic societal violence—ranging from violence against women to gang, school, and other shootings.

Likewise, although Lieberman explores potential mental health problems suffered by the Thurston High shooter, Kip Kinkel, he does not prescribe the need for better mental health care, but his book ends with websites and addresses of various groups that have addressed school safety issues. The failure of the obviously well-intentioned and intelligent Lieberman to address the root causes of the issues he set out to interrogate points to the difficulty men have in seeing the role of guns in male socialization and general problems of how to interpret and deal with problems of mental health. At one point near the end of his studies where he is struggling for general insights and solutions, Lieberman notes how the sciences are carrying out brain research that might provide "neural explanations" in which shooters' "mirror neuron" systems are impaired or defective, creating a "mind-blindness" and lack of empathy (305–306).

Hence, while Athens and Rhodes have an overly sociological and cognitivist take on male rampages and mass murder, there is also a genetic determinist model at play in society that explains violent behavior on genetic or neural factors like brain damage or impairment. Further, as we shall see, some blame tragic murders on Satan or some incomprehensible evil within human nature, views that obviously block understanding of the problem and attempts to grapple with solutions.

Media Culture, Militarism, and Violent Masculinity

In analyzing examples of male violence from the Oklahoma City bombings to the Virginia Tech massacre, I situate these events in the context of a viral media culture, problematic male socialization and constructions of masculinity, and a history of violence and the emergence of domestic terrorism in the United States. The present context also involves the currently hegemonic and highly aggressive militarism and right-wing political forces and policies of the Bush-Cheney administration, as well as violent and aggressive forces in extremist gun cultures.

In his excellent study of escalating militarism from Vietnam to the present Bush-Cheney era, *Imperial Delusions* (2005), Carl Boggs examines the "culture of militarism" in U.S. society (125ff.), with in-depth discussions of patriotism as secular religion, gun culture and civic violence, patriarchy and warrior culture, and Hollywood and the Pentagon—all themes integral to my studies.

Boggs notes that the culture of militarism became especially visible in the 1980s and connects its rise to U.S. military interventions since World War II; an expanding military-industrial complex; and the spread of military values through popular culture, the media, games, and everyday life. Its spread is accompanied by patriotism reinforced through the schools, media, politics, and holidays, often linking patriotism with militarism. In its dangerous forms, patriotism inculcates an "us versus them" Manichean consciousness, xenophobia, and support of aggressive militarism, no matter what the goals and effects—phenomena intensified under the Bush-Cheney administration since 9/11 (see Kellner 2005).

Building on Rhodes's analysis of how "civic violence is typically rooted in human experiences that desensitize people to suffering, pain, and death" (131), Boggs engages the growth of a weapons and warrior subculture, militias, domestic terrorism, the spreading of military values in Hollywood films, and other topics that I also address in this book. He makes the interesting point that many serial killers had military training (140ff.), thus connecting militarism with extreme societal violence. Building on Mary Wertsch and other feminist scholars, Boggs also lays out connections between militarism and patriarchy.

In a book with Tom Pollard, *The Hollywood War Machine* (2007), Boggs explores the relations between Hollywood films, militarism, and the glorification of violent masculinity. Male heroism and celebrations of the assertion of violence, male bonding, and a culture of militarism have been the subject of a vast number of Westerns, war films, and other action-adventure genres. Boggs and Pollard suggest that in the contemporary era of high-tech cinematic spectacle, the products of the "Hollywood war machine" promote U.S. militarism and violent hypermasculinity, providing fantasies for men whose masculinities are in crisis to undertake violent action.

In *Beyond the Spectacle of Terrorism* (2006b), Henry Giroux also explores expanding militarism in U.S. society and culture and interrogates new forms of the spectacle of terrorism. In addressing the ways that a culture of militarism has been undermining democracy, Giroux cites Andrew J. Bacevich, who is concerned that military power is becoming "central to our national identity," and that "Americans in our own time have fallen prey to militarism, manifesting itself in a romanticized view of soldiers, a tendency to see military power as the truest measure of national greatness, and outsized expectations regarding the efficacy of force" (Bacevich quoted in Giroux 2006b: 9).

In his latest book, *The University in Chains: Confronting the Military-Industrial-Academic Complex* (2007), Giroux makes connections between U.S. militarism and the university. Opening with detailed analysis of Dwight D. Eisenhower's prescient warnings about the dangers of a military-industrial complex, Giroux explores how the university and media culture have become part of the complex, and how growing militarism presents threats to democracy.

Building on Debord and other work on the spectacle, including my own, in *Beyond the Spectacle of Terrorism* (2006b) Giroux argues that a new kind of "spectacle of terror" has emerged that is different from Debord's consumer/media spectacle, or the fascist spectacle, which used spectacle to reproduce the power of the existing state and social system. The spectacle of terror, by contrast, comes from outside of the existing social system and is used to demonstrate vulnerability and to inculcate fear. It thus intends to weaken existing societies and has become a force that has been undermining democracy, especially as the Bush-Cheney administration manipulates fear and pushes through an extremist agenda that indeed is highly antidemocratic.

Giroux mainly focuses on spectacles of terror deployed by Islamist radicals, but there is a kinship to the spectacles of terror that I explore in this book, as both forms of terrorism, external and domestic, operate outside the spheres of regular politics and seek to gain media attention, circulate fear, and assault U.S. society. In addressing school shootings and domestic terrorism, I am not, however, offering a causal explanation that one major factor is responsible for these events. Rather, there is a constellation of interacting factors that provokes events like the Oklahoma City bombings or the Blacksburg, Virginia, shootings. The project is thus diagnostic and interpretive, rather than attempting to argue for one master key and to offer simplistic explanations.

Although I argue for a multicausal and multifactor analysis, I want to isolate key elements of domestic terrorism and school shootings and point to some possible solutions to the problems. While I interrogate some of the major sources of violence in U.S. society, there are other sources that I do not explore, such as cultures of violence caused by poverty; military socialization; sports culture and attendant bullying, especially in high school; family violence and abuse; and prisons, which are schools for violence. Occasionally, these topics emerge in my discussions but I want to focus on the primary role of guys and guns amok in the following chapters.[21]

In This Book

> If we do not change our direction, we are likely to end up where we are heading.
>
> *—ancient proverb*

In this book, I first engage the spectacle of the Virginia Tech massacre and put it in the context of the domestic terrorism of the Oklahoma City bombing, the Unabomber, and the Columbine High School and other recent school shootings. From the first days of the Virginia Tech shootings, different ideologues, political forces, and politicians exploited the spectacle, using it to promote their agendas, illustrating my concept of media spectacle as contested terrain. I am highly critical throughout of right-wing commentary and exploitation of the Virginia Tech massacre, the Oklahoma City bombing, and the Columbine shootings. I agree with David Brock (2004) that a right-wing conservative "noise machine" has poisoned our political discourse and undermined our democracy over the past years and I will illustrate this with examples of right-wing exploitation of school shootings and other media spectacles.

Using the resources of critical social theory and cultural studies, I indicate in Chapter 1 how various groups have manipulated the spectacle of the Virginia Tech massacre to advance their own agendas, and I argue against one-sided and reductive explanations of the spectacle and for interpretation from a multiplicity of perspectives.

In Chapter 2, I provide an overview of "The Situation of Contemporary Youth" to make it clear that Seung-Hui Cho should not be used to stigmatize contemporary youth, nor should youth culture be demonized. Although Cho's rampage is an anomaly that is atypical of youth today, it can be seen as a portent of a disturbing set of social problems.

I follow by engaging "Constructing Male Identities and the Spectacle of Terror" in Chapter 3 with discussion of Timothy McVeigh, the Unabomber, and the Columbine shooters, indicating that there are serious problems with alienated youth and young men in contemporary U.S. society that are likely to become more severe, and that alienated youth can emerge from white working- or middle-class cultures, leading me to interrogate race, class, and whiteness in contemporary societal violence. I then return to the Virginia Tech shootings with an analysis of the pressures of masculinity and his Korean American ethnicity on Seung-Hui Cho. In Chapter 3, I also discuss Michael Moore's *Bowling for Columbine* and the debates on the Columbine shootings that provided a template for the media construction and debates over the Virginia Tech shootings. Finally, the concluding chapter "What Is To Be Done?" will follow the debates that have emerged over the Virginia Tech massacre, critically engage proposed solutions, and offer alternative positions on gun control, mental health, school security, militarism, prisons, and ways to address excessive societal violence in the United States.

Let me make it clear that I emphatically do not want to scapegoat youth or any particular group or class of people for the Virginia Tech or other school shootings. I do not support the proliferation of surveillance systems such as followed the Columbine shootings that put metal detectors in buildings and that subjected individuals to the kind of harassment and problematic procedures in place at airports.[22] Schools need to be open institutions of learning and communities where there is a basis of trust. Yet problems need to be acknowledged and addressed concerning school and workplace security that need to be taken very seriously, issues I take up in the conclusion.

I should add also that this is not an antimale polemic. Many of my best friends are men, and it is my position in this book that what the sociocultural and political system has done to men in constructing a model of violent masculinity is the problem, not men per se. Men pay a price for aggressive hypermasculinity. Moreover, Susan Faludi argues in *Stiffed* (1999) that the crisis in masculinity was intensified in the changing socioeconomic conditions since World War II, in which the culture presented false ideals for men to live up to. In a highly sympathetic analysis of men's plight in the postwar economy, Faludi notes that masculine ideals mutated in the postwar era from a prewar Western ideal of the westerner surviving in and controlling the wilderness, often through the gun culture and aggression. This was appropriate to the era of the frontier, but during World War II, a new ideal emerged of the foot-soldier memorialized by Ernie Pyle who fought bravely and valiantly for his country, was part of a unit that worked together, and then returned to be a husband and father to the next generation—an ideal recently put on display in Ken Burns's populist epic *War* (PBS 2007), which focused on ordinary people and their bonding experience during World War II.

Faludi points out that after the war, men were given a new "mission to manhood" with a new frontier (space exploration), a new enemy to fight (Soviet communism), a new brotherhood (corporations and government agencies), and "the promise of a family to provide for and protect" (1999: 26). Men were let down in all of these promises: space exploration was not a unifying ideal and the Russians got into space first with Sputnik, dealing a blow to American manhood; the Cold War got the United States mired in unpopular wars such as Korea and Vietnam with no clear-cut victory, and for many soldiers and their families produced devastation and personal defeat; corporations and government allowed "downsizing, restructuring, union-breaking, contracting-out, and outsourcing" (1999: 30), and thus the loss of job and economic security, as Faludi documents throughout her book. Many men would therefore not be able to provide for their families as they lost their jobs and suffered downward mobility; meanwhile women challenged them in the home during the second wave of feminism.[23]

A personal aside: I was scheduled to lecture at Virginia Tech the week after the shootings. The day of the event, April 16, 2007, I was e-mailing a colleague in Blacksburg concerning what I should focus my public lecture on and then clicked onto the *New York Times* website and learned with horror about the Virginia Tech slaughter. I was extremely concerned when I heard there were shootings in a building where language and humanities classes were being offered since I personally knew people in those departments. I therefore followed the event closely and began analysis as it was unfolding, putting in files material from the traditional media and alternative sources like blogs and a variety of websites, as well as new media sources like MySpace and YouTube. I soon learned that none of my friends there were killed, but I shared the sorrow with the Virginia Tech community and was deeply touched by the event. I therefore decided to write an analysis of the media spectacle of the event that would be critical and diagnostic, rather than simply telling the narrative story of the event.

These school shootings and acts of domestic terrorism are signs of the times and interconnected with fundamental social processes and events of the contemporary era, such as the deadly proliferation of gun and military culture, especially after 9/11 and during the Bush-Cheney administration; the rise of spectacles of murder and terror during a period of expanding media and a tabloidization of news and information, accompanied by proliferating representations of violence and murder on television, film, and new media like the Internet; and an expansion of societal violence on the local and global scale. Since Vietnam, the United States has been engaged in constant military interventions, especially during the Bush-Cheney years, of which the Cho rampage can be seen as part of the escalating societal violence of the era. Since the 1980s there has been an expansion of military culture accompanied by the epidemic of school shootings and domestic terrorism in the 1990s, the threat of which continues apace, and perhaps even more intensely, today.

Rhodes (1999) discusses how killers are desensitized to suffering and "violentized," becoming susceptible to committing acts of violence. It could be that the Vietnam and two Gulf wars and proliferating representations of violence helped produce a "violentized" society and individuals for whom violence is a "normal" mode of conflict resolution and self-assertion, revealing a crisis in values, culture, and consciousness that I will engage throughout this book.

Thus, the societal violence and events under interrogation in the following pages reveal fundamental social conditions, processes, and problems in the United States today. The events are not anomalies, random contingencies, or incomprehensible acts of irrationality and horror entering into an otherwise harmonious and stable society. Rather they are a sign of social problems, conflicts, and pathologies that point to problems that need addressing and social change that needs to be carried out. Hence, their interrogation should provide crucial insights into the present age, and they are part of a critical theory of the contemporary moment on which I have been working for decades.

Although crises of masculinity and male rage will play an important part in my analyses, there is a rational and justified component to rage, if it is rage against injustice, oppression, or violence itself. Rage thus has critical, rational, and oppositional moments when directed toward injustice and negating oppression, but it also has its irrational, destructive, and perhaps even psychotic sides. In *Going Postal* (2005), Mark Ames describes the "rage, murder, and rebellion" in workplace and school shootings since the 1980s as rooted in the selfishness, greed, growing disparities between haves and have nots, and attacks on unions and the working class in the Reagan administration, conditions accelerating dramatically in the Bush-Cheney years. Although one might agree with Ames that school and workplace oppression breed violence in these sites, it is a stretch to overuse comparisons with slave rebellions, as he does (2005: 29ff.), as it is usually innocent coworkers or classmates who are the victims. Although rage against social injustice is certainly justified, certain forms of male rage I will discuss have become extremely dangerous and destructive and, as I suggest, we need to seek ways to deal with this problem by reconstructing masculinity apart from violent and destructive forms.

After my initial analysis of the Virginia Tech massacre, I followed its aftermath on several websites, including the Virginia Tech newspaper, *Collegiate Times,* at http://www.collegiatetimes.com; the *Washington Post,* which has closely followed the story at http://www.washingtonpost.com/wp-dyn/content/linkset/2007/04/16/LI2007041600797.html; a website that collects a variety of "Virginia Tech News" stories at http://thatsthenewthing.com/va_tech; and a Virginia Tech Archive at http://www.april16archive.org/news/ (all accessed on July 19, 2007). There has been, however, a surprising paucity of investigative reporting or informed discussions of the shootings in their aftermath in comparison with, say, the Columbine shootings, which had nearly 10,000 stories dedicated to the event and its aftermath in the 50 largest newspapers (Newman et al., 2004: 49) and was debated for years afterward. Part of the reason may be that many in the Virginia Tech community chose to shun the media and not publicly discuss the event. There will probably be, however, many academic and popular studies of the event, of which this study will be one of the first.[24]

Virginia governor Timothy M. Kaine convened a state panel shortly after the April 16 Virginia Tech shootings to investigate the tragedy, and the panel released its report on August 30, 2007.[25] Described as "hard-hitting" by the *Chronicle of Higher Education,*[26] the 147-page report with multiple appendices sharply criticized the Virginia Tech administration for decisions made before and after the shootings, concluding that university officials missed indications of Cho's mental health problems, misunderstood privacy laws concerning shared information, and could have saved lives if they had immediately warned students after the first shooting. The report made more than 90 recommendations calling for better mental health care; improved communication among medical, legal, and school authorities concerning troubled students; more coordinated emergency preparedness; clearer and tighter gun control laws; and other measures I will discuss in Chapter 4. First, however, I want to discuss the problems of school shootings and domestic terrorism in contemporary U.S. society.

Chapter One

Deconstructing the Spectacle: Race, Guns, and the Culture Wars

IN THIS CHAPTER, I examine the construction of the media spectacle of the "Virginia Tech massacre"; how specific groups and individuals exploited the spectacle for ideological ends; and how race, male rage, youth alienation, school safety, mental health, and guns have emerged as key issues in the event. My analysis unfolds chronologically from the day of the shootings through the first week, before taking up the aftermath and subsequent events in later chapters, where I attempt to contextualize the tragic shootings and indicate the social and cultural conditions out of which they emerge.

The Shootings and the Politics of Race

> "The Virginia Tech killer was Korean, not American."
> —*Bill O'Reilly*

Initial media reports indicated that there was a shooting in a dormitory on the Virginia Tech campus shortly after 7:00 a.m. on April 16, 2007. The first word was that it apparently involved a romantic clash in which a young woman and her resident dorm adviser were shot and the boyfriend was under suspicion. At the initial news conference after the first shooting, Virginia Tech president Charles Steger stated that authorities initially believed the murder in the West Ambler Johnston dormitory was a domestic dispute and that the gunman had left campus.[1] Apparently, police who arrived at the dormitory questioned the roommate of the young woman, Emily Hilscher, who was the first victim of the day. The roommate said that Hilsher's boyfriend had just dropped her off and that he was a well-known gun enthusiast. This led the Virginia Tech police and administrators to believe that it was a lovers' quarrel gone awry, thus falling prey to a stereotype of media culture.

Approximately two hours after the West Ambler Johnson shootings, reports came in that a shooter had entered Norris Hall, which houses the Engineering Science and Mechanics Department and was at the time also the site of many humanities courses, and had begun a killing rampage. Suddenly, it was clear that a major media event was under way, and representatives from all the major U.S. broadcast networks and print publications rushed crews to the scene, as did many foreign media.

Throughout the United States, and indeed the world, websites like www. nytimes.com highlighted reports indicating that over 30 students and faculty were killed and that the gunman had shot himself, setting off a media frenzy that involved old and new media. Virginia Tech information websites like www. Planetblacksburg.com and the student newspaper site, www.collegiatetimes. com, were inundated with hits, and many student observers of the horror posted on these or other Internet sites, or on their Facebook or MySpace pages. One enterprising young student, Jamal Albarghouti, used his mobile phone to capture the sounds of gunshots coming out of Norris Hall and images of the police breaking in. After filming the events, Albarghouti sent his recording to CNN, which placed it on its online I-reports site where it was watched by millions. CNN quickly broadcast it on air, where it was replayed repeatedly and then shown by other networks. Jamal was described by CNN as their "I-reporter," interviewed throughout the day, and featured in a segment on the *Larry King Live* show.

Dan Gilmor, author of the popular citizen journalism text *We The Media,* noted: "We used to say that journalists write the first draft of history. Not so, not any longer. The people on the ground at these events write the first draft."[2] Gilmore perhaps exaggerates, but it is true that old and new media now work in tandem to piece together breaking stories, with "citizen journalists" supplementing regular journalists and bloggers supplementing corporate media pundits.

As people throughout the world accessed traditional media sources and new media, so too did corporate media reporters check out MySpace and YouTube and use material drawn from these and other new media sources. As young people from Virginia Tech circulated cell phone video and images, as well as first-person accounts put up on their own new media spaces, it was clear that new media were now playing an important role in the time of the spectacle by constructing representations of contemporary events. Old media had lost its monopoly and was forced to rely on new media, while a variety of voices and images previously omitted from the corporate media found their own sites of dissemination, discussion, and debate for, as we will see, better and worse.

Every major news corporation rushed crews and top network broadcasting reporters to Blacksburg in one of the most highly saturated media sites of all time. Estimates placed more than 600 reporters and 4 or 5 acres of satellite television trucks on the scene at the peak of the coverage.[3]

The shooter was at first described as an "Asian male," leading to a flurry of speculation. Initial racialized attributions of the killer in a mass-murder spectacle often play on deeply rooted racism. In the Oklahoma City bombings of 1994, initial allegations targeted Arab, Middle Eastern perpetrators, setting off a paroxysm of racism. When it was discovered that the villain was a white American, Timothy McVeigh, who had fought in the Gulf War, there was shock and disbelief (see Chapter 3).

Likewise, on the day of the Virginia Tech shooting, as *Media Matters* reports:

> Right-wing pundit Debbie Schlussel "speculat[ed]" in an April 16 weblog post that the shooter, who had been identified at that point only as a man of Asian descent, might be a "Paki" Muslim and part of "a coordinated terrorist attack." "Paki" is a disparaging term for a person of Pakistani descent.
>
> Schlussel wrote, "The murderer has been identified by law enforcement and media reports as a young Asian male," adding, "The Virginia Tech campus has a very large Muslim community, many of which are from Pakistan." Schlussel continued: "Pakis are considered 'Asian,'" and asked, "Were there two [shooters] and was this a coordinated terrorist attack?" Schlussel asserted that the reason she was "speculating that the 'Asian' gunman is a Pakistani Muslim" was "[b]ecause law enforcement and the media strangely won't tell us more specifically who the gunman is." Schlussel claimed that "[e]ven if it does not turn out that the shooter is Muslim, this is a demonstration to Muslim jihadists all over that it is extremely easy to shoot and kill multiple American college students." (Quoted from http://mediamatters.org/items/200704170006)

Soon after, the media began reporting that the murderer was "a Chinese national here on a student visa,"[4] which led Schlussel and right-wing bloggers to find "[y]et another reason to stop letting in so many foreign students." Some conservative bloggers talked of how young Chinese receive military training and that this could account for the mayhem, while other right-wing websites and commentators argued that the Virginia Tech event showed the need for tougher immigration laws.[5]

When the killer was identified as a "South Korean national," Seung-Hui Cho, and "a South Korean who was a resident alien in the United States," racist comments emerged about the violent authoritarianism of Koreans.[6] Frightened Korean students began leaving the Virginia Tech campus, Korean communities everywhere grieved, and the president of South Korea made a formal apology.[7]

This apology was not enough for the likes of Fox TV's Bill O'Reilly, who argued that "the Virginia Tech killer was Korean, not American."[8] When Jam Sardar, an Iranian American and correspondent for Comcast Network, went on Fox News Channel's *O'Reilly Factor* on April 20, 2007, to discuss the question of whether representation of Cho's ethnicity was overplayed, O'Reilly did most of the talking, argued that Cho's ethnicity deserved top billing, and denied that Arab Americans were victims of any significant backlash after September 11, leading Sardar to comment: "Thanks for letting me listen."

There were also speculations throughout the first day that Cho had not acted alone and that there was a second shooter. On the 8:00 p.m. CNN *Paula Zahn Now* show, Zahn and her CNN correspondent Brianna Keilar repeatedly speculated about a second suspect, confusing what officials described as "a person of interest," probably the boyfriend of the young woman shot in the first dorm murder, with a possible second suspect. Zahn, Keilar, and others on the show spoke of intense anger of Virginia Tech students that there was not an alert by the administration after the first shooting, a theme that disappeared from the media soon thereafter.

Early revelations about the shooter profiled Cho as a loner who seemed to have few if any friends and who generally avoided contact with other students and teachers. There were reports that he had left a rambling note directed against "rich kids," "deceitful charlatans," and "debauchery," which police found in his dorm room and which commentators used to characterize the event as unspecific revenge killings.

The first representation of Cho portrayed a static photo of an unsmiling, shy, sad, and rather ordinary young man in glasses, which replicated a certain stereotype of Asian American males as nerdy, awkward, and self-effacing, but also nonthreatening. Classmates interviewed on television indicated that he rarely spoke and that few knew him. Other reports recounted his extreme alienation, starting in high school. There were reports that in high school Cho was mocked for the way that he spoke. According to a student at Virginia Tech, Chris Davids, who went to high school with Cho:

Once, in English class, the teacher had the students read aloud, and when it was Cho's turn, he just looked down in silence, Davids recalled. Finally, after the teacher threatened him with an F for participation, Cho started to read in a strange, deep voice that sounded "like he had something in his mouth," Davids said.

"As soon as he started reading, the whole class started laughing and pointing and saying, 'Go back to China,'" Davids said.[9]

While there were reports of bullying at middle and high school and in a Christian youth group that Cho participated in,[10] there was no evidence that he was bullied at Virginia Tech where it appears he initially tried to fit in. Yet Cho was obviously haunted by demons and insecurities evident in his writings, two of which from a writing class were posted on the Internet.[11] These texts and previous work in his writing classes had deeply disturbed other students who had access to them, leading one of his teachers to confront the English Department chairman about Cho. Professor Lucinda Roy, a distinguished English professor and then chair of the department, agreed to work with him personally, but Cho was unresponsive, leading Roy and others to advise him to seek campus counseling in 2005, an event to which I will return later in the narrative.

As the media spectacle unfolded during the first days, it was generally overlooked that the massacre could be seen as an attempt by Cho to act out some of his violent fantasies and create a media spectacle in which he appears as producer, director, and star. Just as al-Qaeda has been orchestrating terror events to promote their jihadist agenda, and the Bush-Cheney administration orchestrated a war in Iraq to promote its geopolitical agenda, so too have individuals carried through spectacles of terror to seek attention or revenge or to realize violent fantasies.

In 1995, Timothy McVeigh participated in the bombing of the federal building in Oklahoma City, killing hundreds and unleashing a major media spectacle of the era—linked to the deadly U.S. government attack on a religious compound in Waco a year before (see Chapter 3).[12] Almost exactly four years to the day after the Oklahoma City bombing, two teenage middle-class white boys, Eric Harris and Dylan Klebold, went on a shooting rampage at Columbine High in Littleton, Colorado, before taking their own lives (see Chapter 3). Hence, perhaps not by accident the Columbine High shootings took place on April 20, while the Oklahoma City bombings took place on April 19, 1995, on the anniversary of the government siege of Waco that killed members of a religious community some years before. While Cho's April madness preceded the April 19–20 nexus by a couple of days, he joined a constellation of American domestic male terrorists that call attention to serious social problems of guys and guns amok in contemporary U.S. society that need to be clearly perceived and addressed.

A Convocation and Cho's Multimedia Dossier

> "You have vandalized my heart, raped my soul and torched my conscience. You thought it was one pathetic boy's life you were extinguishing. Thanks to you, I die like Jesus Christ, to inspire generations of the weak and the defenseless people."
>
> —*Seung-Hui Cho*

The cable news networks were covering the "Virginia Tech massacre," as it quickly became designated, in wall-to-wall coverage. When George W. Bush agreed to speak at a convocation at Virginia Tech on April 17, along with the Virginia governor, the two state senators, and a congressional delegation, the major broadcasting networks put aside their soap operas and daytime programming and covered the convocation live, making it a major media event.

Although George W. Bush had avoided going to funerals for victims of his Iraq war for years, he arrived ready to make a speech and then do interviews, with his enabling spouse by his side, with the network broadcasting news anchors who had assembled in Blacksburg for the event. Bush was at a critical time in his presidency. His Iraq policy was opposed by the majority of the public, and the Democrats appeared ready to fight Bush on his failed policy. In the November 2006 congressional elections, Republicans lost control of the House and the Senate, and committees in both chambers were investigating a series of scandals in the Bush administration. Bush's attorney general and one of his closest operatives, Alberto Gonzalez, was caught up in scores of scandals, and there were calls for his resignation that would mushroom by July into calls for Bush's impeachment. Questions concerning Bush's competence were intensifying, and it appeared that his last months in office would be conflicted ones.

Yet, in 1995 it appeared that Bill Clinton's presidency had failed and was collapsing after Republicans won control of Congress in the 1994 off-term elections, and when talk radio was fiercely savaging the Clintons and inventing scandals like the so-called Whitewater affair (see Lyons and Conason 2001). It is believed that after the tragedy of the Oklahoma City bombings Clinton reconnected with the public and his ratings went up steadily from that time, taking him handily through the 1996 presidential elections and enabling him to survive a major sex and impeachment scandal (see Kellner 2003a).

Could Bush also establish himself as mourner in chief, and would the public rally around him as they did after 9/11? Bush's speech, live on all the major U.S. television networks, followed Virginia governor Timothy Kaine's. Kaine took an Old Testament approach, speaking of Job and his sufferings and the mysteries of faith. Bush, by contrast, took a New Testament line, speaking of the love and care of God for his people, suggesting that belief in God and the power of prayer would get them through their ordeal. His carefully crafted sound bite read: "Today our nation grieves with those who have lost loved ones at Virginia Tech. We hold the victims in our hearts. We lift them up in our prayers. And we ask a loving God to comfort those who are suffering." After a few further clichés and generalities from Bush, members of the local Christian, Muslim, Jewish, and even Buddhist faith got a few minutes of national airtime to pitch their religions, before the convocation turned inward to Virginia Tech concerns and the major broadcasting networks cut off their coverage.

Bush and his wife, Laura, were interviewed for the major news networks that night, and it was clear that he was not even going to consider stricter gun control laws. By the weekend, the buzz word for his administration was "mental health," a safe topic that could replace gun control for national debate and political action. It is unlikely that Bush's performance as consoler in chief would help him much, as the following day there were some of the most deadly bombings in the Iraq war. By the end of the week, hundreds of Shiites were dead from terrorist bombings, Shia politicians were pulling out of the government, and it appeared the Iraq debacle was worsening. And on Thursday, April 19, 2007, a congressional grilling of Bush's attorney general Alberto Gonzalez produced such an inept and embarrassingly incompetent performance that even conservative Republicans were calling for his resignation, which eventually led to his resigning in August 2007.

Meanwhile, intense media focus continued to unravel facts about the assassin Cho, his victims and their acts of heroism, and failures of the Virginia Tech administration to deal with Cho and his extreme and eventually explosive problems. A multimedia package that Cho mailed to *NBC News* on April 16, apparently after the first murders in the dorm, and was widely shown on April 18, revealed that Cho indeed had planned a media spectacle in the tradition of the Columbine shooters, whom he celebrated as "martyrs."[13]

A picture and video gallery in the multimedia dossier sent to NBC is said to have contained a DVD that held 27 video clips, 43 captioned still photos, and an 1,800-word document that set out the rant that was reported on the first day.[14] The material made it clear that Cho was planning to carry out a plan that he himself had constructed as the massacre at Virginia Tech. One of the photos in which Cho posed with a hammer in his hand reprises the Korean "Asian Extreme" film *Oldboy* (2004),[15] which itself is a revenge fantasy in which a young Korean inexplicably imprisoned in a room goes out on a rampage of revenge against his captors. Another pose shows Cho pointing a gun at his own head, an iconic image of *Oldboy*, which in turn is quoting Robert de Niro's famous scene in *Taxi Driver* (1976), where he follows a slaughter of perceived villains with a suicidal blowing apart of his head, just as Cho did. Further, as Stephen Hunter argues, much of the iconography in the photo gallery quotes poses in films by Hong Kong action director John Woo, as in the images where Cho holds two guns in his hands or points a gun at a camera. Further, Cho brandishes Beretta and Glock guns of the type featured in Woo's movies, which include *The Killer,* where a professional assassin goes down a corridor, enters a room, and systematically mows down its occupants.[16]

The transformation of Cho's image was striking. The shy, nerdy student was suddenly aggressively staring in the camera with cold and calculating eyes, tightly holding guns, wearing a black baseball cap backward, fingerless black gloves, and a black T-shirt under a khaki photographer-style vest. When he spoke in a mocking monotone, he spit out belligerent taunts and verbal assaults at all and sundry, laced with obscenities. Cho's construction of a violent masculinity is apparent in the gap between the first still photo and his multimedia dossier when he assumes the guises and paraphernalia of an alpha dog, ultramacho man. The very exaggeration and hyperbole of the dossier, hardly a "manifesto" as Brian Williams of NBC described it when he introduced it to a shocked nation, calls attention to the constructedness and artificiality of hypermasculinity in U.S. society. Further, his extreme actions call attention to the potential destructiveness and devastation in assuming an ultramacho identity. Since Cho was apparently not able to construct a normal student and male identity, he obviously resorted to extremity and exaggeration.

Cho's literary expressions in his dossier and personal symbols also point to an aesthetic of excess. Earlier reports indicated that Cho had written in ink "Ismail Ax" on his arm. The "Ismail Ax" reference led some conservatives to conclude that Cho was inspired by Islam. Jonah Goldberg, for instance, speculated that:

> First it was Johnny Muhammad, now it was Cho Sueng [sic] Hui a.k.a. Ismail Ax. Precisely how many mass shooters have to turn out to have adopted Muslim names before we get it? Islam has become the tribe of choice of those who hate American society.... I'm talking about the angry, malignant, narcissist loners who want to reject their community utterly, to throw off their "slave name"

and represent the downtrodden of the earth by shooting their friends and neighbors.

This morning I read that the Virginia Tech shooter died with the name Ismail Ax written in red ink on his arm. The mainstream press doesn't seem to have a clue as to what this might mean. To quote Indiana Jones, "Didn't any of you guys go to Sunday School?"[17]

But on the evening of April 18, NBC reported that the package with the multimedia dossier was addressed as sent from "A. Ishmael." The latter literary spelling of the Old Testament and Koranic "Ismail" could refer to the opening of Herman Melville's classic *Moby Dick,* where the narrator begins with "Call me Ishmael." This reading would position the shooter as on a revenge quest, as was Captain Ahab against the White Whale, Moby Dick. But it also positions Cho himself within the great tradition of American literature, as Ishmael is the narrator of one of the major American novels. Another Internet search noted that the literary character Ishmael is also "tied to James Fenimore Cooper's novel 'The Prairie,' Ishmael Bush is known as an outcast and outlawed warrior, according to an essay written in 1969 by William H. Goetzmann, a University of Texas History professor. In Cooper's book, 'Bush carries the prime symbol of evil—the spoiler's axe,' the professor wrote."[18]

Perhaps the Ismail Ax moniker positions Cho as well in the tradition of Hollywood and Asian Extreme gore films featuring Ax(e) murderers, as other photos in his dossier show him with knives and hammer in hand, iconography familiar from horror and gore films, which he had apparently studied.[19] Yet, Ismail/Ishmael is also a biblical name, prominent in both the Judaic and Muslim religions. As Richard Engel points out: "Ismail is the Koranic name of Abraham's firstborn son. In one of the central stories of the Koran, God orders Abraham (called Ibrahim) to sacrifice Ismail as a test of faith, but then intervenes and replaces him with a sheep. Muslims reenact this story by sacrificing a sheep on Eid al-Adha (feast of the sacrifice) during the Hajj, the annual pilgrimage to Mecca."[20]

Cho's references in his text thus span high and low culture and various religious and literary traditions in a postmodern pastiche.[21] The references to Christ in his rambling "manifesto" position Cho himself as sacrificial and redemptive, although he also blames Jesus for his rampage, writing—in a phrase from the epigraph above—that: "Thanks to you, I die like Jesus Christ, to inspire generations of the weak and the defenseless people." But then: "Jesus loved crucifying me. He loved inducing cancer in my head, terrorizing my heart and ripping my soul all this time."

Another excerpt from his text positions Cho as a domestic terrorist carrying out a revenge fantasy when he writes: "You had a hundred billion chances and ways to have avoided today.... But you decided to spill my blood. You forced me into a corner and gave me only one option. The decision was yours. Now you have blood on your hands that will never wash off." The "you" in the message seems to refer to all the fellow students and teachers who failed to grasp his creative genius and who ridiculed his writings and behavior. "You" also could refer to you and me more generally as part of a culture that Cho could come to violently and psychotically reject, although "you" could also refer to the media as his inspiration, for his sick murder rampage was clearly based on media culture and its vehicle was media spectacle.

Cho thus can be seen as a domestic terrorist assassin in the tradition of Timothy McVeigh, the Unabomber, and the two Columbine shooters (see Chapter 3), the last of whom he mentions in the text as "martyrs." Richard Engel, NBC's Middle East bureau chief, noted in the *MSNBC World Blog* that Cho's "testimony" videos were grimly reminiscent of suicide bombers who left videos explaining their actions and trying to justify themselves with grievances and higher purposes.[22] But Cho also positions himself as a vehicle of class revenge: "You had everything you wanted. Your Mercedes wasn't enough, you brats. Your golden necklaces weren't enough, you snobs. Your trust fund wasn't enough. Your vodka and Cognac weren't enough. All your debaucheries weren't enough. Those weren't enough to fulfill your hedonistic needs. You had everything."

The ensuing media spectacle apparently achieved what the crazed Cho had in mind, a spectacle of terror in the manner of the 9/11 terror attacks that attracted scores of media from all over the world to Blacksburg in saturation coverage of the event. His carefully assembled multimedia package revealed to the world who Cho was and won for him a kind of sick and perverted immortality, or at least tremendous notoriety in the contemporary moment.

There was a fierce, albeit partially hypocritical, backlash against NBC for releasing the media dossier and making a potential hero and martyr out of Cho. No doubt, any network getting such a scoop would broadcast it in the current frenetic competition for media ratings, and all of the networks gave saturation coverage to the dossier, each image of which was burned with the NBC logo, just as earlier video camera footage of the gunshots echoing from Norris Hall all contained the CNN logo.

Cho was media savvy enough to know that NBC (or any television network) would broadcast his material, while it is well known that the police in the Columbine shootings only later released small portions of the killers' videos and writings. It should also be pointed out that Cho's videography and picture posing replicated the form of young people's postings on sites like MySpace or Facebook, while his video is similar to the kinds of postings young people put on YouTube. Previously, Cho's Facebook nom de plume was QuestionMark?, a phrase he also used in text-messaging. Now the world had at least some idea who Seung-Hui Cho really was, although many question marks remain.

Guns and Political Scapegoating

> "Guns have little or nothing to do with juvenile violence .... The causes of youth violence ... are daycare, the teaching of evolution and working mothers who take birth control."
> —*Tom DeLay, former House Republican majority leader and convicted felon*

Every time that there is a significant school, university, or workplace shooting, there is discussion of the need for stricter gun laws, but after some brief discussion the issue disappears. After Virginia governor Timothy Kaine returned to Blacksburg from a Tokyo trade conference on April 17, for the Virginia Tech convocation, he announced that he would appoint a panel at the university's request to review the authorities' handling of the disaster. But, in a widely quoted statement, he warned against making snap judgments and said he had "nothing but loathing" for those who take the tragedy and "make it their political hobby horse to ride."[23]

The progun lobby and right-wing pundits were ready with their ammunition, however, and came out with punditry blazing. Right-wing Internet sites began immediately claiming that the fact that Virginia had banned guns from state universities meant that there were no student shooters able to take down the assailant. I saw this position articulated on MSNBC the day of the shooting itself by a Denver law school professor, with the *MSNBC Live* anchor Amy Robach agreeing that the scale of murder might have been reduced if students were allowed to carry guns. A sane gun authority on the show reacted with horror to the idea of having unrestricted guns on campus, but he was cut off by the anchor and not able to articulate his position. Indeed, consider having a classroom, dormitory, or public university space full of armed students, faculty, or staff who might go off on a sudden whim, and one could easily imagine yet another massacre in a gun-saturated America.

While both sides on the gun controversy tried to get out their points of view, the pro–gun control side was quickly marginalized, as I will show. Initially, however, in Sacha Zimmerman's summary:

Before the blood had even dried at Tech, the gun control debate erupted. Both sides of the issue seemed to be in a race for the first word, for the best spin. "It is irresponsibly dangerous to tell citizens that they may not have guns at schools," said Larry Pratt, executive director of Gun Owners of America. Meanwhile, White House spokeswoman Dana Perino was quick to awkwardly assure the world that the president still believes in the right to bear arms. And Suzanna Hupp, a former Texas state representative and concealed weapons advocate, appeared on CBS's *The Early Show* not 24 hours after the shootings for a debate: "Why are we removing my teachers' right to protect themselves and the children that are in their care?" Her opposition, Paul Helmke, president of the Brady Center to Prevent Gun Violence, swiftly sprung into action: "Let's prevent these folks from getting these guns in the first place.... If they can't get that gun with a high-powered clip that's shooting off that many rounds that quickly, then we're making our community safer."[24]

The corporate broadcasting media, however, allowed few pro–gun control voices to be heard, and few major politicians were speaking out. Representative Carolyn McCarthy (D-NY), whose husband was killed and son seriously injured in a Long Island Rail Road shooting, was on several networks. She urged House leaders to move quickly to push forward stalled legislation that would improve databases that could be used in conducting criminal background checks on potential gun purchasers, an issue she had been pushing for years. While Philip Van Cleave, president of the Virginia Citizens Defense League, conceded that allowing faculty and students to carry guns might not have prevented the rampage, he claimed that at least "they wouldn't die like sheep, ... but more like a wolf with some fangs, able to fight back."[25] The macho right, in fact, attacked the Virginia Tech students for not fighting back more ferociously against the assassin. As *Media Matters* compiled the story:

In the April 18 edition of his daily program notes, called Nealz Nuze and posted on his website, nationally syndicated radio host Neal Boortz asked: "How far have we advanced in the wussification of America?" Boortz was responding to criticism of comments he made on the April 17 broadcast of his radio show regarding the mass shooting at Virginia Tech. During that broadcast, Boortz asked: "How the hell do 25 students allow themselves to be lined up against the wall in a classroom and picked off one by one? How does that happen, when they could have rushed the gunman, the shooter, and most of them would have survived?" In his April 18 program notes, Boortz added: "It seems that standing in terror waiting for your turn to be executed was the right thing to do, and any questions as to why 25 students didn't try to rush and overpower Cho Seung-Hui are just examples of right-wing maniacal bias. Surrender—comply—adjust. The doctrine of the left.... Even the suggestion that young adults should actually engage in an act of self-defense brings howls of protest."

In the April 17 edition of his program notes, Boortz had similarly asked: "Why didn't some of these students fight back? How in the hell do you line students up against a wall (if that's the way it played out) and start picking them off one by one without the students turning on you? You have a choice. Try to rush the killer and get his gun, or stand there and wait to be shot. I would love to hear from some of you who have insight into situations such as this. Was there just not enough time to react? Were they paralyzed with fear? Were they waiting for someone else to take action? Sorry ... I just don't understand."[26]

Boortz and other right-wing macho Rambos dishonor the heroism of professors and students who blocked classroom doors or confronted Cho. For example, a 76-year-old professor, holocaust survivor Liviu Librescu, was killed trying to block the door shut so students could escape out the window. Another professor and his students were able to block the door of their classroom and prevent Cho from entering. Further, there could well be untold tales of heroism, as well as many documented ones.[27] As *Wikipedia* documents, there were many "scenes of mutual help and resistance against the perpetrator":

Professor Liviu Librescu held the door of his classroom, Room 204, shut while Cho attempted to enter it. Librescu was able to prevent the gunman from entering the classroom until his students had escaped through the windows, but was eventually shot five times and killed.

Jocelyne Couture-Nowak tried to save the students in her classroom, after looking Cho in the eye in the hallway. One of the three students who survived from the French class told his family that Couture-Nowak ordered her students to the back of the class for their safety before making an unsuccessful attempt to barricade the door. She was subsequently killed by Cho.

Kevin Granata left his third-floor office of Norris Hall and went down to the second floor as the second round of shootings took place. Reportedly he heard a commotion and went into the hallway to see if he could help anyone. He was killed there by Cho.

Partahi Lumbantoruan attempted to protect fellow students by diving on top of Guillermo Colman. Then Cho walked around the class row by row, shooting people who were apparently still alive, and the second shot killed Lumbantoruan, but Colman was protected by Lumbantoruan's body.

Another student, Zach Petkewicz, barricaded the door of Room 205 with a large table, helping to save 11 lives while Cho shot several times through the door.

Waleed Shaalan, a Ph.D. student in Civil Engineering and Teaching Assistant from Zagazig, Egypt, though badly wounded, distracted the gunman from a nearby student after the gunman had returned to the room a second time in search of signs of life. He was shot a second time and died.

Katelyn Carney, Derek O'Dell, and their friends barricaded the door of the German class after the first attack and attended to the wounded. Cho returned minutes later, but O'Dell and Carney prevented him from reentering the room. Both were injured.[28]

Right-wing response to the Virginia Tech tragedy was both appalling and revealing. As the epigraph to this section indicates, Tom DeLay blamed the Columbine shootings on his favorite liberal targets, and so too did some prominent rightist commentators who took the occasion of the tragedy and intense media spectacle to bash liberals or their favorite ideological targets. *Media Matters* reported that: "On the April 19 broadcast of his nationally syndicated radio show, host Rush Limbaugh declared that the perpetrator of the April 16 Virginia Tech shootings 'had to be a liberal,' adding: 'You start railing against the rich, and all this other—this guy's a liberal. He was turned into a liberal somewhere along the line. So it's liberal that committed this act.'"[29] But it is doubtful Cho had a coherent political ideology, and he clearly inserted himself in the tradition of domestic terrorists including the Columbine shooters and Timothy McVeigh, hardly "liberal," as we shall see.

Professional sixties-basher Thomas Sowell blamed the Virginia Tech and Columbine shootings on 1960s culture and its alleged "collective guilt" that supposedly blamed the urban violence of the decade on society and somehow sent out the message that it was okay to kill people because it's all society's fault.[30] Sowell's failure in argument and reasoning is stunning, as few, if any, make the arguments about the 1960s he claims, and puts on display the simple-minded tendency of right-wing ideologues to blame everything on their own pet peeves and ideological obsessions.

But the most extreme example of rank hypocrisy and political exploitation of the Virginia Tech tragedy was a dual intervention by *Washington Post* columnist Charles Krauthammer. Krauthammer, one of the most enthusiastic advocates of the Iraq war to this day, reasonably wrote in his April 19 *Washington Post* column that it is terribly inappropriate to exploit tragedies like the Virginia Tech shootings to make ideological arguments. But later in the day and less than 48 hours after the shooting, Krauthammer was on *Fox News* exploiting the shootings to promote one of his personal hobby horses. As Glen Green-wald notes in his *Salon* blog, Krauthammer just couldn't help running to *Fox News* "to explain why the Virginia Tech shootings and the killer's 'manifesto' are connected to Al Jazeera, the Palestinians and other Muslim Enemies who dominate Krauthammer's political agenda":

> KRAUTHAMMER: What you can say, just—not as a psychiatrist, but as some-body who's lived through the past seven or eight years, is that if you look at that picture, *it draws its inspiration from the manifestos, the iconic photographs of the Islamic suicide bombers over the last half decade in Palestine, in Iraq and elsewhere.*
>
> That's what they end up leaving behind, either on Al Jazeera or Palestinian TV. And he, it seems, as if his inspiration for leaving the message behind in that way, might have been this kind of suicide attack, which, of course, his was. And he did leave the return address return "Ismail Ax." "Ismail Ax." *I suspect it has some more to do with Islamic terror and the inspiration* than it does with the opening line of Moby Dick [emphasis in original].[31]

In fact, the "Ismail" and "Ishmael" references in Cho's testimony could refer to the Ishmael character in either the Old Testament or the Koran, or it could refer to Moby Dick's narrator, or a hybridized fantasy of Cho's disordered mind. Krauthammer's blaming the massacre on "Al Jazeera, the Palestinians and other Muslim Enemies" gives us insight into Krauthammer's deranged and disordered mind that sees his Muslim enemies at work everywhere from Iraq to Blacksburg, Virginia.

Never missing an opportunity to attack pharmaceuticals, the "church" of Scientology blamed Cho's reported use of antidepressants for the rampage and sent twenty of its "ministers" to Blacksburg to help with the "healing" process. A scientologist spokesperson, Sylvia Stannard, claimed that the killings demonstrate "these mind-altering drugs" make "you numb to other people's suffering. You really have to be drugged up to coldly kill people like that." Indeed, according to a report by George Rush and Joanna Rush Molloy: "Even before Cho's name was released, the Citizens Commission on Human Rights, a group founded by the church [of Scientology], said in a press release that 'media and law enforcement must move quickly to investigate the Virginia shooter's psychiatric drug history—a common factor amongst school shooters.'"[32]

Obviously, Cho had major mental health issues, and serious psychiatrists saw clinical evidence in Cho's dossier, writings, and behavior of classical paranoid schizophrenia,[33] which itself could be genetically generated or the product of some terrible brain disorder, while others saw evidence of depression, acute autism, or various forms of psychosis, or claimed that there was no evidence he suffered from any specific mental illness.[34] Yet such disease may have a multiplicity of causes, and it is often impossible to pinpoint the exact causal etiology, just as shootings like the Columbine rampage have a multiplicity of causes. For instance, medical explanations for individual violence cover over the social problems that school shootings and societal violence call attention to, just as do the repeated evocations by pundits that Cho was simply "insane," and this explains everything, or that he was an exemplar of "radical evil," another popular conservative (mis)explanation.[35]

After school or workplace shootings or similar events that become media spectacles, demands are made for simple explanations, scapegoats, and actions. After the Columbine shootings, certain pundits attacked the Internet, Marilyn Manson, and various forms of goth or punk music and culture, violent films and television, video games, and just about every form of youth culture except bowling. In Cho's case, his alleged earlier interest in video games, his deep Internet fascination, and his seeming affinity for violent movies could lead some to scapegoat these forms of youth culture. This would be, I believe, a serious mistake. Rather than ban media culture from the lives of youth and its study from schools, I would advocate critical media literacy as an essential part of education from early grade school through the university level (see Kellner 1995 and Chapter 4 of this book).

In addition, however, I want to argue for multicausal and multiperspectivist interpretations of events like the Virginia Tech massacre or the Columbine shootings (or, for that matter, political events like the Iraq war [see Kellner 2005]). We still do not know exactly why the Columbine shootings took place and there are no doubt multiple factors ranging from the experiences at school of the extremely alienated teenage boys, to any number of cultural influences, including the culture of violence and violent gun culture in the United States, or to specific familial or individual experiences. As Michael Moore and a father of one of the teenagers shot at Columbine concluded in the film *Bowling for Columbine* (2002), there's no one simple answer to why there is so much gun violence in the United States, but rather a variety of interacting causes, requiring multicausal explanation (see Chapter 3).

Likewise, we may never know why Cho chose to engineer and orchestrate the Virginia Tech massacre, but from his multimedia dossier it is clear that there was a range of influences spanning violent Korean and Asian films, the Columbine shooters to whom he referred as "martyrs," religious texts and references ranging from the Koran to both the Old and New Testaments of the Bible, to possible literary influences. Reports of his life indicate that earlier he was devoted to basketball and video games, and his dorm-mates noted that he spent hours on the computer, often listening repeatedly to certain songs. Such reports were used to attack Internet games,[36] but few criticized his alleged one-time basketball obsession as fuelling murderous fantasies. Moreover, one report indicated that he wrote the lyrics to his favorite Collective Soul song, "Shine," on the walls of his dorm room:

> Teach me how to speak
> Teach me how to share
> Teach me where to go
> Tell me will love be there[37]

While the disappointment of such yearning could inspire rage, it is ludicrous to blame the music, or any one of Cho's media cultural influences, for the Virginia Tech massacre, and pundits who pick out any single influence, usually one of their favorite targets, are irresponsible. Complex events always have a multiplicity of causes and to attempt to produce a single-factor explanation or solution is simplistic and reductive. As noted, Cho also had creative ambitions, understood the workings of the media and media spectacle, and carefully planned his moments of infamy. Virginia governor Kaine's *Report of the Review Panel: Mass Shootings at Virginia Tech* (2007), suggests some other possible reasons for Cho's rampage. Cho's sister told the panel that in his second and third year in college he undertook to become a writer, worked hard on a manuscript, sent a book outline to a New York publisher, and was extremely dejected when it was rejected (*Report of the Review Panel* 2007: 40ff.). A forensic behavioral scientist asked to profile Cho, whose findings were included in the report (Appendix N-1-4), speculated that in this period Cho was consumed by a driving ambition to become a great writer and "probably was devastated" when his proposal was returned "rejected."[38]

No doubt more facts and information may emerge concerning Cho's influences, motivations, and warped actions, but it would be wrong at this time to try to provide a one-sided interpretation or explanation. Yet there is no doubt that Cho became obsessed with guns and violent gun culture during his last days. There are reports that he had thoroughly immersed himself in the culture of gun violence, buying one gun from a local store and another over the Internet, where the seller indicated he appeared to be a highly knowledgeable gun consumer. Cho bought ammunition from the Internet, went to a gym to buff himself up, went to a shooting range to engage in target practice, and thoroughly immersed himself in ultramasculinist gun culture. He was obviously suffering a crisis of masculinity and resolved to overcome it through his ultraviolent shooting spree. Indeed, as I will explore in Chapter 3, there were multiple discernible factors in Cho's life situation that likely drove him to his rampage and infamy.

School and Workplace Security: The Debate Begins

> "It is irresponsibly dangerous to tell citizens that they may not have guns at schools."
> —*Larry Pratt, executive director of Gun Owners of America*

> "Let's prevent these folks from getting these guns in the first place.... If they can't get that gun with a high-powered clip that's shooting off that many rounds that quickly, then we're making our community safer."
> —*Paul Helmke, president of the Brady Center to Prevent Gun Violence*

While right-wing ideologues raved and served up their ideological explanations, serious investigative reporting was attempting to uncover how Cho got his guns and ammunition so readily, why his dangerously explosive alienation was not detected, what institutional measures could be taken to improve school and workplace safety, and what better mental health care could be put in place.

On April 19, there were shocking revelations concerning what university and state officials knew about Cho's disturbing problems. A *New York Times* article by Shaila Dewan and Marc Santora, "Officials Knew Troubled State of Killer in '05," indicated that on November 27, 2005, a female student reported to campus police that Cho had made unwelcome telephone calls and personal communications to her, but she declined to press charges. On December 12, 2005, a second woman asked the police to stop Cho from sending instant messages to her, but she also declined to press charges. Later in the day of the second complaint, an acquaintance of Cho notified the police that he might be suicidal and a medical intervention ensued.[39]

> Mr. Cho went voluntarily to the Police Department, which referred him to a mental health agency off campus, Chief Flinchum said. A counselor recommended involuntary commitment, and a judge signed an order saying that he "presents an imminent danger to self or others" and sent him to Carilion St. Albans Psychiatric Hospital in Radford for an evaluation.

"Affect is flat and mood is depressed," a doctor there wrote. "He denies suicidal ideations. He does not acknowledge symptoms of a thought disorder. His insight and judgment are sound."

The doctor determined that Mr. Cho was mentally ill, but not an imminent danger, and the judge declined to commit him, instead ordering outpatient treatment.

Officials said they did not know whether Mr. Cho had received subsequent counseling.[40]

It had been widely reported that also during 2005 and 2006 a number of Cho's literature professors had tried to seek help for him and reported his aberrant behavior to campus police and administrative authorities. An April 20 article by Marc Santora and Christine Hauser indicated that as many as eight of Cho's teachers in the previous 18 months "had formed what one called a 'task force' to discuss how to handle him, gathering twice on the subject and frequently communicating among themselves." Furthermore: "On at least two separate occasions they reached out to university officials, telling them as recently as this September that Mr. Cho was trouble. They made little headway, however, and no action was taken by school administrators in response to their concerns."[41]

It is astonishing that despite Cho's well-established campus, legal, and institutional mental health record, when complaints were made in 2006 to the Virginia Tech administration by professors in the English Department, no intervention was made on Cho's and the community's behalf. This failure to "connect the dots" is similar to the lack of communication among the FBI, CIA, INS, FAA, and other authorities within the Bush-Cheney administration, who could not connect the disparate information about the terrorists who committed the 9/11 attacks.

A similarly tragic failure of communication appears to have occurred at Virginia Tech, where information about Cho amassed by university police, counselors, and local judicial and mental health authorities was not shared. Virginia Tech seemed to have no central data collection in place concerning its students, and according to the *Report of the Review Panel* (2007), members of the Virginia Tech administration misunderstood the privacy restrictions and did not share or compile Cho's medical records, and many of his medical records turned out to be lost.[42] A failure to cross-reference database information would also become relevant in explaining how Cho was so readily able to buy guns and ammunition, with some, as we see below, arguing that legally he should never have been sold his instruments of murder in the first place.

There were indeed many signs that Cho was deeply and dangerously disturbed; his professors who noted upsetting symptoms in his writing and behavior attempted to engage him. One of his professors concluded that Cho's writings in 2006 became "increasingly unhinged. He submitted two plays to Prof. Edward C. Falco's class that had so much profanity and violent imagery that the other students refused to read and analyze his work. Professor Falco said he was so concerned that he spoke with several faculty members who had taught Mr. Cho."[43]

Another of Cho's professors, Lisa Norris, "who taught Mr. Cho in a 10-student creative writing workshop last fall, was disturbed enough by his writings that she contacted the associate dean of students, Mary Ann Lewis. Ms. Norris said the faculty was instructed to report problem students to Ms. Lewis."[44] According to Norris, Lewis claimed she had no record of any problems with Cho, despite his well-documented classroom and stalking problems. "Ms. Lewis, associate dean of the College of Liberal Arts and Human Sciences, said Wednesday night that she would not comment on Ms. Norris's statement."[45]

It appears that the faculty of the English Department at Virginia Tech acted in a completely responsible manner, but that the university administration is going to have to answer some serious questions on why Cho was not better monitored, documented, and cared for, and why the many reports on his behavior were not shared with the faculty—points all raised in the *Report of the Review Panel* (2007).

In addition, there were reports that there were two bomb threats at Virginia Tech during the two weeks before the massacre that were taken seriously enough to cause class evacuations, and that Cho himself was found with a bomb threat note in his pocket.[46] In the light of these dangers, it is inexplicable why Virginia Tech did not immediately cancel classes and inform the community after the first dorm shooting, instead buying into the story that the incident was a lovers' quarrel turned violent.

A debate also emerged concerning the police response to the shootings. On May 21, 2007, Virginia state police officials announced that Cho was armed with at least 377 rounds of ammunition when he entered Norris Hall. Police said that Cho had fired 174 rounds in the building, killing 30 and wounding 24, and that police recovered 203 live rounds on Cho or scattered on the floor, indicating that he could have killed more people had the police not intervened when they did.[47] While spokesmen for the police claimed that their rapid entry had saved lives, it had previously been reported that approximately nine minutes passed from the time of Cho's first shots in Norris and his suicide, evidently brought on by the police entry, and that five of the minutes were spent breaking through the chains Cho had assembled to lock the door and on planning an assault. Some security analysts, however, indicated that the response should have been faster and more lives would have been saved.[48] As we will see in Chapter 3, one of the scandals of the Columbine shootings was the amount of time it took police to penetrate the buildings, but it appeared that the Virginia Tech police learned from Columbine and attempted to break into Norris Hall immediately once the shooting began.

Mourning, Copycats, and Ideological Manipulation

> "But the tragedies of Virginia Tech—and Columbine, and Nickel Mines, Pennsylvania, where five girls were shot at an Amish school last year—are not the full measure of the curse of guns. More bleakly terrible is America's annual harvest of gun deaths that are not mass murders: some 14,000 routine killings committed in 2005 with guns, to which must be added 16,000 suicides by firearm and 650 fatal accidents (2004 figures). Many of these, especially the suicides, would have happened anyway: but guns make them much easier."
>
> —*Editorial, "America's Tragedy,"* Economist, *April 19, 2007*

There is always a danger of copycat shooting after a major media spectacle like the Virginia Tech massacre, and the day after the shootings there were reports of bomb and shooting threats throughout the country, and schools and campuses were closed in Oklahoma, Tennessee, Texas, and Louisiana.[49] There was danger that impressionable high school students would imitate Cho's rampage, and thus schools and colleges of all types felt threatened. The pattern continued throughout the week, and on Saturday, April 21, 2007, the *Los Angeles Times* reported that "fear of violence at dozens of campuses across California puts people on edge as some arrests are made and schools are closed."[50]

Meanwhile, at Virginia Tech, after the shock of the shooting and while the widespread showing of Cho's video was being absorbed, signs began appearing telling the media that it was time to leave—with one iconic handwritten sign saying: "VT Stay Strong. Media Stay Away." Another student group sent an e-mail to the media telling them it was time for them to leave and for the community to start taking back their campus.[51]

On Friday, April 21, 2007, there was a national day of mourning to honor those massacred at Virginia Tech with memorial services at the university and across the nation. On Saturday, April 21, 2007, the *New York Times* published a story suggesting that "U.S. rules made killer ineligible to purchase gun." The story suggests that Cho should not have been able to purchase the guns he so easily acquired under U.S. gun laws, dramatizing the need both for better laws and stricter enforcement:

> Under federal law, the Virginia Tech gunman Seung-Hui Cho should have been prohibited from buying a gun after a Virginia court declared him to be a danger to himself in late 2005 and sent him for psychiatric treatment, a state official and several legal experts said Friday.
>
> Federal law prohibits anyone who has been "adjudicated as a mental defective," as well as those who have been involuntarily committed to a mental health facility, from buying a gun.
>
> The special justice's order in late 2005 that directed Mr. Cho to seek outpatient treatment and declared him to be mentally ill and an imminent danger to himself fits the federal criteria and should have immediately disqualified him, said Richard J. Bonnie, chairman of the Supreme Court of Virginia's Commission on Mental Health Law Reform.[52]

Obviously, federal and state gun laws are complicated, obscure, and not clear even to authorities. As Representative Carolyn McCarthy (D-NY) has been arguing for years, thousands of guns purchased by mentally instable and otherwise unbalanced people are being found in the hands of people who use them to shoot and kill innocents. Politicians of both parties have been reluctant to take up any gun control debates because of the power of the NRA and gun lobby to the shame of our nation.

The shameful nation was fully on display on the weekend talk shows of April 21–22, where the topic of the moment was the Virginia Tech massacre. On Saturday, April 21, during his weekly broadcast, George W. Bush emphasized that the issue was "mental health," and his right-wing confederates used this topic to decenter the gun control issue. Yet some "no gun control" extremists continued to insist that the problem at Virginia Tech was that it was a "gun-free zone" and that had there been guns allowed, someone could have taken out the shooter. The shameless Newt Gingrich made this argument on the ABC's *This Week* Sunday talk show on April 22, citing examples of towns where shooters were taken down by a local armed citizen. Gingrich was also unembarrassed by a graphic that quoted him after the Columbine shootings in 1999, blaming the tragedy on the "culture of liberalism."[53]

Throughout the afternoon of April 21, similar arguments were made on CNN's *Glen Beck Show,* which featured a bevy of progun spokesmen who blamed the tragedy on the prohibition of guns on campus and provided anecdotal examples of how towns without restrictions on gun use had dealt with would-be assassins.[54] This invocation of the Wild West was followed by an array of cultural conservatives on Beck's shameful show who blamed the shootings on popular culture. These right-to-lifers were passionate in their defense of fetuses and in their assaults on media and youth culture, but they had no sympathy for any gun control (nor would they likely say anything against capital punishment or wars like Iraq, showing the rank and shameless hypocrisy in their "right to life" or "prolife" arguments).

On the *Fox News* Sunday shows the line pushed by Brit Hume and other right-wing ideologues was that the Virginia Tech tragedy was caused by excessive regard for "privacy" and "disability rights," as if Virginia Tech had coddled Cho to preserve his rights (as opposed to being simply incompetent, or not having policies and institutional structures in place to deal with problem students). CNN and Fox commentators also decried "gun-free zones" as a menace to public safety, "the culture of moral relativism," and campus "PC" (i.e., "political correctness" that supposedly allowed the kind of writing in which Cho indulged—whereas, in fact, professors and students in at least four of his writing classes stood up and drew the line against Cho's disturbed rantings).

Monitoring network talk shows for several hours on Sunday, April 22, 2007, revealed almost unopposed supremacy of the right-wing slogans of the day, with only one gun control advocate portrayed, in a brief segment on ABC's *This Week* in which Senator Charles Schumer (D-NY) said that there was now House and Senate bipartisan support for stricter controls on making guns available to individuals with mental health problems.

Tim Russert on NBC's *Meet the Press* can always be counted on to advance the Republican Party talking points of the moment, and Sunday April 22, 2007, was no exception. After some tough questions to Virginia Tech president Charles Steger, Russert talked to two conservative members of the newly appointed Commission on the Virginia Tech Shooting, created by Virginia governor Timothy Kaine, and two cabinet members of the Bush administration who had been appointed as spokespeople for the issue. None of these guests mentioned gun control or had anything constructive to say about the serious problems of school safety evoked by the tragedy, suggesting that it is highly unlikely that establishment politicians will contribute anything to making the schools and country more secure.

After Russert's conservative establishment figures delivered their talking points, *Meet the Press* did have a discussion of whether politicians would take up the issue of gun control, but the panel generally made the point that neither party had any interest in reforming gun laws.[55] While Russert and his guests did not make the point, in fact, the absence of any major politician of either party raising gun control as an issue points to the frightening power of the NRA and gun lobby and the shameful cowardice and lack of principle of leading presidential candidates in both parties. Of the multitude of pundits on the Saturday and Sunday network TV talk shows, almost all were highly conservative and partisan, and I did not see anyone who gave a coherent account of the tragedy on any of the network talk shows. Different right-wing commentators had their special ideological hobbyhorses to ride, but there was no serious debate and no intelligent analysis of the event or serious proposals concerning possible solutions. The corporate media proved themselves to be utterly morally and intellectually bankrupt and a national disgrace, proving the irrelevancy of network corporate television to issues of national importance.

While the corporate media in the United States, especially broadcast media, had little discussion of gun control or criticism of U.S. gun culture, in the foreign press this theme was major. The Virginia Tech massacre was a global spectacle, with front-page news stories and intense broadcasting coverage throughout the world. The BBC, for example, garnered a record number of Internet hits on its website coverage of the story. There were victims of the shootings from five continents and varied commentary on the event from all over the world.[56]

In the neoliberal British *Economist* magazine, an article entitled "America's Tragedy: Its Politicians Are Still Running Away from a Debate about Guns" noted that no major U.S. politician spoke up about gun control after the Virginia Tech tragedy. It indicated that, while disturbed people existed in every society, the difference,

> as everyone knows but no one in authority was saying this week, is that in America such individuals have easy access to weapons of terrible destructive power. Cho killed his victims with two guns, one of them a Glock 9mm semi-automatic pistol, a rapid-fire weapon that is available only to police in virtually every other country, but which can legally be bought over the counter in thousands of gunshops in America. There are estimated to be some 240m[illion] guns in America, considerably more than there are adults, and around a third of them are handguns, easy to conceal and use. Had powerful guns not been available to him, the deranged Cho would have killed fewer people, and perhaps none at all.

Further: "Since the killing of John Kennedy in 1963, more Americans have died by American gunfire than perished on foreign battlefields in the whole of the 20th century. In 2005 more than 400 children were murdered with guns."[57]

Criticisms of U.S. gun laws were echoed in articles and commentary throughout the world, with *Le Monde* (April 17, 2007) noting that for George

W. Bush the tragedy at Blacksburg was just the aberration of an individual that had nothing to do with gun laws. The conservative *London Times* commented on April 18, 2007:

> Perhaps of all the elements of American exceptionalism—those factors, positive or negative, that make the U.S. such a different country, politically, socially, culturally, from the rest of the civilised world—it is the gun culture that foreigners find so hard to understand.
>
> The country's religiosity, so at odds with the rest of the developed world these days; its economic system which seems to tolerate vast disparities of income; even all those strange sports Americans enjoy—all of these can at least be understood by the rest of us, even if not shared.[58]

An editorial in the *Press* (Christchurch, New Zealand, April 19, 2007), indicated that from the great distance of its country's perspective "no-one will doubt the true reason why so much mayhem could be unleashed by an apparently disaffected and socially inept student: the gun culture which is deeply embedded in American life." While expressing sympathy for the victims, the editorial criticized "the absurd willingness with which America allows its citizens to arm themselves. In Virginia itself, about the only constraints on buying firearms, we learn, are a criminal record and a restriction to buying one weapon a month. Perhaps somebody in America can pose a rational, convincing argument as to why that should be so." The editorial unleashed a volley of responses collected on a Nexis-Lexis page ranging from attacks on Kiwis for criticizing their American friends at such a time, to raving defenses of unrestricted gun laws by both New Zealanders and Americans, to attempts to produce a rational discourse on the topic.

A biting critique by an ex-U.S. diplomat, John Brown, however, dared to talk of "the Cho in the White House," suggesting that George W. Bush's reckless and catastrophic invasion and destruction of Iraq was as insane and even more consequential than Cho's violent killing rampage: "As Cho disrupted a small, defenseless college town in Virginia that welcomed him, Bush has dislocated a whole society that was not threatening the United States. Seen from an overseas perspective, there is, as with Cho and his 'enemy,' something megalomaniacal as well as delusional about the President's identification of a vast Soviet-style Islamofascist foe that the U.S. Armed Forces are supposed to face down in the Global War on Terror."[59]

Perhaps both Bush and Cho had "good" intentions or sincerely believed they were fighting "evil," but both were seriously deluded and their actions had terrible destructive consequences. I have previously argued that Bush and bin Laden shared an absolutist and dualistic Manichean vision that saw the world as a battle between good and evil, identified themselves as good, saw their other as evil, projected their own aggressive and violent tendencies upon a foreign "Other," and justified violent extermination of innocents as part of their absolutist Terror War.[60] In his media manifesto, Cho, too, was highly moralistic, excoriating contemporary forms of evil and immorality, while projecting his own confused and aggressive impulses on the world in an utterly pathological paroxysm of hypermasculinity run amok.

Only the alternative press, of course, would compare Cho with Bush, or the deluded invasion of Iraq with Cho's demented murder spree—although Keith Olbermann on his April 17, 2007, MSNBC *Countdown* show did, to his credit, raise the issue of why the country is willing to pay so much attention to a school shooting, while ignoring the fact that as many Americans and far more Iraqis are killing each other almost every day in the shameful Iraq war.[61] Indeed, Iraq and an explosion of global and domestic violence provide the context in which the Virginia Tech massacre took place. Since the ill-fated Bush-Cheney invasion of Iraq in March 2003 there had been a Pandora's box of horrors on nightly television and hundreds of thousands of people killed and displaced in Iraq as refugees. In addition, American cable TV networks, local TV news, and the growing genre of "true crime" documentaries had saturated the country with violence. Cho would thus become one more media icon of America the Violent.

Already by the end of the first week, however, it was clear that conservatives and hard-core gun advocates would make the Virginia Tech massacre an issue of mental health and "privacy" laws, which they were completely willing to exploit to deflect focus from gun culture. As noted, George W. Bush sounded the theme of "mental health" in his weekend address and the right-wing noise machine on Fox, CNN, and other sources were taking up the theme. In a Sunday, April 29, report on CBS's *60 Minutes,* the main spokesman for the NRA made it clear that they would support a ban on selling weapons to those who had been determined by a court to be "mentally incompetent," although *60 Minutes* that day had a representative of a further right-wing extremist gun group who wanted no restrictions on to whom guns could be sold!

A representative of the mental health community on *60 Minutes,* however, indicated that there is a very difficult issue to negotiate concerning what mental health information may be made public to what federal or local agencies, as the information could be misused and abused and might make individuals resist getting needed mental health treatment. As with the issue of individual rights and freedoms versus security, there were hard choices to be made between security and rights concerning federal databases, but it was not clear that any politicians were willing to take on these difficult issues and come up with reasonable solutions.

In the next chapter, I present an analysis of the situation of contemporary youth to indicate that Cho is obviously atypical and that youth culture should not be demonized for his aberrant behavior, but that youth alienation is a serious problem that must be engaged. In Chapter 3, I put Cho in the context of domestic terrorism and male rage, indicating some examples of young men becoming completely alienated and constructing their identities through violent behavior, depicting the emergence of several varieties of the crisis of masculinity and homegrown domestic terrorism. In Chapter 4, I return to the aftermath of the Virginia Tech massacre, indicate how it has been exploited by certain conservative groups and ideologues, and suggest some solutions to the problems posed by events from the Oklahoma City bombings to the Virginia Tech massacre.

Chapter Two

The Situation of Contemporary Youth

COMPREHENDING HORRIFIC EVENTS like the Columbine school shootings and the Virginia Tech massacre requires better understanding of the situation of contemporary youth. Youth are of special importance because it is they who will further shape the world to come. The offspring of the Baby Boomers born in the 1940s and 1950s, their identities are indelibly marked as "post"—post-Boomer, post-1960s, or postmodern. Yet they live in a present marred by extreme uncertainty, facing a future that is murky and unpredictable.

For youth today, change is the name of the game, and they are forced to adapt to a rapidly mutating and crisis-ridden world characterized by novel information, computer, and genetic technologies; a complex and fragile global economy; and a frightening era of war and terrorism. According to dominant discourses in the media, politics, and academic research, the everyday life of growing segments of youth is increasingly unstable, violent, and dangerous. For some, the situation of youth is today marked by the dissolution of the family; growing child abuse and domestic conflict; drug and alcohol abuse; sexually transmitted diseases; poor education and crumbling schools; and escalating criminalization, imprisonment, and even state execution. These alarming assaults on youth are combined with federal cutbacks of programs that might give youth a chance to succeed in an increasingly difficult world.

Hence, today's youth are at risk in a growing number of ways, and survival is a challenge. Ready or not, they will inherit a social world that is increasingly deteriorating and a natural world that is ever more savaged by industrial forces. Yet they also have access to exciting realms of cyberspace and the possibilities of technologies, identities, and entrepreneurial adventures unimagined by previous generations. Contemporary youth in the United States include the best-educated generation in history, the most technically sophisticated, and the most diverse and multicultural—making generalizations about youth in the present day precarious.

To illuminate the situation of contemporary youth, we need a *critical theory of youth* that articulates positive, negative, and ambiguous aspects in their current situation. The situation of youth is analyzed in terms of both hopes and prospects and problems and challenges. A critical theory also delineates some of the defining features of the condition of contemporary youth to indicate the ways that they are encountering the problems and challenges facing them, and to suggest how these might best be engaged.

Obviously a wide diversity of youth experiences exists, involving varying genders, races, classes, sexualities, and social groups. Thus there are major differences within youth groups today, as well as situations that they share in common. In particular, in addition to differences of class and race, there are gender differences between young men and women with very different socialization processes, gender ideals, and relations of power and domination. In the following pages I will first focus generally on the situation of youth and then indicate how some general determinants of the situation of contemporary youth produce male rage and a crisis of masculinity, a theme I explore in this chapter. Although some conservatives blame many of the problems of the contemporary era on youth, I want to make clear in this chapter that it is the situation of contemporary youth that produces many problems for youth and thus for society. Further, while some youth, usually male, become school shooters and domestic terrorists, there are many positive features and examples of youth today who have potential for a better future, as well as dangers of not being able to meet the challenges of the contemporary era.

Within the present social situation, there are grave dangers for youth, but also some enhanced freedoms and opportunities. More positive futures cannot be created, however, unless youth are able to achieve a variety of forms of literacies, including print, media, computer, and multiple literacies that will enable them to engage and help construct contemporary culture and society, a project requiring a reconstruction of education (see Kellner 2002, 2004, and Chapter 4).

Many of today's youth are privileged subjects of the contemporary era because they are the first generation to live intensely in the transformative realms of cyberspace and hyperreality, where media culture, computers, genetic engineering, and other emerging technologies are dramatically transforming all aspects of life (see Best and Kellner 2001). It is a world not only where multimedia technologies are changing the very nature of work, education, and the textures of everyday life but also where previous boundaries are dissolving. Global capitalism is re-structuring and entering an era of crisis, war, and terrorism, and uncertainty, ambiguity, cynicism, and pessimism are becoming dominant moods.

Consequently, the youth of the new millennium are the first generation to live the themes of postmodern theory.[1] Entropy, chaos, indeterminacy, contingency, simulation, and hyperreality are not just concepts they might encounter in a seminar, but forces that constitute the very texture of their experience, as they deal with corporate downsizing and the disappearance of good jobs, economic recession, information and media overload, the demands of a high-tech computer society, crime and violence, identity crises, terrorism, war, and an increasingly unpredictable future. For youth, contemporary life is a wild and dangerous ride, a rapid roller coaster of thrills and spills plunging into the unknown.

In the following section, I discuss some of the labels that have been applied to successive generations of youth in the United States since World War II. Al-though calling some of the dominant sociological labels discussed below into question, I am using the categories and debates about youth to try to clarify the situation of contemporary youth. The goal is to contribute to a critical theory of youth that illuminates both the negative aspects and perils of youth today, as well as hopes and possibilities for a better future, elucidating contradictions in the situation of youth today.

From Boomers to Busters

> "Perhaps the cruelest joke played on our generation is the general belief that if you went to college, you'll get a job and be upwardly mobile."
> —*Steven Gibb*

The prospects for youth have always been problematic, dependent on class, gender, race, nationality, and the concrete sociohistorical environment of the day. "Youth" itself is a social construct that takes on different connotations at different periods in history. As the social historian Philippe Aries reminds us (1962), "childhood" and "youth" are socially constructed conceptions of age and not biological givens. Yet, proving his famous point that childhood is unknown, Rhodes (1999) claims that Aries's *Centuries of Childhood* is "shockingly mistaken" (235). Aries claims that medieval childhood was free and innocent, because childhood was unknown, while modern times brought increasing brutality. Rhodes finds this view completely romanticized and cites the historian Lloyd deMause, who has a sharp critique of Aries's idealization of childhood, writing:

> Of over two hundred statements of advice on child rearing prior to the eighteenth century which I have examined, most approved of beating children severely, and all allowed beating in varying circumstances.... Of the seventy children prior to the eighteenth century whose lives [this is, letters biographies, autobiographies] I have found, all were beaten except one ... [a German scholar's] extensive survey of the literature on beating reaches similar conclusions to mine.... The beatings described in the sources were generally severe, involved bruising and bloodying of the body, began early and were a regular part of the child's life (deMause, cited in Rhodes 1999: 236).

Thus deMause argues that the Western history of childhood "is a nightmare from which we have only recently begun to awaken. The further back in history one goes, the lower the level of child care, and the more likely children are to be killed, abandoned, beaten, terrorized and sexually abused" (cited in Rhodes: 236). As noted in Chapter 1, conservatives often find targets to blame for school shootings and youth killings, such as permissive liberalism, a hedonistic mass culture, godlessness in a secular society, or other favorite scapegoats. DeMause, Rhodes, and others, however, criticize conservative child-rearing philosophies that involve harsh punishment as producing violentization and potential killers (Rhodes 1999: 237ff.), a topic that I will return to later in these studies.

Further, the idea that a transitional period of youth occurs between childhood and adulthood is a relatively recent invention, beginning perhaps with Rousseau's *Emile* (1662 [1979]) in mid-eighteenth-century Europe that celebrated childhood and delineated stages of youth. Sociological labels like "The Lost Generations" for the 1920s or "The Silent Generation" for a post–World War II, 1950s generation began emerging in the twentieth century. During the post–World War II period, "youth culture" was widely used to describe the rising beat and rock culture and the consumer and fashion styles of the era that quickly mutated into the counterculture in the 1960s (see Savage 2007).

Since then, there has been a flourishing industry in designing terms like "Baby Boomer" to describe persons born after World War II into the relative affluence of the 1950s and 1960s.[2] This generation was the beneficiary of an unprecedented economic expansion and a highly self-conscious sense of generation because it went through the turbulent 1960s together and emerged in many cases to prosperity and success in corporate, academic, and political life in the 1970s and beyond.

What is striking about the post-Boomers and the contemporary situation of youth is the totalizing and derogatory terms used to describe them. Post-Boomer youth have been tagged with terms such as the "Postponed Generation," the "13th Generation," the "New Lost Generation," the "Nowhere Generation," or, most frequently, "Generation X," as well as "the Scapegoat Generation," "GenNet," "GenNext," and other catch phrases.[3] Such terms were first applied to the 80 million Americans born between the mid-1960s and the 1980s, who follow the "Boomer" generation.

While there have been attempts to present post-Boomers as a coherent generation,[4] in fact, contemporary youth embrace a wide array of young people, and youth culture is equally heterogeneous. Post-Boomers include those who helped create the Internet and the culture of video gaming; the latchkey kids who are home alone and the mall rats noshing fast food in the palaces of consumption; the young activists who helped generate the antiglobalization and emerging peace and antiwar movements; the cafe slackers, klub kidz, computer nerds, and sales clerks; a generation committed to health, exercise, sustainability, ethical dietary practices, and animal rights, as well as anorexics and bulimics in thrall to the ideals of the beauty and fashion industries. Today's youth also include creators of exciting 'zines and diverse multimedia such as can be found on sites like MySpace, Facebook, and YouTube; the bike ponies, valley girls, and skinheads; skaters, gangstas, low-riders, riot grrls, and hip-hoppers; all accompanied by a diverse and heterogeneous grouping of multicultural, racial, and hybridized individuals seeking a viable identity.

By the 1990s, new forms of "postmodern culture" became a central part of youth culture.[5] Originating during this period, the style of MTV has come to influence postmodern media culture on the whole—normalizing a cultural style that seeks to absorb and echo as pastiche anything and everything, while it turns oppositional cultural forms such as hip-hop and grunge into seductive hooks for fashion and advertising. The postmodern media and consumer culture is alluring, fragmented, and superficial, inviting its audiences to enter the seductive game of consumption, style, and identity through the construction of look and image. Postmodern cultural forms are becoming dominant—at least for youth—with the breaking down of fixed categories between generic boundaries a recurrent feature of contemporary film and TV, as are pastiche, sampling, and hyperirony. For example, *Six Feet Under* is sometimes referred to as a "dramedy" since it combines comedy and drama, and mixes genres like the family melodrama, youth-growing-up genre, and various kinds of romantic dramas, including a gay relationship between the family son and an African American man.

Novel forms of electronic music such as techno and rave also produce cultural artifacts through which youth can intensely experience postmodern culture, as they indulge in designer drugs, chemical and herbal ecstasy, and psychotropic drinks. In a different register, youth can produce their own music or forms of culture and post them on YouTube, Facebook, or other sites, share music with each other in P2P file-sharing, and create new forms of music by mixing previous forms and "sampling" other work into their own. Thus, for contemporary youth, postmodernism is not merely an avant-garde aesthetic or academic topic, but it is the form and texture of their everyday lives.

Most crucially, perhaps, experiences of the Internet have brought postmodern culture into the homes and lives of contemporary youth. Hooking into the World Wide Web, individuals can access myriad forms of culture, engage in discussions, create their own cultural forums and sites, establish relationships, and create novel identities and social relations in a unique cyberspace (see Turkle 1995). Internet culture is, on the whole, more fragmented, diverse, and interactive than previous media culture, and as sight and sound become more integral parts of the Internet experience, individuals will increasingly live in a space significantly different from previous print and media culture. Being propelled into a new cultural matrix is thus an integral part of the contemporary adventure, with unforeseen results.

Youth culture is thus intersected by media and computer technologies, and the current generation has grown up in postmodern culture. Media culture has indeed extended and prolonged youth culture as 1960s rockers like Mick Jagger, Tina Turner, and Bob Dylan continue to strut their stuff, and youth has become an ever more obsessive ideal in U.S. culture. The mass marketing of plastic surgery and medicine like Viagra support a highly sexualized mass culture that idealizes the youthful libido as a satisfying state of being ideally obtainable by every person. Yet in opposition to the dominant media and consumer culture, resistant youth subcultures have emerged that provide autonomous spaces where youth can define themselves and create their own identities and communities (Kahn and Kellner 2003). Youth subcultures can be merely cultures of consumption where young people come together to consume cultural products, like rock music, that bind them together as a community. Yet youth subcultures can also be countercultures in which youth define themselves against the dominant culture, such as in punk, goth, grrl, or hip-hop culture.[6]

Youth subcultures can compose an entire way of life, encompassing clothes, styles, attitudes, and practices, and be all-involving ways of living. Youth subcultures contain potential spaces of resistance, though these can take various forms ranging from narcissistic and apolitical to anarchist and punk cultures, to activist environmental, animal rights, and Vegan groups, to right-wing skinheads and Islamist jihadists. Thus, although there might be elements of opposition and resistance to mainstream culture in youth subcultures, such counterculture might not be progressive and must be interrogated in specific cases concerning its politics and effects.

Certainly, in the age range of 15 to 30-something, in young men and women, and in various classes and races, there are important differences to note in an increasingly complex and hybridized matrix of contemporary youth, but they also have crucial things in common. In standard media and sociopolitical representations, youth are pejoratively represented as cynical, confused, apolitical (or conservative), ignorant, bibliophobic, obsessively focused on image and seeing and being seen on this level, and narcissistic. Youth are typically portrayed in media culture as whining slackers and malcontents suffering from severe attention deficit disorder induced by MTV, remote-control channel surfing, net cruising, and video and computer games, and tempered by Ritalin, Prozac, and the favored drug of the moment. Indeed, cohorts of American youth over the past couple of decades have been widely stigmatized as the "doofus generation," the "tuned-out generation," the "numb generation," the "blank generation," a generation of "self-centered know-nothings," and "Generation Ecch!" From the right, Allan Bloom (1986) infamously excoriated youth as illiterate and inarticulate adolescents blithely enjoying the achievements of modern science and the Enlightenment while in the throes of a Dionysian frenzy, drugged by music videos, rock and roll, and illegal substances, and ushering in "the closing of the American mind," the endgame of Enlightenment values. Such jeremiads constitute only the tip of the iceberg of hostility and resentment toward contemporary youth by older generations, reopening a "generation gap" as wide as that between 1960s youth and "the establishment."

Such negative labels and characterizations of youth are falsely totalizing. They eliminate, for example, young political activists and volunteers, bright students in opposition to the values of media culture, and the technical wizards who developed much computer software and pioneered the Internet. Moreover, pejorative characterizations of youth fail to understand that whatever undesirable features this generation possesses were in large part shaped by their present and past, and how the younger generation is an unwitting victim of the economic recession and the global restructuring of capitalism and the decline of democracy. As a young writer and promoter of his cohort as "the Free Generation," rejecting the label "Generation X," Geoffrey Holtz writes: "We are, perhaps more than any previous generation, a product of the societal trends of our times and of the times that immediately preceded us. The years in which we were raised—the sixties, seventies, and eighties—saw unprecedented changes in the political, social, and economic environment that, for the first time in American history, have made the future of society's young members uncertain" (1995: 1).

There is no widespread agreement concerning what concepts best characterize contemporary youth. During the 1980s and into the 1990s, the term "Generation X," popularized by Canadian writer Douglas Coupland (1991) was widely adopted. The "X" could signify the crossroads upon which the present generation stands between the modern and the postmodern. It suggests an unknown and indeterminate future, a fluidity of identities that are being redefined by new technologies and cultural experiences, and a situation of uncertainty and social chaos. Yet if one needs a label to characterize this generation, then perhaps not "Generation X," which is vague and widely rejected by those it is supposed to characterize,[7] but "post-Boomers" is preferable because they are the successors to those Americans born between 1945 and 1960, and their identities in large part are shaped in reaction to the Boomers and their times. Moreover, they are the first generation to grow up in the post-1960s cold war era, characterized by the unfolding of the postindustrial society and postmodern culture, and they have been living in the tensions and conflicts of the "post."

The post-Boomer generation could also be labeled as "Busters," for with this generation the American dream, enjoyed by many Boomers, went bust, and they were thrown into a world of uncertainty, disorder, and decline. The Baby Boomers came of age during the optimism that followed World War II with the rise of suburbia, cheap education, good job opportunities, abundant housing, the Age of Affluence, and the exciting and turbulent events of the 1960s. Their children, in contrast, matured during more troubled times marked by recession, diminishing expectations, the conservative reaction led by Ronald Reagan and George Bush Senior, an explosion of shallow greed and materialism, the disillusioning drama of a dot-com boom rapidly followed by a dot-com bust, and the horrors of the Bush-Cheney years.

The e-boom was a boom period for youth and by youth—and was quite significant for this reason. Though ballooned out of proportion by the financial industries, the Internet boom represented a new economy led by a young vanguard. The Bush-Cheney regime, by contrast, can be seen in many ways as a return to the old guard, the old extraction-based economy that sees economic advancement as a win-loss game best advanced through imperialist expansion—a shift from the consumer-, innovation-, and service-driven economy that envisioned (at least) a win-win global economy based on national comparative advantage and world trade. Thus, the restoration of the old order is also an attack on the Young Turks, which also has the flavor, in many ways, of revenge.

Moreover, dramatically worsening social conditions in the current situation emerged following the September 11, 2001, terrorist attack on the United States and the subsequent "war against terrorism." After declaring war against an "axis of evil" in his 2002 State of the Union speech, in early 2003 Son of Bush assembled his father's legion of doom and a gigantic military machine to wage war against Iraq in an unfolding millennium of perennial war, one that will sacrifice many in another generation of youth (see Kellner 2005).

Hence, today's post-Boomer youth face a life that is more complex, insecure, risky, and unpredictable than Boomer youth, and today's youth face ever more dangerous and anxious times with threats of terrorism, war, and large-scale apocalypse on the horizon, as nature revolts against abuse and global warming and environmental crisis loom large, and as the global economy sputters and possibilities for a better life diminish. Post-Boomer youth have lived through the fallout of the rising expectations of the "new economy" and globalization, finding that dot-com bust, terrorism, and a reactionary U.S. administration bent on a return to the past and threatening unending war has imperiled their future as well as the prospects for survival of the human species.

Post-Boomers and Contemporary Youth

"We grew up as America, in many ways, fell down."
—*Rob Nelson and Jon Cowan*

Ultimately, it will be up to the contemporary generation to define itself. It's time today for a dialogue among teachers, parents, youth, and other interested parties concerning the situation of contemporary youth, both in terms of prospects and problems, and hopes and challenges. While the term "post-Boomer" helps indicate the experience of coming after the Boomer generation and living out the drama of the "post," the new millennium produces novel social conditions for today's youth who are engaging innovative and challenging cultural forms, and a dramatically worsening economic and political situation, and ever more complex and unpredictable life. This generation faces the challenges of forging careers in a declining economy, surviving the threats of war and terrorism, and overcoming the conservative hegemony that threatens their future.

There were earlier signs that post-Boomers were coming to resent the elderly, the "G.I." and "Silent" generations, born respectively from 1901–1924 and

1925–1942, who, through various federal programs, have grown richer as youth have grown poorer, and today's youth are bracing for a shock when 56 million Boomers retire in 2010, seeking social and medical benefits that are becoming increasingly costly and scarce.[8] Moreover, the post-Boomer generation has been stuck with the highest federal deficit in history, which it will be forced to pay off. In addition, escalating prices for higher education and easy to obtain but high-interest loans have put many students into terrible debt.[9]

Despite efforts of the Clinton administration to cut back on the federal deficit and to produce a surplus for the years to come, future youth face paying off trillions of dollars of debt by the year 2020, more than twenty times what it was in 1960. This enormous mortgaging of the future is arguably the product of unwise and unfair government spending that benefited upper and middle classes over lower classes, and the middle-aged and elderly over the young. During the two Reagan administrations, the national debt doubled and the Bush Senior administration managed to further double the deficit in one term. Moreover, the Bush-Cheney administration racked up a record $304 billion deficit for 2003 and $422 billion for 2004, raising the national deficit to $8.2 trillion by 2006.[10] Consequently, future generations will be forced to pay for the parties for the rich and greedy thrown by two Reagan and three Bush administrations and will have to clean up the mess.

And so contemporary youth share in common a difficult future. As Holtz realized (1995), whatever new freedoms and possibilities are available to contemporary youth—from education to jobs to housing—the opportunities to enjoy them are vanishing. The post-Boomers are not only the largest and most diverse of all American generations, they are "the only generation born since the Civil War to come of age unlikely to match their parents' economic fortune" (Holtz 1995: 7). The brief exception of the dot-com boom put Holtz's analysis in temporary question, but unfortunately his subsequent comment seems appropriate where he describes the current generation as "the only one born this century to grow up personifying (to others) not the advance, but the decline of their society's greatness" (Holtz 1995: 7).

Whereas Americans once viewed a better future as a birthright, they now see growing up in an age of decline as a rite of passage. Indeed, various statistics add up to a grim picture of decay that shapes the cynicism and pessimism of many post-Boomers and contemporary youth. From the cradle to the seminar room, their lives have been far more difficult and troubled than past generations. Childhood poverty rates, family divorces, rising living and education costs, taxes, staggering debts, escalating violence and incarceration rates, teen pregnancy, mental illness, higher drug use and arrests, obesity, cigarette smoking, and suicide rates are way *up,* as school performance, job prospects, median weekly earnings, unemployment benefits, and prospects of future home ownership rates are *down.*[11]

By the time the Boomers' children reached adolescence, optimism had thus given way to pessimism, boom to bust, opportunity to crisis, and they were "lost" in the shuffle. For many, youth was artificially prolonged as even college graduates could not get good jobs, or lost their jobs after the dot-com bust or the disasters of the post-Enron corporate collapse and catastrophe of Bushonomics. Many young people have been forced to go back to live with their parents and a second adolescence, as the perks of adulthood become ever more difficult to achieve.

Yet for Holtz and others of the post-Boomer generation, the situation is not entirely negative. He prefers to call contemporary youth—much too optimistically—the Free Generation because "with the breakdown of many gender-based traditions and racial stereotypes, we enjoy a much broader range of lifestyle and career choices than any generation that preceded us" (1995: 3). But he also realizes that this generation is "free" of any social, cultural, or political defining generational experience that provides a common collective identity.

Indeed, in many ways, the current generation of youth is living in an especially depressing political environment. Where the Boomers had the idealism of the Civil Rights movement, the anti–Vietnam War movement, the counterculture, solidarity with groups involved in liberation struggles, and dreams of social revolution, their children had Watergate, the Iran hostage crisis, the Iran-Contra affair, CIA wars in Central America, accelerating S&L scandals, cynical conservatism, dreary materialism, anxious narcissism, 9/11 and the paranoia of additional terrorist attacks, the perils of a cycle of Terror Wars, and the retrogression of the Bush-Cheney regime.

Boomers watched Neil Armstrong plant a flag on the moon; post-Boomers and contemporary youth witnessed the *Challenger* and *Columbia* space shuttle explosions. Boomers faced the threat of bullies in the schoolyard, post-Boomers pass by metal detectors and security guards on their way into school and face shootings such as the Columbine shooting in high school and the Virginia Tech massacre in college. Where the Boomers enjoyed Woodstock and the utopia of free love, their children had Woodstock II and then the simulacrum of Woodstock III, a soulless, commodified parody of the original, orchestrated by MTV; as well as "safe sex" necessitated by the specter of AIDS in a world where Eros and Thanatos are increasingly fused.

Perhaps most crucially, while Boomers enjoyed the luxury of well-funded government services, contemporary youth in the United States must now live with the consequences of the 1996 so-called welfare reform bill, which began the process of making deep cuts in funding for women, children, and education, followed by continued redistribution of wealth from poorer and middle classes to the rich under the Bush-Cheney administration. Of course, there are gains and advantages shared by the current generation, and generational experience varies according to class, gender, race, region, and individual. While racism continues to fester and racial differences intensify, many youth of color have opportunities today that were denied to their parents. Although sexism continues to prevail, many younger women have absorbed feminist consciousness into their everyday lives and also have more opportunities for independence than their mothers and grandmothers. And while homophobia continues to oppress gays, gay youth are out in record number and enjoying solidarity and support denied to previous generations. Also, there are proliferating spaces of youth subcultures, including cyberspace, which provide opportunities for self-expression and participation denied many in the previous generations (Kahn and Kellner 2003, 2005).

Yet the post-Boomers and contemporary youth share a common identity—as products and users of mass media and information technologies and citizens within a common social and political environment. Today's youth are not the first TV generation (their Boomer parents had that honor),[12] but their media experience is far more intensive and extensive. Where Boomers were introduced to a TV world with limited channels in black and white, post-Boomers experienced the cornucopia of 100-plus channels in living color transmitted by cable and satellite television, a wealth of video cassettes, remote control and wireless devices, massively multiplayer video games, DVDs, BitTorrent, MySpace, and YouTube. Whereas much Boomer TV watching was rigorously supervised and circumscribed by concerned parents, post-Boomers were parked in front of the TV as a pacifier, often with both parents at work, indulging themselves in a media orgy supplemented by video and computer games.

Post-Boomers therefore have watched much more TV than Boomers, competing with the time they spend in school and with other forms of media consumption. The shows post-Boomers watch are of a far different nature, often filled with images of sex and violence the likes of which were not seen in the 1950s and early 1960s, substituting shows like *Law and Order,* the *CSI* series, and *The Sopranos* for *Ozzie and Harriet, Dobie Gillis,* and *Lassie.* Younger viewers of the past decade have watched shows like *The OC* and *Grey's Anatomy* (for teens) and *SpongeBob SquarePants* and *Fairly Odd Parents* (for preteens) compared to the likes of *The Howdy Doody Show, The Mickey Mouse Club,* and *Mr. Ed,* which entertained young Boomers. On the other hand, while young Boomers made the nightly news iconic, post-Boomers prefer the comedic critique of *The Daily Show,* before turning to follow the superficial antics of *American Idol,* or follow the dramas of celebrities like Paris Hilton, Britney Spears, Justin Timberlake, and Lindsay Lohan.

The current wave of "reality TV" shows feature young contestants struggling for survival, prizes, and celebrity against older players in *Survivor,* locked up in a panopticon of surveillance in *Big Brother,* and subject to the degradations of sexual and social rejection in the highly competitive personality/sex contests of *Temptation Island, The Bachelor, The Bachelorette, Joe Millionaire,* or MTV's *The Real World.* CBS's 2007 "reality" series *Kid Nation* takes forty kids and dumps them into an abandoned New Mexico desert town to see how they organize a society and comport themselves, leading critics to decry child exploitation and the mistreatment of minors. Many of the "reality" shows feature narcissism and sadism, depicting a highly Darwinist neoliberal struggle for the survival of the fittest and sexiest, while losers are rejected and cast aside as unworthy.

But post-Boomers are also the first generation to grow up with personal computers, CD-Roms, the Internet, the World Wide Web, DVDs, iPods, and iPhones, providing for exciting adventures in cyberspace and proliferating technological skills, making this generation the most technologically literate in history and offering unprecedented opportunities for them to become engaged politically and create their *own* culture. Peer-to-peer (P2P) sharing of music, video, computer programs, and other digitized products represents more communal and social sharing than is evident in the reality TV shows, and programs like BitTorrent, MySpace, Facebook, and YouTube represent social technologies designed by youth to create a participatory and shared digital youth culture, one currently at war against the adult world of copyright litigation and the government net police who try to bust kids for downloading and sharing copywrited material.

There are also signs of a repoliticization of youth in the face of the Iraq War and multiple horrors of the Bush-Cheney administration. A 2007 poll by the *New York Times, CBS News,* and MTV indicated that young Americans are leaning left and "are more likely than the general public to favor a government-run universal health care insurance system, an open-door policy on immigration and the legalization of gay marriage."[13] The poll indicated that the young "have continued a long-term drift away from the Republican Party," are concerned about the direction of the country, and believe that "their votes can make a difference."

A story by Christopher Phelps (2007), "The New SDS," reports on growing student activism, indicating that "angry at the Iraq debacle, emboldened by the Bush-Cheney tailspin, a new student radicalism is emerging whose concerns include immigrants' rights, global warming and the uncertainties facing debt-ridden graduates." Describing emergent SDS (Students for a Democratic Society) groups on campuses throughout the country with more than 2,000 members, Phelps discusses how different groups are producing their own philosophies and activism as a response to deteriorating social conditions and the prospects for youth in the United States.

Contemporary youth are thus active in producing their own technology, culture, politics, and identities. Hence, one needs to distinguish between a youth culture produced by youth itself that articulates its own visions, passions, and anxieties, and media culture about youth produced by adults to be consumed by youth. One also needs to distinguish between youth cultures that are lived and involve immediate, participatory experience as opposed to mediated cultural experience and consumption, and to be aware that youth cultures involve both poles. Moreover, one should resist either reducing youth cultures merely to cultures of consumption, or glorifying youth culture as the force of resistance. It is best instead to ferret out the contradictions and the ways that youth cultures are constructed by media and consumer culture contrasted with the ways that youth in turn constructs its own communities and culture.

Youth Alienation, Violence, and the War against Youth

> "'Youth' is when you blame your troubles on your parents; maturity is when you learn that everything is the fault of the younger generation."
>
> —*Bertolt Brecht*

The Virginia Tech shootings, as with the earlier Columbine High School shootings that I examine in the next chapter, dramatize the problem of the alienation of youth in the contemporary era. During the conservative 1950s and era of the "mass society," the "organization man," and "other-directedness" described by major sociologists, youth alienation was described in terms of nonconformity and individual rebellion, or as anomie (Durkheim), activities described negatively by the conservative society. But in the 1960s, precisely nonconformity, rebellion, and "doing your own thing" were positive signs of a youth counterculture that seemed to provide its own antidotes against alienation by producing its own novel forms of subjectivity, culture, and ways of life.

During the 1970s and the 1980s the discourse of youth alienation subsided, but new forms of normativity have emerged, as Tyson Lewis (2006) argues in "Risky Youth and the Psychology of Security." Alienation was traditionally marked as deviance from normality and conformity, but in a regime of "flexible normality" that accompanies the more flexible economy and labor of contemporary capitalism, "normality" is expanded in ways that allow more variety and difference. This includes extreme play of male aggression and violence, forms reproduced and amplified by media culture. As Klein and Chancer argue, "Hypermale expectations tend to be made 'normal' in three specific ways: accepting a 'boys will be boys' ideology, tolerating violence, and condoning misogynist and homophobic attitudes and acts" (2000, 146).

In all the cases I examine of domestic terrorists and school shooters, hypermasculinity found outlets in violent gun culture and forms of male identity present in media culture with tragic results. The expansion of societal violence and aggression as a consequence of more flexible normality provoked a conservative backlash. From the 1980s onward, as an outgrowth of the culture wars of the 1960s, a war on youth was beginning that concerned how some sociologists, politicians, educators, and journalists began depicting and talking about contemporary youth.

Conservative attacks against youth culture, particularly forms like heavy metal, punk, grunge, and so-called alternative music, began circulating during the Reagan era, and the attack in the 1980s and 1990s was broadened against rap and hip-hop, as well as video and computer games and Internet culture. But the fiercest attacks began coming in the 1990s by right-wing ideologues like John DiIulio, who later became head of the Bush-Cheney administration's Office of Faith-Based and Community Initiatives. DiIulio warned of the emergence of a new breed of juvenile delinquents, the so-called superpredators.[14] As Razzano, Skalli, and McQuill put it:

> In contrast to girls, boys and young men are seen as violent and dangerous "superpredators"—"a 'generational wolfpack' of 'fatherless, Godless, and jobless' youth." The superpredator is a conservative political and cultural construct that links male youth of color to the inevitability of crime and violence. In mobilizing this concept, politicians have helped create a "youth control complex,"[15] [Victor Rios] wherein youth are suspects across a range of cultural spaces, including the justice system, the street, school, and family. Such a system that assumes youth's criminality works to "manage, control, and incapacitate black and Latino youth."[16] [ibid.] In so doing, the possibilities, real and imagined, for these youth are severely curtailed.[17]

The Struggle against "The War on Youth"

> "It has become common to think of kids as a threat to the existing social order and for kids to be blamed for the problems they experience. We slide from kids in trouble, kids have problems, and kids are threatened, to kids as trouble, kids as problems, and kids as threatening."
> —*Lawrence Grossberg (2005: 16)*

Against the war on youth, Donna Gaines, Toby Miller, Mike Males, Henry Giroux, Lawrence Grossberg, Ruth Wilson Gilmore, Angela Davis, and others have been attacking the right wing, and other ideologues who scapegoat and denigrate youth, by amassing counterarguments and statistics. As Grossberg notes in the epigram above, youth have been increasingly blamed for a variety of social ills. Hence, whereas youth were once the hope of the future, now they are stigmatized and demonized.[18]

Sociologist Donna Gaines's *Teenage Wasteland: Suburbia's Dead-End Kids* (1998) explored the alienated lives of suburban youth. Working as a freelance journalist investigating a story about four teenagers in northern New Jersey who in 1987 killed themselves in a suicide pact, Gaines won access to the "teenage wasteland" of a group of so-called burnouts of Bergenfield, New Jersey. This began a sociological odyssey whereby Gaines began interviewing contemporary youth and finding recurrent stories of abuse and violence, alienation from parents, school, and environment, and subcultural refuge in countercultures. In an interview with Benjamin Frymer (2006), Gaines describes her project:

> My purpose in writing *Teenage Wasteland* had been to take on the adult authority structure, which is basically my Baby Boom generation—the parents—but more so mental health practitioners, school officials, legislators ... and just say look, "Here's a big wake-up call. This is what's happening. Kids aren't thriving. You're blaming them. You're saying they're subliterate. You're calling them burnouts, dirtbags, and losers. What are you really giving to them? You're neglecting them. You're starving them—emotionally, physically, psychologically—you're giving them no resources and then you're blaming them. So, what's up with that?"

In his book *Framing Youth: Ten Myths about the Next Generation* (1999), Mike Males lays out in detail that, contrary to myth, teenage abuse of alcohol and drugs, teen pregnancy, and teen crime are down, and that statistics concerning their parents' Boomer generation's abuse of drugs, alcohol, sexual violence, and crime are far higher.[19] Males excoriates the media and liberal and conservative ideologues and politicians alike for perpetrating myths against youth, during a period when drug and alcohol use, teen pregnancy, and violent crime among youth have been steadily declining.[20]

Males argues that generations of youth from the 1980s to the present provide a convenient scapegoat for the problems of U.S. society in his book *The Scapegoat Generation: America's War on Adolescents* (1996), where he describes how young people are blamed for a broad array of problems. Critiques of Males's analysis indicate that he does not adequately articulate the differences in the situations of richer and poorer youth and underplays the specificities of race,[21] but, in fact, he does note how poorer and youth of color are more susceptible to violent crime. Yet it can be argued that Males tends to exaggerate the roles of liberals in demonizing youth and he himself tends to scapegoat older Americans who are said to defend their own Social Security, Medicare, and pensions more aggressively than they support programs helping youth. On the other hand, Males is probably right that some liberals do indeed buy into the demonization of youth and it is not surprising that seniors are well organized in promoting their interests while youth are generally unorganized.

Du Boff and Herman, and other critics of Males's work like Henry Giroux, indicate that Males does not adequately implicate the role of advertising, consumer and media culture, and corporate capitalism in the exploitation of youth, leading youth into concern with style, fashion, and triviality at the expense of more serious pursuits. While Males's work is largely sociological, Giroux situates the war on youth within the broader currents of consumer capitalism, neoliberalism, accelerating militarism, and the ways that media culture and public discourse, as well as academic discourse, position youth as an enemy.

In the light of the ongoing attack on youth and youth culture in the contemporary post-Columbine conjuncture, it is interesting to read in Giroux's 1996 *Fugitive Cultures* analyses of how media were then scapegoating youth, especially youth of color, as the source of social problems and the escalation of violence in society. Giroux cites the disturbing statistic that already in the mid-1990s "close to 12 U.S. children aged 19 and under die from gunfire each day. According to the National Center for Health Statistics, 'Firearm homicide is the leading cause of death of African American teenage boys and the second leading cause of death of high school age children in the United States'" (cited in Giroux 1996b: 28).

In particular, Giroux shows how media representations of blacks stigmatize youth and, more broadly, people of color. Racial coding of violence and the association of crime with youth of color was evident in the attacks on rap music and hip-hop culture that circulated throughout the 1990s, and that continue to the present.[22] As an example, Giroux cites the hypocrisy of Republican Senate majority leader and 1996 Republican presidential candidate Bob Dole's attack on rap and on Hollywood films' depiction of violence, drugs, and urban terror. Yet Dole refused to criticize violence in the films of the Hollywood right, such as those of Republicans Bruce Willis and Arnold Schwarzenegger. Moreover, Dole was a fervent supporter of the NRA and critic of stricter gun laws, and failed to address the ways that poverty and worsening social conditions generated violence (produced in part by Republican policies that Dole spearheaded as a leader of the Republican Congress in the 1980s and early 1990s). Moreover, Dole had often not even seen the films nor heard the music he attacked (1996b: 67ff.).

Clearly pointing to the political consequences of such cultural and political discourses and representations, Giroux notes that "such racist stereotyping produces more than prejudice and fear in the white collective sensibility. Racist representations of violence also feed the increasing public outcry for tougher crime bills designed to build more prisons and legislate get-tough policies with minorities of color and class" (1996b: 67). Hence, racist and brutal depictions of people of color in media culture contribute to intensification of the culture of violence and fuel campaigns by right-wing organizations that stigmatize racial groups. Such representations also promote social and political conditions that aggravate rather than ameliorate problems of crime, urban decay, and violence.

Indeed, throughout the 1990s and continuing into the new millennium there have been copious media spectacles featuring dangerous blacks, including sustained attacks on rap music and hip-hop culture, black gangs and crime, and urban violence in communities of color. Latinos are also stigmatized with political (mis)measures such as Proposition 187 "which assigns increasing crime, welfare abuse, moral decay, and social disorder to the flood of Mexican immigrants streaming across the borders of the United States" (Giroux 1996b: 66). Social scientists contribute to the stigmatization in books like *The Bell Curve* (1994) that assert black inferiority and provide "a respectable intellectual position" for racist discourse in the national debate on race (1996b: 67).

Hollywood films and entertainment media contribute as well to negative national depictions of people of color. In his discussion of Hollywood cinematic portrayals of inner-city youth, Giroux analyzes how communities of color are shown as disruptive forces in public schools, contributing to white moral panic that youth of color are predatory, violent, and destroying the moral and social fabric of the country. Films like *Boyz N the Hood* (1991), *Juice* (1992), *Menace II Society* (1993), and *Clockers* (1995) present negative representations of African American youth that Giroux argues feed into right-wing moral panics and help mobilize support for harsher policing and incarceration of ghetto youth. Against these prejudicial and sensationalistic fictional representations, Giroux valorizes Jonathan Stack's documentary *Harlem Diary* (1996) in which urban youth are themselves provided with cameras and cinematic education to explore their situations and to give voice to their own fears and aspirations (1997: 62).

Giroux correctly notes that the proliferating media stories about youth and violence at the time generally avoided critical commentary on the connections between the escalation of violence in society and the role of poverty and social conditions in promoting violence—a blind spot that continues into the present. In addition, he astutely notes that the media scapegoating of youth also neglects dissection of the roles of white men in generating violence and destruction, such as "the gruesome toll of the drunk driver who is typically white" (1996b: 37).

At the same time, working-class youth and youth of color are being represented in the media and conservative discourses as predators—as threats to existing law, order, and morality. Most disturbingly, at the very time that poverty and division between the haves and the have-nots are growing, a conservative-dominated neoliberal polity is cutting back the very programs—public education, job training, food stamps, health and welfare support—that provide the sustenance to create opportunities and hope for youth at risk. Giroux correctly rejects the family values and moralistic critique of media culture of such conservatives who lead the assault on the state and welfare programs while supporting prisons, harsher punishment, and a "zero tolerance" for youthful transgressions.

Instead of stigmatizing adults as enemies of youth, as does Males, Giroux targets the corporations that circulate problematic images of youth and the right-wing social forces that scapegoat youth for social programs at the same time they attack programs and institutions that might actually help youth. Giroux correctly perceives media culture as pedagogy and calls upon cultural critics to see the pedagogical and political functions of such cultural forms that position youth as objects of fear or desire. In a series of studies, Giroux notes how corporations exploit the bodies of youth to sell products, manufacturing desires for certain products and constructing youth as consumers.

Giroux's *Channel Surfing* (1997) and *Stealing Innocence* (2000) provide examples of critical pedagogy that demonstrate that "childhood" and "youth" are social constructions and sites of struggle between opposing political ideologies and forces. "Children" and "youth" in Giroux's view are a complex site of hope and possibility, as well as domination and exploitation. Giroux critically delineates pedagogies in locales ranging from schooling to media culture and everyday life that shape youth. In particular, he provides sustained critique of representations that scapegoat youth for public problems at the same time that the political and media establishments carry out attacks on public schools and on programs and policies that provide opportunities and hope for youth. Giroux criticizes representations of youth such as are found in Calvin Klein ads, depictions of irresponsible sex and drug use in films like Larry Clark's *Kids* (1996), and a variety of urban films that especially vilify youth of color and help foster public images of youth as decadent, corrupt, and in need of discipline and control.

In subsequent books like *Public Spaces, Private Lives* (2001) and *The Abandoned Generation* (2003), Giroux discusses the war on youth in the context of escalating conservatism, militarism, and draconian criminalization and incarceration of youth. In the study "Disposable Youth and the Politics of Domestic Militarization: Mis/Education in the Age of Zero Tolerance" (2001: 29ff.), Giroux criticizes conservative discourses and policies that villainize youth as the source of contemporary disorder. Since the Bush administration policies on education and "faith-based charity" programs are guided by principles of "zero tolerance," Giroux's critique engages a particularly noxious discourse and politics with which contemporary educators and citizens have been confronted in the following years. Crucially, Giroux shows how discourses of "zero tolerance" mesh with right-wing policies that support authoritarian education, the prison-industrial complex as the solution to social problems, and punitive punishment for youthful misbehavior.

Despite declining statistics for violent crime committed by youth, incarceration and executions of youth escalated after the 9/11 terror attacks, which generated a new politics of fear and militarism that affects youth in important ways. In recent work, Giroux has been engaging the implications of policies of zero tolerance and domestic militarization in making youth disposable. Giroux notes that the "zero tolerance laws that have swept the nation since the 1980s, and gained full legislative strength with the passage of the Violent Crime Control and Law Enforcement Act of 1994" have disproportionately forced the imprisonment of youth and people of color, often for minor crimes or infringements of drug law, under the provisions of a draconian "three strikes and you're out" law (Giroux 2006a: 157).

Giroux follows Ruth Wilson Gilmore in her notion of "domestic militarism" in stressing growing police attacks on youth, arrests, and incarceration. As Gilmore puts it: "The new State is shedding social welfare in favor of domestic militarization. Programs that provide for people's welfare, protect the environment, or regulate corporate behavior have been delegitimized and jettisoned. There is a new consensus among the powers that be that focuses the domestic State on defense against enemies, both foreign and U.S.-born. What's new is the scale of militarism being directed at people inside the U.S., and the scope for what comes into the crosshairs of the prison industrial complex rather than some helping agency" (cited in Giroux 2001: 39).

Indeed, youth are at risk today of being preyed upon by a military that has returned thousands of dead soldiers in body bags from U.S. interventions in Afghanistan and Iraq, and thousands more injured, often seriously. To be sure, young people wind up in the military for a variety of reasons, "ranging from economic pressure to the desire to escape a dead-end situation at home to the promise of citizenship."[23] When mandatory military service was replaced by a volunteer military in 1973, the term "poverty draft" gained currency. An article by Jorge Mariscal Sojourners, "The Making of an American Soldier: Why Young People Join the Military," indicates how the military recruits a large percentage of poor people, focusing heavily on inner-city areas, which has led to a movement to keep military recruiters out of schools. In addition, Sojourners points out that the military prowls local community colleges, where recruiters try to convince students that they are in a dead-end situation and should join the military for career advancement.

Tragically, when many working-class youth or youth of color return from military service, they are not offered adequate social services and are targets of a war on youth. In the introduction to *Abandoned Generation* (2003), "The War against Youth in the Post-9/11 Era," Giroux notes how young people have been more frequently portrayed as a danger to U.S. society and how contemporary anxieties concerning race, class, and sexuality have been projected onto youth. In his words, "Youth occupy a degraded borderland within the economic and cultural geography of neoliberal capitalism, in which the spectacle of commodification exists side by side with the imposing threat of the prison-industrial complex. The war against youth can, in part, be understood as part of the fundamental values and practices of a rapacious neoliberal capitalism; moreover, the consequences of this complex cultural and economic assault can no longer be ignored by educators, parents, and other concerned citizens" (2003, p. xvi).

Against the scapegoating and commercialization of youth, and the promotion of attitudes of cynicism, despair, and hopelessness, Giroux wants to foster an ethic of hope and possibility, conceptualizing youth as a contested terrain, as an arena both of oppression and struggle. Giroux argues that by criticizing misrepresentations of youth in media culture and the scapegoating of youth through negative media images and discourses, we are combating an attack on youth used to justify cutbacks in education, harsher criminal penalties, and other punitive measures that are arguably part of the problem rather than the solution. I will take up the issue of the reconstruction of education, and possible solutions to the problems of the war on youth and the prison-industrial complex, in the concluding chapter.

In *Caught in the Crossfire* (2005), Lawrence Grossberg provides an engrossing account of "America's war on its children," describing the ways youth are being oppressed, the discourses and rhetorics that attack and scapegoat youth, and the multiple challenges that youth face today. In a far-reaching analysis in Chapter 3, "Accounting for the Kids," Grossberg assesses the one-sided tendencies to blame the media, racism, parents, capitalism, or the crisis in family values for the problems of youth today. Grossberg indicates that all of these factors contribute, but that one needs to contextualize the situation of youth in terms of far-reaching changes going on in the economy, polity, society, and culture. He outlines various responses to the changes in Part II, "The Contemporary Political Field," in which he assesses neoliberalism, the new conservativism, and liberalism and the Left, none of which adequately engage problems of youth in a productive way. The third part dissects youth in a coming "new American modernity" and offers perspectives on the reconstruction of political culture, economic life, and cultural life in ways that youth can more democratically participate in society and culture. A concluding chapter calls for a democratic conversation on these topics and a revitalization of democracy.

Grossberg is right to provide a contextualist analysis in terms of fundamental changes in U.S. society and culture to understand problems of youth today and to use social theory and history to contextualize the situation of youth. He is correct to advance a multicausal and multiperspectivist model on the problems of youth and to avoid one-sided explanations (and solutions) to the problems confronted by youth. Grossberg's approach is thus very much similar to my own multiperspectivist and multicausal model that contextualizes spectacular acts of societal violence from the Oklahoma City bombings to the Virginia Tech massacre within social conditions and crises of contemporary U.S. society.

In Chapter 4, I will offer some very specific discussion on the need for reconstructing education, reconstructing masculinity, increasing mental health care, curbing a gun culture run amok, reforming a punitive prison system, and fighting escalating militarism, all of which I see as key issues for the revitalization of democracy and addressing the problems of youth and of violence on which I focus in these studies. To dramatize the problems at hand, I want to wrap up this chapter on the situation of youth by indicating that youth today are seriously imperiled, although not for the reasons that conservatives and other establishment figures indicate.

Perils of Youth

"Children are the future of any society. If you want to know the future of any society look at the eyes of the children. If you want to maim the future of any society, you simply maim the children. The struggle for the survival of our children is the struggle for the survival of our future. The quantity and quality of that survival is the measurement of the development of our society."

—*Ngugi Wa Thion'o (cited in Grossberg 2005: 187)*

In an era in which unprecedented numbers of youth are incarcerated and executed and sent to war, youth today are in constant peril. Of course, depending on one's class, race, and region, perils are of different degrees and sorts. In this chapter, attempting to delineate the situation of youth, I have noted the growing economic, political, and social challenges to youth, but also the achievements and potential of youth to create a better future.

But the perils are many. As Jackson Katz points out in *The Macho Paradox* (2006), the dominant forms of male socialization and the ultramacho concept of masculinity dominant in U.S. culture from sports through the military and media are dangerous to both men and women. Katz's focus is on male violence against women, but macho male socialization is equally dangerous to victims and perpetrators alike, as violence begets violence. The macho notion of manhood in which men come to assert their masculinity with guns, violence, and even murder puts everyone in peril. This dominant concept of masculinity threatens both men and women alike, and until the cycle of male socialization and violence is broken, we will all be in peril.

While the project of gender and social reconstruction is of crucial importance (see Chapter 4), we need to face resolutely the perils youth confront today. To delineate these threats I want to cite some examples from recent work of Larry Grossberg, Jackson Katz, Donna Gaines, Toby Miller, Henry Giroux, Rhonda Hammer, and Angela Davis. Grossberg has written:

In most states in the United States, at 16 today, you cannot get your ears pierced without the permission of your parents. You cannot get a tattoo, and you cannot buy cigarettes. In fact, people under 16 cannot go to the Mall of America in Minnesota (the largest shopping mall in the country) after 6 p.m. on Friday or Saturday without a parent. But you can be tried and jailed as an adult, and more and more kids are. And in a growing number of states, you can be put to death as a penalty. Think of that—you can't get your ears pierced, but you can be put to death.[24]

As Jackson Katz reminds us:

- *JAMA: The Journal of the American Medical Association* published one study in 2001 which found that 20 percent of adolescent girls were physically or sexually abused by a date.
- Nearly one-third of American women report being physically or sexually abused by a husband or boyfriend at some point in their lives.
- An estimated 17.7 million women in the United States, nearly 18 percent, have been raped or have been the victim of attempted rape.
- Studies show that 15 to 38 percent of women and 5 to 16 percent of men experienced some form of sexual abuse as children.
- The average age of entry into prostitution is thirteen or fourteen.
- Studies suggest that between 3.3 and 10 million children witness some form of domestic violence annually. (2006: 21–22)

Summarizing her *Teenage Wasteland* (1998) research and pointing to the epidemic of teen suicide, Donna Gaines writes:

"Teenage suicide" was a virtually nonexistent category prior to 1960. At the time of the Bergenfield suicides it was described as the second leading cause of death among America's young people; "accidents" were the first. More than 400,000 adolescents attempt suicide each year. The rate of teenage suicide (ages fifteen to twenty-four is the statistical category for teenage suicide) has tripled in the past thirty years. The suicide rate for younger children (ages ten through fourteen) has more than doubled over the last fifteen. The actual suicide rate among teens is estimated to be even higher, underreported because of social stigma. Then there are the murky numbers derived from drug overdoses and car crashes, recorded as accidents. To date, teen suicides account for 14 percent of youth mortalities. (2000: 107)

As Toby Miller puts it:

Meanwhile, a succession of judicial decisions has further disenfranchised them, with conservative justices contemptuous of privacy rights for children, and the U.S. repeatedly establishing new records amongst developed countries for the execution of people under 18, with the longstanding support of the Supreme Court, half of which favored killing those aged under 15 until a 2005 decision (Males 1996: 7, 35). Young people lost free-speech protection, because the Supreme Court differentiated youthful from adult citizens, permitting state governments to legislate in ways that would be unconstitutional if applied to adults (*Ginsberg v. New York*, 390 U.S. 629). Today's capacity of the FBI and the Customs Service to utilize body-language profiling to identify potential terrorists, with agents trained to notice 'exceptional nervousness' via visible carotid arteries, chapped lips, 'fleeting smiles,' 'darting eyes[,] and hand tremors' derives from a 1968 decision of the Court, which established that young people could be arrested because they 'didn't look right' to officials. And while it protects adults from being treated with psychotropics against their will, this protection does not exist for the young in the majority of U.S. jurisdictions, who have also been subject to genetic testing on the grounds that it can disclose future classroom disobedience. Only two nations deny children rights, other than to counsel and due process in criminal cases. One is Somalia. You are encouraged to guess the identity of the latter, with the hint that the Kansas Juvenile Code incorporates parental rights as part of creepy Christianity's horror in the face of children's citizenship. (Miller, forthcoming)

Reflecting on some of the hidden horrors of militarism and the abuse of women, Henry Giroux notes:

The popular demonization and "dangerousation" of the young now justifies responses to youth that were unthinkable 20 years ago, including criminalization and imprisonment, the prescription of psychotropic drugs, psychiatric confinement, and zero tolerance policies that model schools after prisons. In the latter case, the No Child Left Behind policy now provides financial incentives to schools that implement zero tolerance policies, in spite of their proven racial and class biases; In addition, drug-sniffing dogs, metal detectors, and cameras have become common features in schools, and administrators willingly comply with federal laws that give military recruiters the right to access the names, addresses, and telephone numbers of students in both public schools and higher education—even though there have been numerous cases of rape and sexual abuse by recruiters who used their power to commit criminal acts against teenagers. For instance, a report by the Associated Press revealed that over 100 young women in 2005 were preyed upon sexually by military recruiters. The six-month investigation found that "Women were raped on recruiting office couches, assaulted in government cars and groped en route to entrance exams [and that at] least 35 Army recruiters, 18 Marine Corps recruiters, 18 Navy recruiters and 12 Air Force recruiters were disciplined for sexual misconduct or other inappropriate behavior with potential enlistees in 2005."[25] Trust and respect now give way to fear, disdain, and suspicion, creating an environment in which critical pedagogical practices wither, while pedagogies of surveillance flourish.[26]

Taking up the theme of violence against women and children during an era of global war, Rhonda Hammer writes.

Violence against women and children has been intensifying dramatically in Iraq since the Bush/Blair military intervention and occupation of April 2003. Alexander Cockburn notes that primary victims include: "the weakest in our midst: no money for food, for shelter, for the kids." In these ways, he asserts, "do we nourish the next generation of Enemy Combatants." ... Moreover, an international rights group, "Anti-Slavery International" reported to the United Nations session on slavery in March 2002 that there were at least 27 million people forced into slavery in the world today. These figures are growing, due in large part to the escalating poverty, and sexual exploitation and forced labour of children." (Reuters in *Metro Today,* May 27, 2002). In addition, the Amnesty International *Children's Report for the 2000 Campaign to Stamp out Torture* provides us with a shocking pronouncement on the global state of violence against children: "Violence against children is endemic: children are tortured by the police or security forces; detained in appalling conditions; beaten or sexually abused by parents, teachers or employers; maimed, killed or turned into killers by war. Some are victims many times over, first of the chronic poverty and discrimination that renders them vulnerable to torture and ill-treatment, then to the injustice and impunity that allows it to continue unpunished" (www. stoptorture.org). (2004: 90ff.)

Pointing to escalation of imprisonment and execution of youth in the prison-industrial complex, Angela Davis writes:

The prison-industrial complex embraces a vast set of institutions, from the obvious ones, such as the prisons and the various places of incarceration such as jails, "jails in Indian country," immigrant detention centers, and military prisons to corporations that profit from prison labor or from the sale of products that enable imprisonment, media, other government agencies, etc. Ideologies play a central role in consolidating the prison-industrial-complex—for example, the marketing of the idea that prisons are necessary to democracy and that they are a major component of the solution of social problems. Throughout the world, racism has become embedded in imprisonment practices: whether in the U.S., Australia, or Europe, you will discover a disproportionate number of people of color and people from the Global South incarcerated in jails and prisons. The everyday tortures experienced by the inhabitants of domestic prisons in the U.S. have enabled the justification of the treatment meted out to prisoners in Abu Ghraib and Guantánamo.... It was hardly accidental that a U.S. prison guard like Charles Graner was recruited to work in Abu Ghraib. He was already familiar with the many ways prison objectifies and dehumanizes its inhabitants. (2005: 69)

Of course, young men and young women face different challenges in negotiating the perils of youth, as members of different classes, races and ethnicities, regions, and sexualities. In the next chapter, I want to focus on crises of masculinity and the ways that dominant modes of macho socialization imperil young men, as well as the rest of society. I will focus on how ultramasculinist socialization, a violent guns-and-weapons culture, and a powerful and often violent media culture impacted on Timothy McVeigh, Terry Nichols, and the Oklahoma City bombings; on the strange excursion into violence of the Unabomber Ted Kaczynski; on the Columbine High School shooters Dylan Klebold and Eric Harris; and on Seung-Hui Cho and the Virginia Tech massacre. My argument will be that a wide range of specifiable and determinant factors together in the context of the current social organization and politics in the United States cause school shootings, terrorism, and violent behavior that require multiple solutions, rather than citing one dominant cause and one magic solution.

Chapter Three

Constructing Male Identities and the Spectacle of Terror

CONTEMPORARY YOUTH ARE A DISPARATE GROUP who construct identities in many different ways. Some conform to their specific dominant culture while others seek alternative identities in youth subcultures or create their own personal styles and identities that often mutate over time. Identities in the present age are more flexible and malleable than previous eras and young people try on a variety of cultural styles and references, often from media culture, to construct identities and lifestyles (Kellner 1995).

In an era of media spectacle, producing acts of violence and terror is one way to guarantee maximum media coverage and achieve celebrity. Intense media focus on the spectacles of the day gains saturation TV coverage on the 24/7 cable television networks and instant notoriety on the Internet. In an era of faux celebrity, where ordinary people become stars of "reality television," or of new websites like MySpace, Facebook, or YouTube, the craving for celebrity becomes acute, and acts of violence and terror are a way to guarantee instant celebrity.

Further, the construction of male identities in traditional ways has been problematized and made more difficult in the contemporary era, as discussed in previous chapters. In following pages, I compare the construction of male identities in four sets of individuals who have sought to produce ultramasculine identities through producing spectacles of terror that achieve notoriety and media celebrity. I begin with a discussion of "white male identity politics" and illustrate the concept with discussion of right-wing extremist militia groups and Timothy McVeigh, found guilty of and later executed for the Oklahoma City bombings of 1995. This analysis provides an opportunity to interrogate white male identity politics and right-wing gun culture and political extremism, and examine some specific crises in masculinity and dangerous attempts at resolution through creation of violent male identities. Then I look at the Unabomber, Ted Kaczynski, who produced another kind of bizarre media identity through mailing bombs to targeted individuals from 1978 until his capture in 1996.

To continue the interrogation of contemporary youth, I examine the Columbine shootings through the construction of the media spectacle of the shootings and the fierce debate in its aftermath of the cause of the school shootings; this discussion is followed by analysis of Michael Moore's *Bowling for Columbine* (2002), which I will suggest is immensely relevant for understanding school shootings and violence in the United States. I conclude this chapter with an analysis of how these spectacles of terror and male identity construction compare with Seung-Hui Cho in the Virginia Tech massacre.

There are, to be sure, significant differences between the four cases that I will interrogate in this chapter in terms of class, race, socialization, politics, and acts of terror. Yet, they exhibit in common crises in masculinity, obsession with guns and weapons culture, and the creation of mediated identities through spectacles of terror that qualify as examples of homegrown domestic terrorism.

White Male Identity Politics[1]

Until the 1960s, white male identity appeared to be fairly secure and unreflectively given, with white males a relatively uncontested ruling group. Since the founding of the United States, the importation of black slaves from Africa, and subjugation of native indigenous people, white men have been, and continue to be, the ruling power, presiding over the lives and consciousness of oppressed groups within and beyond the national borders. White men also have ruled for centuries over women, who legally and culturally have been the "second sex," the "other," and "object" to the white male "subject" (de Beauvoir 1952). Whereas white men are born with gender and race (though not necessarily class) privilege, other individuals are born members of subordinate or disadvantaged groups: One is born of color, a woman, poor, or with physical disabilities, and subsequent life experiences position individuals in relationships of subordination to which they are often forced to submit or to contest. Likewise, such constraints limit the choices one can make. White males, by contrast, are the dominant group, and while they too may be limited by class or other factors, when members of the ruling group feel threatened and besieged, they often seek identities that take on aggressive and extreme forms.

"Whiteness" itself is not a natural condition, but is a social construct. By itself, white skin color is an absence and lack that only takes on meaning in the presence of color—black, brown, yellow—which then creates a system of color differences that can become the basis of a system of racial hierarchies generating ideologies for racial oppression. When whites are the dominant race, they produce racial hierarchies in which "white" is the normal, the good, the superior, and people of various colors are the "other" and are denominated as racially different and often inferior. "Whiteness" in turn remains nameless, obliterating through silence traces of its construction and domination, until members of oppressed racial groups challenge its hegemony, attack its domi-nance, and attempt to undermine its legitimating ideologies. Then, whiteness must defend itself, members of white groups are put on the defensive, and there is a struggle over the social construction of race and attempts to redefine racial meanings.

When the once-dominant group is under attack, its members often turn on other groups with intense hostility and defend their own prerogatives with extremist racist ideologies and/or violent expressions of hypermasculin-ity—such as are now proliferating in the contemporary situation. Whiteness is, however, a curious identity marker, and some white men who identify with "their race" most fervently are, in fact, often quite tanned and dark-skinned "rednecks" who are sometimes darker than members of some "colored" and "nonwhite" races.[2] The fragility of racial skin markers thus requires bizarre racial ideologies to legitimate the superiority of whiteness and generates violent attitudes and actions against members of other races to bond "whites" together in a shared identity.

White men formerly were able to gain secure identities in terms of their position in the economy, as breadwinners, providers of the family, and by virtue of their economic class position, as well as the right of male privilege in a patriarchal society. Wealthy white men were admired as paragons of economic success and power, whereas middle-class and working-class white men could achieve positive male identities in terms of upward mobility and their abilities to provide for their families. Even poor white men still had an identity that made them superior to women and minorities, serving as rulers of their own domestic sphere and asserting their superiority over peoples of color. This form of white patriarchal male identity allowed them to identify with other white men in the ruling class over and against women and people from other races within their own social class.

Things began changing in the 1960s, with the intensification of social turmoil and challenges to the class, gender, sexual, and racial status quo by feminist groups, black and brown power groups, gay and lesbian groups, revolutionary movements in the third world, and a counterculture that contested heretofore existing institutions, practices, and values. Perhaps for the first time, straight white men were forced to seriously confront who they were and their relations to other groups. To make matters worse, beginning in the 1970s with a declining inflationary economy and the global restructuring of capital, working-class white men lost their breadwinner identities as their places of work closed down and jobs were eliminated or relocated to the developing world. In addition, affirmative action programs began hiring and promoting women and minorities for positions and jobs that formerly might have gone to white men. Farms were also foreclosed upon in record numbers during the predatory Reagan-Bush Senior period of the 1980s and early 1990s when capital was able to do whatever it wanted and received support or a turn back from the state, making farmers susceptible to hate politics that targeted Jews, blacks, or other minority groups as the enemy.

Overall, these complex cultural, political, and economic changes robbed white men of positive identities (as family providers, farmers, union members, and so on) and left them feeling besieged and confused. With women, gays and lesbians, and minority groups so proudly and defiantly championing their newfound identities, uncovering their hidden histories, and bonding together in exuberant and dynamic ways, white men felt compelled to respond. Many made the transformation smoothly, expressing solidarity with other groups and identities in an egalitarian spirit, and constructed identities that were multiple, flexible, and politically progressive.

Other white men, however, felt threatened and reacted against these changes. The combined effects of political upheaval, identity politics, affirmative action, multiculturalism, and economic decline led many white men to adopt a victim mentality that previously was characteristic of oppressed groups, and to blame the government and minorities for their plight. This situation gave rise to a new strain of white male identity politics fueled by intense rage, resentment, paranoia, and apocalyptic visions, often exploding into violence and finding solidarity in militia movements, right-wing hate and extremist groups, Christian fundamentalism, survivalist sects, and talk radio and Internet subcultures.

Thus, white male identities are challenged in an economy that is rapidly depriving white working-class men of the jobs that provided them with dignity and identity, as the economy moves to a global and high-tech form of capitalism. With the end of the industrial era and displacement of family farms with big agribusiness, the sorts of jobs that depended on male strength and skills are declining, while industrial labor is increasingly exported to the developing countries. In addition, computers and automation are taking over and displacing manual and skilled labor in a variety of sectors in the new high-tech economy, thus dispensing with male labor power.

Furthermore, white men are growing fearful of being replaced as the dominant group. The rise of militia, neo-Nazi, and other extremist movements in the United States, as elsewhere, is related both to the growing economic crisis and the rise of ethnicity and multiculturalism.[3] While racial minorities are still literally "minorities" in the United States as a whole, in many cities such as Los Angeles and Washington, D.C., blacks, Hispanics, and Asian Americans outnumber whites to form the oxymoron of "minority majorities."[4] As a result of the growing influx of ethnic minorities and their expanding economic, political, and cultural power, conservative whites and the extreme right fear an irretrievable loss of identity, tradition, jobs, and, in extreme form, even genetic "purity." This fear, in combination with the widespread revolt of women against male domination and a widely perceived view that women, blacks, and other groups are largely the beneficiaries of government affirmative action and welfare programs, has created an explosive situation where white male identities and power are threatened, with many reacting violently.

As a result, many dispossessed white men join militia movements or rightwing hate and extremist groups in order to reconstruct their political identities, often engaging in bizarre and sometimes violent behavior. Extremist movements empower disempowered people and provide a sense of meaning, purpose, and even destiny to confused and alienated individuals, the victims of undereducation and a high-tech global capitalism undergoing dramatic restructuring that no longer needs their labor power. Working-class and middle-class men often join militias, which give them a sense of purpose and empowerment, like the Arizona Vipers militia group arrested and incarcerated in 1996.[5] Millions of men of various backgrounds and ethnicities join groups like the Promise Keepers, who fill sports stadiums to reassert their male power and privileges in revivalist spectacles that combine conservative patriarchy with religion (see Diamond 1995). Similarly, Louis Farrakhan's October 1995 "Million Man March" on Washington, coming soon after the racial passions engendered by the O. J. Simpson verdict, empowered black men, providing a sense of purpose and direction, however dubious. And as I write in June 2007, there have been new sorts of threats from homegrown Muslim terrorists, including alleged plots to blow up Fort Dix and the JFK airport (although the government may have wildly exaggerated the operationality and viability of these attacks).[6]

The turn to white male (and in some cases black male or Muslim male) identity politics represents in part a rejection of modernity, combining premodern with postmodern motifs. Many of the men under siege turn to premodern ideologies like fundamentalist Christianity, Islam, archaic racism, survivalist and back-to-nature repudiations of modern life, and a variety of bizarre extremist ideologies. Many of these ideologies take the form of a postmodern pastiche, parallel in structure to postmodern cultural objects and theory that mix and combine aspects of past ideological discourses.[7] Many extremist militia, for instance, blend fundamentalist Christian beliefs with the speculations of religious sects, racism, National Socialism, and other bits of past discourses, assembling the pieces into new ideologies that empower and provide meaning and identity to their followers. Many of these discourses are extremely shallow and superficial, disconnected, and even schizophrenic, as are the postmodern artifacts that Jameson describes (1991).

Both the theories and the politics of many strains of white male identity politics thus take the form of a postmodern pastiche, combining premodern atavistic religious ideologies with modern racism, and forms of political organization with high-tech explosives and weapons and the use of advanced communications technologies like the Internet to disseminate their views and justify their actions. Yet the new ideologies, ranging from militia extremism to the Unabomber or Islamist terrorists, are often virulently antimodern, attacking modernist values, secularism, and institutions, and calling for a return to a simpler way of life. A pervasive mindset of white male identity politics is extreme paranoia, projecting confusion and anxiety over the tumultuous changes of the present age onto cosmic forces (evil, the Devil) or scapegoated villains, such as other races, "the new world order," or, in the Bush-Cheney years, "liberals" and secularists. There is also emphasis on chaos and disorder, and a nihilistic repudiation of modern discourses—key features of the postmodern paradigm articulated in *The Postmodern Turn* (Best and Kellner 1997: Chap. 6). Indeed, dominant white male identity ideologies are antimodern, antisecular, antidemocracy, often antiurban, and extremely antistatist and antiglobalist in scope. They build on prior anticommunist ideologies that exhibited fanaticism and a rigidly Manichean mindset, dividing the world into good and evil and "us" and "them." But this time a variety of figures (Jews, people of color, the state, the U.N., a world Zionist conspiracy, Islamist terrorists, or Mexican and other immigrants, and so on) stand for the evil "them" that threatens "us" and "good" white American values and people.

The new white male identity politics thus constitute a form of post–cold war ideologies, building on anticommunism, but shifting the animus to new targets. The extent of antistatism in the new right-wing ideologies is especially curious. Rightists during the cold war era were strongly pro-state, and were often deeply patriotic, defending the American way of life and its institutions against its "foreign" enemies and threats. But with the fall of communism, hatred of the enemy was projected inward, against the state, and especially the U.S. government and its institutions. Likewise, the warrior ethos that has been boiling in the cauldron of male frustration and paranoia has displaced its violence against foreign enemies to domestic targets, especially U.S. institutions like the government, the FBI, the IRS, the ATF, and other alphabetic targets of rightist hate and paranoia during the Clinton era, and to terrorists, Muslims, gays and lesbians, and liberals and Democrats in the Bush-Cheney era. Yet both the anticommunist ideology of the older right and the demonizations of the contemporary extremist right engaged in conspiracy theories that scapegoated alleged enemies, projecting all evil onto the imagined villains and covering over the real sources of domestic suffering and misery.

Militia, Right-Wing Extremism, and Terrorist Bombings

> "These were no soft-bellied, conservative businessmen assembled for some Masonic mumbo-jumbo; no loudmouthed, beery rednecks letting off a little ritualized steam about 'the goddam niggers'; no pious, frightened churchgoers whining for the guidance or protection of an anthropomorphic deity. These were *real men, White* men ... the best my race has produced ... combin[ing] fiery passion and icy discipline, deep intelligence and instant readiness for action ... They are the vanguard of the coming New Era, the pioneers who will lead our race out of its present depths ... And I am *one* with them!"
> —*William Pierce*, The Turner Diaries

The rise of militia and extremist white male identity politics and the attendant antistatism in the 1990s thus attests to the decline of national identity and the nation state in the face of identity politics, globalization, increased focus on the local community, and assaults on the state from left and right. It also attests to, as Carl Boggs (2000) has argued, to a decline of democratic politics and rise of a panorama of "antipolitics" ranging from militia and survivalists to cult and spiritualist groups, a wide array of (anti)political forces that Boggs explores in his *The End of Politics*.

These new forms of antipolitical politics undercut and challenge traditional political culture and democracy. There are thus some parallels between the belief of the extreme right, anarchism, and some varieties of postmodern politics. Although rightists sharply differ from left-wing anarchists in their rejection of socialist revolution, secular values, and in their embrace of racism and separatist politics, they share the classical anarchist animus against the validity of centralized government. The Posse Comitatus movement, for example, holds that any form of government higher than the local sheriff is invalid and most extremist groups reject as well the right of the government to impose taxes. Some groups seek formal separation from the government and threaten to shoot any trespassers on their property. For example, the intimidation tactics of the Freemen group in rural Montana effectively deterred both local and federal officials from serving them warrants for illegal acts, with government forces wary of another Ruby Ridge debacle.[8] Eventually, in April 1996, government forces moved on the Freemen compound to serve arrest warrants for financial fraud and threatening government officials, and after a tense 81-day standoff, the Freemen surrendered.

Unlike most left anarchists, except for those espousing "propaganda of the deed," the survivalists are committed to violence and terrorism as legitimate political tactics. An FBI raid on a right-wing religious commune on the Arkansas-Missouri border called the Covenant, the Sword, and the Arm of the Lord uncovered 30 gallons of raw cyanide intended for poisoning the water supply of a large urban center (Coates 1987). During 1996, a Georgia militia group was arrested for plans to disrupt the Olympic Games in Atlanta; two Arizona groups and a Washington group were arrested for plans to destroy government buildings; and there were waves of bombings and the burning of churches in the United States that has continued to the present.[9]

Oddly, the extreme right has absorbed some of the most radical positions and tactics associated with the ultraleft in the 1960s, including virulent anti-statism, domestic terrorism, and bombings. In an interesting reversal, once it was sectors of the Left like the Weather Underground that robbed banks and armored cars and planted bombs, but by the 1990s this is the signature of the extreme right.[10] One of the most popularized militia strategies is that devised by Louis Beam, a Christian Identity leader, who developed a concept of "leaderless resistance" which calls for a "cell system" of conspiratorial groups—a direct and acknowledged appropriation of Leninism. Moreover, where members of the counterculture once lived on farms and espoused the use of alternative medicine and lifestyles, now we find this characteristic of the survivalist movement. To complete the irony, where leftists once dedicated themselves to free speech, many now call for censorship or regulation of speech, while members of the right are sometimes impassioned defenders of freedom of hate speech, attacking government attempts at censorship. However, segments of both the right and the Left today are preaching a separatist identity politics.

Male rage and paranoia and the rise of white male identity politics have been some decades in the making. The U.S. defeat in Vietnam created a sense of the loss of manhood and diminished American males, especially those who fought in the war and were rejected upon their return (Jeffords 1989). Men sought compensation for loss of power in warrior fantasies, nurtured by media culture and a whole subculture of pulp literature, guns, conventions, weekend survivalist camps, and an exotic profusion of paramilitary culture (see Gibson 1994; Kellner 1995; and Boggs 2005). As Gibson states: "American men—lacking confidence in the government and the economy, troubled by changing relations between the sexes, uncertain of their identity or their future—began to dream, to fantasize about the powers and features of another kind of man who could retake and reorder the world" (1994: 11).

The crisis in masculinity drove many men to seek solace in guns and weapons. Gun and military culture in particular fetishize weapons as an important part of male virility and power, treating guns as objects of almost religious veneration and devotion. In this constellation, the expression of violence through guns and the use of weapons is perceived as an expression of manhood. In recent years, however, gun culture has mutated into a more defuse military culture where explosives and more lethal weapons are deployed by extremist white male groups and individuals to try to reconstruct even more exaggerated hypermale identities.

Such a constellation provides a lethal mix when combined with right-wing extremist ideology. Indeed, during the past two decades, rightist hate groups have been sporadically active, testifying to the fragmentation of contemporary U.S. society into a battleground between warring groups and ideologies. Beginning with the killing of Denver talk show host Alan Berg in 1984 (who made the fatal mistake of taunting neo-Nazis on the air), continuing through a series of daring armed robberies (where the Order, a neo-Nazi commando movement, netted millions of dollars to fund other groups in the movement), galvanized by the government attacks on white supremacist Randy Weaver and his family in 1992 and David Koresh's Branch Davidian Church in Waco in 1993, and culminating with the bombing of the Alfred P. Murrah Federal Building in Oklahoma City in 1995, it has become clear that the extremist right is willing to fight, kill, and die for its cause.

The actions of the radical right are not only based on visceral hatred of Jews and minorities, but are informed by an extensive body of literature and complex ideology. Besides Genesis, which they ludicrously distort to legitimate their bizarre interpretations of history and the origins of the races, and the Book of Revelation, which underpins their apocalyptic vision, William Pierce's *The Turner Diaries* (1978) has had a major impact on right-wing extremists, providing inspiration for counterfeiting, assassinations, armored car and bank robberies, and, perhaps, even the bombing of the federal building in Oklahoma City. The bomb used in Oklahoma, like the one evoked by Pierce, contained a mixture of fuel oil and ammonium nitrate fertilizer, was similar in size to the one that Pierce's terrorist "hero" detonated at the FBI building in Washington, D.C., and went off at approximately the same hour in the morning.

Further, it is well documented that Timothy McVeigh, found guilty of the Oklahoma City bombings in June 1997, was deeply influenced by *The Turner Diaries* (see below). The dementia of the extreme right is also informed by an apocalyptic vision of a nuclear Armageddon, a worldwide domination by Jewish capitalists through ZOG (the Zionist Occupation Government), and the eclipse of the white race and the United States through the growth of immigrant and minority populations. Strongly rooted in the Book of Revelations, these extremists uphold the prophesy of a final battle between Good, the White Race, and Evil, consisting of Jews and racial minorities, and are obsessed with the Tribulation, manifesting trials and suffering in the few years before Armageddon, the final battle between Good and Evil, Good and Satan (see Dyer 1997).

This apocalyptic Armageddon was depicted in a best-selling series of novels, *Left Behind*, by Christian evangelist Tim LaHaye and Jerry B. Jenkins. Beginning in 1995, the series of 10 novels has been accompanied by three films: *Left Behind: The Movie* (2001), *Left Behind 2: Tribulation Force* (2003) and *Left Behind 3: World at War* (2005). The story line concerns the Rapture, which comes and takes away good Christians, presumably to a life in Heaven with Jesus and God the Father, but the narrative deals with the trials and tribulations, pardon the pun, of those left behind. *Left Behind: The Movie* (2001) focuses on Global News Network reporter Buck Williams (Kirk Cameron), who learns the truth—that the explanation for the mysterious disappearance of scores of people is the Rapture, and that the salvation of those left behind lies with becoming a true Christian and joining a resistance movement against the forces of darkness who are creating a secular society.

The story line of the films and novels depicts Christians finding each other and forming a "tribulation force," resistant to the secular reign of the

Antichrist, who uses the United Nations to form a Global Community (GC) that gets sovereign nations like the United States to give up their weapons and sovereign power in the name of world peace. *Left Behind 2: Tribulation Force* (2003) explores the horrors of the tribulation and the evil Antichrist Nicolae Carpathia gaining world power, but shows the rise of a Christian community and hopes for salvation of the believers.

Left Behind 3: World at War (2005) has U.S. President Fitzhugh (Lou Gossett Jr.) come to realize that Nicolae is the Antichrist and that he plans to destroy the United States. In an early scene, an oppositional militia, eventually coded as positive resistance forces, attacks the president's caravan, since he has in their view betrayed the country by ceding power to the Global Community. The film puts on display right-wing fears of global power and legitimates violent resistance against a state that it believes is ungodly and betraying U.S. interests. Exploiting fears of terrorism after 9/11, the film shows the Antichrist Carpathia putting anthrax in Bibles to spread a deadly virus among the Christian community, that learns, too late for the survival of some of the main characters, that wine drunk in the Christian sacrament is the antidote.

For real-world evangelical Christians and those who believe in a coming Rapture, the battle between the forces of Light and Darkness is expected to culminate in nuclear war.[11] Hence, many survivalists and other extremists retreat to living in compounds well supplied with food, water, medicine, and guns, where they think they have a better chance of survival than in urban centers. This confers on them the added advantages of distance from dreaded minorities and being able to organize for coming battles, whether it be against racial minorities or the government. After the war is over, they hope to rebuild civilization as a white nation. For now, the leadership of the survivalist right urges its members to join in an exodus to the states of Wyoming, Montana, Idaho, Washington, and Oregon, a migration they call the "Northwest Territorial Imperative."

All too literally, the disturbed fantasies of the apocalyptic right provide literary mappings for others to follow. Radical right-wing discourse is also a feature of talk radio with hosts like Rush Limbaugh, G. Gordon Liddy, Oliver North, Michael Savage, and others advocating extremist politics. Moreover, the radical right has invaded cyberspace with a vengeance in order to promote its hate politics, having opened up numerous computer lists, websites, and blogs that supplement their use of audio- and videotapes, telephone "hot lines," and newsletters—constituting a form of the postmodernization of political discourse in the new public sphere of cyberspace (see Kellner 1997a; and Kahn and Kellner 2005). The Internet in particular has proved a fertile recruiting ground for white supremacists and neo-Nazis with many websites, bulletin boards, discussion lists, and chat lines for those in extremist groups.

The Internet has also been efficacious in recruiting youth to the movement. Extremist websites provide rock music for young "Aryan Youth," online youth magazines with movie reviews (*Pulp Fiction* is described as "better than a cold beer on a hot Auschwitz afternoon!"), ads for Ku Klux Klan Kollectibles, racist news "suppressed by the mainstream press," and electronic sales of rightist literature, music, and other products.[12] Of course, the youth cultures of evangelical Christians, Muslims, leftists, feminists, and others of all political temperaments are also available on the Internet, so cyberspace is becoming more and more a contested terrain, a site of cultural and political struggle for the present and the future.

Yet, it is ironic that many extremist right-wing groups openly assail modernity and modern values, asserting religious fundamentalism, premodern atavism, and bizarre irrationalist ideologies—while using advanced technology to disseminate their messages. The right-wing groups are intensely paranoid, suggesting that the paranoia that Thomas Pynchon depicts in his novels like *Gravity's Rainbow* (1967) has permeated everyday life and taken extreme forms—though of a form one could call "clinical" rather than "creative" paranoia, as in Pynchon's concept (see Best and Kellner 2001: Chap. 1). The right fears such things as the United Nations takeover of the United States, the elimination of rights to own guns and practice religion, and the disappearance of the white race. Their paranoia is so profound as to see anticounterfeiting strips on $20 bills as government radio transmitters, to fear the markings on the back of interstate road signs as signals for the U.N. army of occupation (directed from black helicopters), and the implantation of anal spy systems in the buttocks of every person who has had any contact with the federal system (Coates 1987). And during the mid-1990s the right constantly blamed the U.S. government for terrorist acts that its own members had carried out.

Home-Grown Terrorism: Timothy McVeigh and the Oklahoma City Bombing

"The tree of liberty must be refreshed from time to time with the blood of patriots and tyrants."
—*Abraham Lincoln (on the back of a T-shirt worn by Timothy McVeigh)*

The right-wing extremist movements were galvanized and driven to violence by two specific events. A 1992 government attack against separatist and white supremacist Randy Weaver left his wife and son dead in a botched attempt to arrest him for refusing to stand trial for illegal gun sales. Weaver and his family had left Iowa for Idaho, where they purchased their own land, built a house, and, when they ran out of money, got into illegal activities such as petty crime and illegally selling guns. Deeply immersed in fundamentalist Christianity, Weaver also got involved with neo-Nazi groups and attracted the attention of the FBI, who apparently used him in a sting operation when he was arrested for attempting to sell illegal sawed-off shotguns. Refusing to surrender to a warrant for his arrest, Weaver fortified himself and his family in his Ruby Ridge homestead and in an infamous raid—which won Weaver martyr status among the extreme right—federal agents shot and killed his wife and young son (see Walter 1995; and Spence 1995).

Another U.S. government assault, on the Branch Davidian religious cult in Waco from February 28 to April 19, 1993, resulted in the death of around 80 men, women, and children, convincing the extreme right that the U.S. government was evil and radicalizing their hatred of it. The Branch Davidians preached a version of apocalyptic Christianity and in preparation for the end of the world and Second Coming of Christ—and perhaps federal assaults on their property—stocked up on guns and weapons in a compound near Waco, Texas. When federal agents raided the property, the Branch Davidians fought back and four federal agents were killed in the gunfire. A 70-day siege followed, ended by a deadly conflagration in which a fire ignited during a government assault killed most of those in the compound, including many women and children.[13]

Many rightists interpreted the assault on the Waco Branch Davidian sect as an attack by the government on religious freedom and the right to carry guns and responded passionately to the FBI siege of the compound and the resultant fire that killed most of the occupants. It is widely believed that the Oklahoma bombing, which took place on the second anniversary of the Waco assault, was intended as revenge against the U.S. government for such acts—the event also overlapped with the second anniversary of the Ruby Ridge siege, the execution of a white supremacist, and the anniversary of the beginning of the Battle of Lexington that began the U.S. Revolutionary War. Video footage shown nationally in April 1996 depicted Timothy McVeigh, one of the suspects in the Oklahoma bombings, handing out extremist literature in Waco during the FBI siege against the Branch Davidians, and many who knew him indicated that he had gone to Waco and was extremely upset by government actions there. There were many threats by extremist groups to get revenge against the government for killing members of Weaver's family and the Branch Davidians, who became martyrs in the extreme right's iconography.

In any case, on April 19, 1995, the largest terrorist bomb in U.S. history went off in Oklahoma City at 9:02 a.m. It was estimated that the truck bomb contained over 6,000 pounds of explosives and the blast resulted in the complete destruction of the federal building and claimed 168 lives, including 19 children, while injuring and maiming many more victims.[14] At first the suspects were believed to be Middle Eastern in origin. For over 24 hours, CNN repeatedly played sketches of Middle Eastern suspects said to have been seen in the vicinity of the bombing and interviewed one terrorist specialist after another who speculated that a Middle Eastern group had targeted U.S. domestic sites for terrorist activities. Pundits in the mainstream press took up this position and urged that military special forces be used against "potential terrorists." "Shoot them now, before they get us," *New York Newsday* columnist Jeff Kame urged in an op-ed piece, while Mike Royko ranted in his syndicated *Chicago Tribune* column: "I would have no objection if we picked out a country that is a likely suspect and bombed some oil fields, refineries, bridges, highways, industrial complexes.... If it happens to be the wrong country, well, too bad, but it's likely it did something to deserve it anyway."[15]

However, the day after the bombing a picture was released of two white male suspects, and it was announced on April 21 that Oklahoma police held in custody one of the suspects, John Doe #1, who apparently turned out to be Timothy McVeigh.[16] Later that day, Terry Nichols, a friend of McVeigh who had served in the military with him and shared his antigovernment views, surrendered himself and later was also formally charged in the bombing. From what we know of McVeigh and Nichols, they are salient examples of white male identity politics whereby alienated men construct their identities through the production of spectacles of terror. It was widely reported that Timothy McVeigh, the main suspect in the Oklahoma bombing who was declared guilty of the crimes by a jury in June 1997, was an avid reader of *The Turner Diaries* and other extreme rightist literature. McVeigh promoted the book among friends and acquaintances and sold it during gun shows.[17] In many ways, the Oklahoma bombing, even down to the chemical composition of the bomb and time of the explosion, copied the scenario of *The Turner Diaries,* where guerilla resistance forces formed revolutionary cells and carried out acts of violence, connected with other groups in an underground network.

McVeigh and Nichols were known for their love of guns, and McVeigh evidently supported himself by selling weapons at gun shows. Both McVeigh and Nichols served in the Gulf War, had military training, and dabbled in explosives, experimenting with explosive devices at Nichols's brother's farm in northern Michigan. Both violently opposed any gun control or restrictions and were paranoid that the Brady Bill, which proposed restrictions on assault weapons and tightened checks on proposed gun owners, was the first step in taking away citizens' Second Amendment gun rights.[18]

Both McVeigh and Nichols were classic losers, adrift in contemporary society, and evidently empowered themselves through use of weapons and associations with right-wing extremist groups and ideologies, gaining identities through such associations and fantasies. In addition, McVeigh repeatedly saw antigovernment Waco videotapes and was seen and videotaped himself giving out antigovernment literature at the site of the Waco siege.

Further, McVeigh had frequently checked out from video rental stores John Milius's *Red Dawn* (1984),[19] a fantasy of a communist invasion of the United States countered by young teenagers who go to the mountains and organize themselves as a guerilla army. Milius is an especially reactionary and masculinist director who equates manhood and virility with the use of weapons, assertion of male violence and power, and using violence to triumph over adversity. His teenage revolutionaries called themselves the "Wolverines" and coincidentally the Michigan militia, with which McVeigh and the Nichols brothers were allegedly associated, adopted the Wolverine as its symbol.

McVeigh later told two reporters working on a biography of him that he saw himself as Luke Skywalker attacking the Death Star to undermine the Evil Empire, as in the original *Star Wars* (1977) (see Michel and Herbeck 2001: 224ff.). McVeigh noticed that the *Star Wars* films showed clerical workers sitting around computer consoles on Darth Vader's Death Star, and noted other workers who enabled the Evil Empire to function: "When Luke blew up the Death Star those people became inevitable casualties. When the Death Star exploded, the movie audiences cheered. The bad guys were beaten: that was all that really mattered. As an adult, McVeigh found himself able to dismiss the killings of secretaries, receptionists, and other personnel in the Murrah Building with equally cold-blooded calculation. They were all part of the Evil Empire" (225).[20]

In an interesting analysis of how the media makes terrorists celebrities, Brigitte Nacos (2007) indicates how both McVeigh and Osama bin Laden were made into major celebrities by media framing and presentation. In a detailed account of McVeigh's achieving celebrity status in the six months before his execution, Nacos cites how MSNBC presented a program about McVeigh and the Oklahoma City bombing on its series *Headliners and Legends,* usually devoted to celebrities and stars, thus calling attention to McVeigh's transformation into a celebrity. She also cites Neil Gabler's analysis of celebrity and entertainment, indicating how a *Newsweek* color photo by Eddie Adams, the famed Vietnam War photographer, made a romanticized McVeigh appear "more like a typical Gen-Xer than a deranged loner, much less a terrorist" (Gabler, cited in Nacos: 97), while the actual article and interview "was pure *Photoplay*: gushy, reverent, excited" (ibid.).

Responding to his media celebrity treatment, women sent McVeigh nude photos of themselves, marriage proposals, and money—angering families of the victims (Nacos 2007: 98). Moreover, Nacos indicates, it was not just TV and news magazines that helped McVeigh achieve fame and celebrity. In a similar fashion, newspapers carried frequent articles on him, such that during the last six months of his life he "received almost a third as many mentions as the President George W. Bush, and stories about him far exceeded the volume of coverage devoted to Vice President Dick Cheney, who was widely seen as equally influential and important as the president" (100).[21]

McVeigh thus became the fantasy figure he dreamed about. And it appears that McVeigh, many right-wing militia members, and the school shooters who would carry out the Columbine and Virginia Tech spectacles of terror were all living in a fantasy world generated by novels, films, and right-wing literature. Identifying with the figures and apparitions of pulp fiction and media culture, these disempowered males find identity and empowerment in the construction of extremist politics and violent acts, often living out their fantasies in bizarre and dangerous forms, or as fantasy revenge turned into real horror.[22] The way that contemporary pulp literature and films provide inspiration and maps to the actions of the extremist right testifies to both the power of cultural artifacts and the poverty of the right-wing imagination, which needs to follow a book plot or film scenario to undertake effective action. Moreover, the participants in the Oklahoma bombing were also trained by the military and had thus undergone military socialization. Timothy McVeigh and Terry Nichols were socialized in the military and by media culture to be warrior heroes, to achieve great acts of violence. When frustrated, such ideals can take very explosive forms, as seemed to have happened in the Oklahoma bombing.[23]

Likewise, both Nichols and McVeigh were deeply immersed in paramilitary and gun culture and appeared to be empowered by their use of guns. Both were extremely angry and paranoid that the government was going to take away their guns and were prepared to fight to the death to prevent this, taking "preemptive action" in the strike on the Oklahoma City federal building. Evidently, the Clinton administration's passing of the Brady Bill assault weapons ban in 1994 created tremendous anger and paranoia on the gun-culture right, and McVeigh and Nichols in particular were outraged and angry (see Stickney 1996: 151).

It is striking how many of the major political assassins, school shooters, and serial killers in recent U.S. history had military training or were gun enthusiasts.[24] Lee Harvey Oswald, age 24 at the time of John F. Kennedy's assassination in 1963, had both paramilitary training (Air Cadets) and military experience (U.S. Marine Corps); Sirhan Sirhan, age 24 at the time of Robert Kennedy's assassination in 1968, had paramilitary experience (California Cadets), received weapons training, and owned .38 and .22 caliber handguns. Charles Whitman, a former Marine, put his love of guns and sniper training to work in 1966 at the University of Texas, Austin, to become one of the first infamous school shooters.[25] Arthur Bremer, age 22 when he attempted to assassinate George Wallace in 1972, was the son of a U.S. military man and was fascinated with paramilitary organizations; he collected guns and owned .38 and 9-mm handguns—the .38 was used to shoot Wallace. Mark David Chapman, age 25 at the time of his assassination of former Beatle John Lennon in 1980, was the son of a career Air Force enlisted man, underwent weapons training, and used his .38 handgun to assassinate Lennon. John Hinckley, age 25 at the time of the assassination attempt on Ronald Reagan, held neo-Nazi and white supremacist beliefs and had planned to assassinate President Carter approximately six months before his attempt to assassinate Reagan on March 30, 1981. He collected guns and owned a .38 handgun, which he used in the assassination attempt on Reagan.

McVeigh, who was 26 at the time of the Oklahoma City bombing, joined the Army and participated in the 1991 Gulf War. He allegedly became depressed after failing to be accepted into the Special Forces. McVeigh had some connections to paramilitary antigovernment groups, and was, as we have seen, a major gun enthusiast and antigovernment activist. All of these young men suffered from male rage and crises of masculinity, used weapons and violent action to create a hypermasculinity, and produced media spectacles to assert themselves and gain celebrity.

McVeigh appears to have been highly conscious that he was producing a major media event and was eager to use the media to circulate his extremist ideas and present himself as an antigovernment freedom fighter. In any case, the suspects in the Oklahoma bombings and many other infamous assassins and domestic terrorists have been involved in a form of white male identity politics connected with right-wing extremism and gun culture, using media spectacle to promote their agendas. The phenomenon of homegrown domestic terrorism with U.S.-based groups engaging in terrorism against the state is a relatively recent phenomenon, especially for the right. It appears that after the end of the cold war and the fall of communism, the symbolic universe of the right collapsed and they were thrown into a situation of chaos and indeterminacy in which many forces appeared threatening, but without the rigid and firm boundaries between "us" and "them," good Americans and evil communists, that maintained the cold war Manichean vision that Ronald Reagan so perfectly articulated and upheld.[26]

Reagan, in retrospect, successfully kept frustrated white males focused on the external communist enemy, as George H. W. Bush attempted to do with his wars on Panama's Manuel Noriega and Iraq's Saddam Hussein. Bush Senior failed to articulate and sustain a feared foreign "Other," however, as well as failing to provide a viable economic program. Bush and his national security advisor Brent Scowcroft also made the mistake of disseminating a notion of the "new world order" after the Gulf War, in which countries would bind together to fight aggressors and bullies (under American leadership, of course). In fact, the concept of a "new world order" was earlier promoted by Italian fascism and German National Socialism (see Kellner 1992). But the extremist right in the United States interpreted the term to indicate a new world government that would take away its religious freedom and gun ownership rights.

Thus, the antistatism of the right began in earnest during the first Bush regime and intensified under the Clinton administration.[27] Lacking a clear-cut enemy, white male identity politics has a whole range of antagonists, ranging from people of color to federal bureaucrats, gays and lesbians, feminists, liberals, Jews, and the state, all the way to the "new world order." The great diversity of targets of extremist hatred leads to eclectic postmodern ideological pastiches that cobble together a variety of discourses promulgated by the various rightist groups. And while white male paranoia fears conspiracies and growing chaos, the more extremist groups themselves have been forming conspiracies and fomenting chaos. Following the example of *The Turner Diaries,* in which antigovernment rebels counterfeit money and rob banks, the Montana Freemen engaged in a series of bogus check-writing schemes, mail frauds, and other crimes to finance the extremist right before their arrest in June 1996.[28] A Freeman document exhorted individuals to sever ties to government by not paying taxes or recognizing any U.S. government authority. The document proclaimed that "free white males" have lost control of the country and that, "We the People are now ruled by foreigners/aliens."[29]

Harvest of Rage

"Tears of rage, tears of grief."

—*The Band*

Threatened white males—and some white women—thus create empowering identities by appropriating bizarre ideologies and projecting evil onto threatening external forces, which in the 1990s took radically antistatist forms. Such views are a casebook example of white male paranoia and identity politics. Indeed, militia and radical right paranoia has been so extreme that from the beginning militia members insisted that the U.S. government itself perpetrated the Oklahoma bombing as an excuse to suppress the militia movements.[30] Yet precisely such paranoid extremism and the proliferation of a premodern warrior culture is ironic at the very time that the traditional warrior is militarily obsolete in the new era of cyborg-technowar (Best and Kellner 2001: Chap. 2). The violent hysteria of the extreme right, and its turn to weapons and violence, is a retrograde and irrational attempt to turn back history, to desperately resist its own obsolescence in an era when white males' labor power and military power are of less and less use in a high-tech society.

Yet right-wing extremism is also an expression of genuine suffering and the devastation wrought upon entire regions of the country by the global restructuring of capital. Recent years have seen a tremendous increase in suffering in rural America, exhibiting a massive failure of government to provide a safety net, especially for rural individuals not visible in the media or supported by government institutions. The process of the restructuring of capital has not only brought devastation to urban areas and created problems for the prospects of youth, as described in the previous chapter, but has also devastated entire regions of the country. The global restructuring of capital brought first "the deindustrialization of America" (Bluestone and Harrison 1982), in which industrial jobs were exported abroad; factory regions were shut down, forming ugly "rustbelts" in once prosperous industrial regions and devastating inner cities dependent on the wages of industrial labor.

Capitalist restructuring during the 1980s and beyond brought about devastation to the rural heartland of America (see Dyer 1997). Large corporations and agribusiness took over family farms, displacing entire generations of farmers, creating tremendous despair and misery (and a questionable food supply for the rest of us). Whereas the U.S. government once subsidized small farmers and banks, and government and banks readily provided generous loans to support the family farm, suddenly in the 1980s agricultural policies were reversed and farmers and rural regions were left to fend for themselves. There were massive cutbacks in rural health programs, schools, and other programs (Dyer 1997), with both major political parties focusing on urban problems and serving largely middle- and upper-class urban and suburban constituencies.

With the rationalization of industrial labor and agriculture, accompanied by deindustrialization and the monopolization of agribusiness, both industrial labor and agricultural labor became significantly less central to the production process, producing the devastation of the rustbelt and then rural America. The logic of capital is ruthless and as the need for industrial and agricultural labor declined in an era of high tech and automation entire regions were displaced and devastated, with consequences not yet over. Agricultural labor, like industrial labor, of the old sort is just not needed, or less is needed and it is done by part-time, unorganized groups, often migrant workers, that can be more easily exploited. Traditional factory towns and the family farm are thus both gone with the wind, blown away by shifts in global corporate production, giant agribusiness, and the complicity of the capitalist state. This causes massive suffering, including loss of identity for workers and farmers, and by the 2000s had created white male resentment against immigrant workers, especially undocumented ones (although this is a story for another time).

Thus, capital in conjunction with new high-tech computerization and automation relentlessly eliminates traces of the premodern, but also distinguishing features of modernity—that is, industrial regions and labor, the family farm and rural communities, and vibrant inner-city neighborhoods for the poor. Entire regions and ways of life are eliminated as capital restructures. Both the rustbelt and farmbelt have been devastated, although these regions tend to be "the invisible America," neglected by mainstream media and politics, producing a fertile ground for white male extremist politics. While one can sympathize with the victims of capitalist restructuring, displaced rural and industrial workers should know that their problems are not caused by Jews, ZOG, the United Nations, immigrants, or the U.S. government—though the last contributes to their sufferings to the extent that it is a capitalist tool in the hands of highly greedy conservative forces and seems to be cutting back on even minimal safety nets for the victims of capitalist restructuring in the Reagan/Bush/Clinton/Bush era. Rather, it is the global restructuring of capital that is causing the devastation and not any specific conspiracies, except to the extent that ruling groups and interests always conspire to advance their interests.

What Dyer calls "the harvest of rage" (1997) continued to sow its seeds in the aftermath of the Oklahoma City bombing. During the succeeding years, there have been attacks on the Amtrack railroad system and federal buildings all over the United States, plots to disrupt the 1996 Olympics in Atlanta with terrorism, assaults on the White House, a kidnapping and confrontation with state authorities by the Republic of Texas, the bombing of abortion clinics, and a wave of burnings of black and other churches, with an especially shocking wave of black church burning in the South in 2006.[31] There are many militia movements in existence throughout the United States, as well as other extremist groups and individuals loosely affiliated with the movement.[32]

It is, however, difficult to assess the actual forces and dangers of the extremist movements. On one hand, some of the most visible aspects of the militia movement declined in the years just following the Oklahoma City bombing. In the years just after the bombing, there was a drop in some categories of gun sales, membership in some militia and rightist extremist groups, decline in subscription to right-wing periodicals, and a less blatant new warrior culture.[33] Yet the drop right after the bombings, indicating a decline in "wannabe" white male warrior culture, might have covered a shift underground to more serious and less visible extremist groups that may have grown during subsequent years.

It could also be the case that the two presidential terms of George W. Bush lessened right-wing extremist fervor because many of its own found themselves in positions of power, and the policies of the Bush-Cheney regime were more in tune with rightist sympathies, especially on guns and war. After the 9/11 terror attacks, the Bush-Cheney administration was successfully able to mobilize fear and anger against Islamic and foreign terrorists, undercutting anti–U.S. government rhetoric and anger and providing an enemy and target for right-wing rage.

It remains an open question whether the worsening economic situation for many, and demoralization with the Bush administration because of its Iraq debacle, its many scandals, and incompetence, will once again generate violent right-wing extremism. Right-wing talk radio demonized Bill Clinton and his administration in the 1990s and has been an even more ferocious attack dog against liberal Democrats in the Bush-Cheney era (see Brock 2004). The number of threats and level of security already mobilized behind 2008 presidential Democratic Party candidates Hillary Rodham Clinton and Barack Obama may point to a festering resentment on the right that may well seek domestic targets, as in the past.

Further, as Morris Dees and the Southern Poverty Law Center have long documented, hate groups and crimes continue to emerge, with 844 active hate groups located on the Center's latest map in 2007, a 40 percent rise since the start of the millennium and up 5 percent from the previous year.[34]

Anti-immigration recruitments have reportedly brought new members into so-called nativist and patriot groups as well as white supremacist hate groups like the Ku Klux Klan, racist skinheads, and white nationalists with one, the Minutemen, advising supporters to get together survival supplies and threatening that "hundreds of thousands of Americans will consider this [a liberalized immigration bill] the final straw, violent civil disobedience will break out all over the country if this legislation gets passed."[35]

In any case, it appears that white male extremist politics today is more diffuse, fragmented, and perhaps underground than before. The Internet has replaced print media publications for some right-wing extremists, while others are just more secretive and less obvious, harder to document and follow. It could be argued that new communications technologies intensify the power and effect of extremist groups, which have countless websites, Internet discussion lists, talk radio shows, print publications, and audio and videotapes. Indeed, an HBO documentary, *Hate.com: Extremists on the Internet* (2000), portrayed a growing right-wing extremist and gun culture present in cyberspace, and the latest count by the Southern Poverty Law Center lists 566 U.S.-based hate sites on the World Wide Web in 2006, up from 522 a year earlier.[36]

Thus, the number of right-wing extremist sympathizers may outnumber their hard-core members, and constitutes a disturbing new political force in the United States and other societies that allow unrestricted gun ownership and freedom of speech. Moreover, as diffusion of computer and other new communication technologies expands, there is potentially a growing base of recruitment for extremist groups.

The combination of male rage, right-wing paranoia and identity politics, and a culture of violence is extremely lethal. The Branch Davidian obsession with weapons that attracted the attention of the federal government in Waco in the first place, the Oklahoma and other terrorist bombings, the mail bombs sent by the Unabomber to representatives of the high-tech society, and the high school and college shootings at Columbine, Virginia Tech, and elsewhere disclose the obsession with guns, violence, and weapons in U.S. society and the ways that men use violence to create identities, gain meaning, and assert their power. Indeed, the depiction of violence as a mode of solving problems and empowering males is also a standard trope of media culture, which in recent years has accelerated positive representations of violence in popular film and television, as well as rap music (see Kellner 1995).[37] Media culture extols violence in many of its genres, which show violence as the most efficacious mode of eliminating "evil" and resolving problems while celebrating violent male heroes as icons of masculinity.

As noted, many extremist groups espouse violent hatred of other social groups and exhibit paranoia that conspiracies abound to further rob them of their rights and power. The hyperrealization of this paranoia via talk radio, Internet discussion lists and websites, audio- and videotapes, and other technologies lends credence and force to these fantasies. In a high-tech society, messages acquire an aura and power via their dissemination over electronic media. As McLuhan (1964) pointed out, radio is a tribal drum that intensifies the power and prestige of the message and the messenger. Indeed, extremists from Hitler to Rush Limbaugh who articulate the anger, paranoia, and frustrations of the underlying population through the electronic tribal drum attain cult status and a wide following. This vision is fully evident in the power of talk radio that in many ways is another major feature of postmodern politics. In talk radio, the ordinary citizen, denied a voice in party politics and official media discourse, finds articulated his or her hatreds, fears, rage, and insecurity. The world of talk radio is a hyperreal world of the "ecstasy of communication" (see Baudrillard 1983) where views hitherto taboo are spoken and the alienated and marginalized can find community with those who share their perspectives.

Although talk radio could make possible genuine democratic debate and dialogue, allowing a full range of views usually excluded from ordinary political expression, in fact it is usually the extreme right that is allowed talk radio venues; white men compose over 80 percent of the talk radio hosts around the country and the majority of them are conservative (see Boggs and Dirmann 1999). This is partly because of corporate control and ownership of broadcast media, which find left-wing views anathema, and partly a function of a commercial broadcast system that operates under the perception that the majority of the audience is on the right side of the political spectrum. Consequently, when more progressive voices slip into the spectrum, they are subject to corporate control and the threat that low ratings will result in their termination.[38]

Moreover, while talk radio appears to be a direct expression of public discourses, it is in fact carefully constructed and restricted. Calls are monitored by controllers who allow only those voices in tune with the ethos of the show on the air, and the host can cut off callers at anytime. In addition, there is an implosion between politics and entertainment, with talk radio hosts like Rush Limbaugh, Howard Stern, or Don Imus providing shock entertainment rather than informed public dialogue. And to some extent, audiences are pulled into the spectacle, either via their calls and mediated participation, or their passionate responses in private or public sites where individuals gather to hear their favorite shows and to cheer on the hosts.

In April 2006, just before the Virginia Tech massacre, radio talk show provocateur Don Imus found himself under fierce attack for stigmatizing members of the highly successful Rutgers women's basketball team as "nappy-headed hos." After a few days of impassioned denunciation by blogs and civil rights groups, the traditional media picked up the issue, and when the articulate and poised Rutgers women basketball players appeared with their coach in a nationally televised press conference, Imus's rancid goose was cooked. For years, a vehicle of white male rage and sexism, racism, homophobia, and just plain nastiness, Imus played an angry white guy with cowboy hat, longish hair, and defuse rage. His vilification of young women athletes and college students, many African American, however, caused some of his major sponsors to drop him. These pressures, along with anger within the media outlets that carried him and escalating negative public opinion, caused MSNBC to drop the televised part of his talk radio show, and soon after CBS cancelled the show itself.

Talk radio and Internet sites and discussion groups thus reveal the ugly face of white male rage in a society more and more fragmented into conflicting social groups. White male rage and paranoia is also evident in films like *Falling Down* (1993) and any number of Stallone-Willis-Schwarzenegger Planet Hollywood brainless brawn films. *Falling Down* shows a mid-level defense worker, played by Michael Douglas, losing his job and going on a rampage in Los Angeles against Latinos, Koreans, blacks, neo-Nazis, and his former wife, who rejected him. The license plate of his car reads "DeFens," short for the defense industry job that gave him his identity and pride; without this job, he becomes unhinged, thus putting on display the "falling down" of white males in a recessionary economy and affirmative action society. The film touched raw nerves and became part of a discourse about white male paranoia and rage.[39]

Hence, the media and new technologies rapidly circulate extremist ideologies and provide examples of redemptive violence—a major theme of contemporary Hollywood film. Moreover, the rapid proliferation of new technologies has had significant effects and is creating a new realm of politics, experience, and social turbulence. In a media society that systematically nurtures fantasies of violence, vengeance, and destruction, it is not surprising that domestic terrorism has permeated the United States. Disaffected individuals are able to create meaning and identity for themselves through affiliation with extremist groups and the execution of dramatic acts that in turn are disseminated via the media. These acts encourage others inclined to act out their identity fantasies and help advance a culture of violence and extremism. Such acts, of course, also produce a backlash and further divide and fragment the society. Consequently, intense fragmentation, the acting out of culture wars through the media and new technologies, and escalating social violence are defining characteristics of our present moment.

The Unabomber and the Politics of Terror

"In order to get our message before the public with some chance of making a lasting impression, we've had to kill people."
—*Unabomber Manifesto* (1996)[40]

While Timothy McVeigh had grandiose fantasies of being a crusader against evil, created a diabolical media spectacle, and wanted to take credit as the supreme architect of the destruction, covering up for possible co-conspirators, Theodore J. Kaczynski, who won renown as the Unabomber, sent bombs through the mail to those who he believed were perpetuating the technological society and sought anonymity until he was finally captured in 1996, after an almost 20-year campaign of terror. Yet Kaczynski, too, used the media to popularize his ideas, to publish his manifesto, and ultimately to make himself a celebrity.

The Unabomber was eventually convicted of carrying out 16 mail bombings and attempted bombings in 7 states, from 1978 through the mid-1990s, injuring 10 people and killing 3. His victims were university professors who promoted technology and computers, airline officials, a computer store owner, a public relations official, and an official of the California Forestry Association, all of whom he believed were advancing the interests of the technological society.

Although the so-called Unabomber appears not to have belonged to any specific political group, the phenomenon provides another example of white male identity politics in which a frustrated and deeply alienated man creates meaning and identity through violent acts that are widely disseminated through the media. In a series of terrorist bombings from 1978 to his capture in a remote Montana cabin in 1996, he unleashed one of the largest manhunts in history and was the number one public enemy on the FBI list. In addition, the Unabomber published a long manifesto that contains an assault on modernity and a call for a return to premodern ways of life. Yet he used deadly explosives to send out his "message" and did not hesitate to exploit the media to promulgate his views. Thus, the Unabomber is a bizarre example of white male rage and the attempt through a demented form of (anti)political action to produce spectacles of terror that advance his politics.

The Unabomber and the white male extremists have in common contempt for politics as usual and pursue politics by other means, combining violent acts with attempts to manipulate the media to get out their "message." They practice a form of media and identity politics in which they assert their power and constitute their social identity through their actions that they seek to have presented and circulated in the media. Both the Unabomber and extremist militia groups use lethal forms of violence as vehicles for their politics that attract high-intensity media coverage. As for the Unabomber, he first made evident his goals in a letter to the *New York Times* postmarked April 20, 1995, in which he described himself as an anarchist who would "like to break down all society into very small, completely autonomous units. Regrettably, we don't see any clear road to this goal, so we leave it to the indefinite future. Our more immediate goal, which we think may be attainable at some time during the next several decades, is the destruction of the worldwide industrial system. Through our bombings we hope to promote social instability in industrial society, propagate anti-industrial ideas and give encouragement to those who hate the industrial system."[41]

The Unabomber had begun by planting small-scale explosives at Northwestern University in 1978 and 1979, and then mailed a bomb that exploded on an American Airlines flight in 1979, forcing the plane to land prematurely and injuring 12. He next mailed a package bomb to the president of United Airlines in 1980 and to university professors in Utah, Nashville, and Berkeley during the following years. This led the FBI to name the suspect the "Unabom" because he seemed to be targeting university campuses and the airlines industry. Over the next 15 years, he sent off 16 bombs, eventually killed 3 people, and injured and maimed many others.[42]

After the Oklahoma bombing in April 1995, the Unabomber upped his ante, sending off a bomb shortly after the Oklahoma blast that killed a member of the California Forestry Association. He also threatened to blow up an airline in California and sent letters to the media taunting the FBI and demanding that major newspapers publish his 35,000-word manifesto within three months or he would kill someone else in retaliation.[43] On June 28, 1995, the Unabomber's manifesto arrived in the offices of the *New York Times* and was received the next day at the *Washington Post*. After much deliberation and debate, the *Post* published it in fall 1995, with both papers sharing expenses and responsibility. The manifesto quickly circulated through the Internet, was published by a small California press, and occasioned discussion throughout the traditional and alternative media.

In the "manifesto," its author justified his terrorist actions in terms of an assault on modern technological society, which he claimed was destroying the earth, producing destructive and life-negating technologies, and robbing human life of its savor. The stilted academic prose attacks modernity and industrial-technological civilization as a whole; calls for revolution, not reform, but attacks "Modern Leftism"; and, although the author claims he is an anarchist, lacks a real vision of a self-organizing society and democratic community. The text opens:

> The industrial revolution and its consequences have been a disaster for the human race. They have greatly increased the life expectancy of those of us who will live in "advanced" countries, but they have destabilized society, have made life unfulfilling, have subjected human beings to indignities, have led to widespread psychological suffering (in the Third World to physical suffering as well) and have inflicted severe damage on the natural world. The continued development of technology will worsen the situation. It will certainly subject human beings to greater indignities and inflict greater damage on the natural world, it will probably lead to greater social disruption and psychological suffering, and it may lead to increased physical suffering even in "advanced" countries (1).

The Unabomber's manifesto is a quirky technophobic discourse that takes the form of a postmodern pastiche, cobbling together elements of various antitechnology discourses, much as he crafted his bombs out of found material. He appears scornful and resentful of progressive movements that practice "political correctness," putting him in the camp of antileftist technophobes and anarchists. Throughout the manifesto, he appropriates French thinker Jacques Ellul's antitechnology discourse,[44] following Ellul (1964) in the opening paragraph just cited in arguing how the beneficial aspects of technology cannot be separated from harmful and destructive elements, thus arguing as per Ellul that the good and bad elements of technology are inseparable.

Yet the Unabomber seems to find no good elements in technology, and thus the discourse is an extreme form of technophobia that fears and hates all technology. There are echoes in the manifesto of 1960s countercultural theorists like Theodore Roszak (1968) and Charles Reich (1970) who reject the "system" as a whole; of Herbert Marcuse's 1964 attack on technological civilization in *One-Dimensional Man*; and of a variety of back-to-nature ideologies and celebration of "wild nature." The author claims that "primitive man suffered from less stress and frustration and was better satisfied with his way of life than modern man is" (45). Technology for the Unabomber has thus been "a disaster for the human race," breaking down social order and "creating a sense of purposelessness" (1). His only positive ideal is advocacy of withdrawal into wild nature, a world "independent of human management and free of human interference and control" (183). In his premodern vision, people should become "peasants or herdsmen or fishermen or hunter, etc." (184).

There is also an activist component in the Unabomber's manifesto: Action must be taken to restore humanity to a "positive ideal." "The factories should be destroyed ... technical books burned" (166). To some extent, the Unabomber's discourse derives from the Luddite tradition, although, as Kirkpatrick Sales argues (1995), he has at best superficial knowledge of this tradition and directs his attack on modern leftism. Thus, while the text appears to derive from left countercultural attacks on technology and technological civilization, the position is actually closer to rightist survivalism and antimodern technophobia. The Unabomber's ideological kinship is thus with alienated militia types who withdraw from civilization, rail against the society they left behind, and violently attack it and its representatives. In this sense, the Unabomber is congruent with the shift in antigovernment and antisystem tactics and ideology from left to right, and the use of violence in pursuit of a white male identity politics.

 In a sense, violence and white male identity politics go hand in hand, since identity politics is involved in constituting one's self-image, gaining attention, acting out one's grievances, and playing to the media. White male identity politics thus involves an externalization of rage and resentment in public acts that often take violent forms, such as seems to be the case of the Unabomber and domestic terrorism. Men are socialized to find validation in self-assertion, and media culture has progressively celebrated violence as a means of constructing masculinity. Since dramatic and violent actions gain maximum media attention, they can be emulated, becoming models to be imitated, thus white male identity politics finds itself caught up in a spiral of violence, as in the case of the militia, the Unabomber, and other forms.

Although there is no overt racism in the Unabomber manifesto, the taunts against "political correctness" and "minority movements" reveal yet another frustrated white male angry about the course of contemporary society and politics. While the militia groups form organizations and communities, and even Timothy McVeigh seems to have attempted to get others to share his fantasies and to participate in his spectacle of terror, the Unabomber appears to have been totally isolated and alienated from peer groups, women, family, and community.[45] Whereas militia paranoia is primarily focused on the U.S. government, the Unabomber's paranoia is focused on technological civilization as a whole. Both deployed violence, however, to carry out their agendas and both represent a new sort of identity politics that exhibits white male rage and paranoia.

The Unabomber is also caught in the contradiction of claiming to be antimedia and technology and yet using technology and the media to carry out his agenda. He condemns "black-and-white" binary thinking (186), yet views technology only in this way. Advocating peace and harmony, the Unabomber has devoted his life to violence and murder. The Unabomber complains how modern industrial civilization renders individuals powerless and steals autonomy from them, blocking what he calls the "power process," and yet "empowers" himself in an extremely bizarre fashion through a form of media politics in which he asserts his "autonomy" by breaking society's deepest taboo against murdering other individuals.

One of the more tantalizing debates concerns the impact of Joseph Conrad's *The Secret Agent* (1907) on the Unabomber. Kaczynski's brother David, who turned him in, found an uncanny resemblance between the plot of the novel, known to be one of his brother's favorites, and the Unabomber's terrorist activity. The novel was allegedly found on the suspect's premises, and in a 1984 letter to his family Kaczynski indicated that he was reading Conrad's novels for "about the dozenth time."[46] There were also reports that FBI agents were told that Kaczynski used the name "Conrad" or "Konrad" to check into hotels in northern California where he was carrying out his bomb attacks (See Gibbs et al. 1996: 136).

The Secret Agent, published in 1907, concerns a professor who gives up his career to move to a small, dingy house, where he dedicates himself to making bombs and attacking representatives of science and mathematics. If the Unabomber was indeed influenced by Conrad's novel, as McVeigh seems to have been by *The Turner Diaries,* this would provide another example of the power of literature, though it would also indicate a lack of literary training on the part of the Unabomber/Kaczynski who would have missed Conrad's bitter irony and attack on "a purely Utopian revolutionism" had he indeed taken the novel as a model for his life.

Obviously, the Unabomber's use of murder and the media to get his "message" across represents a new sort of media politics and spectacle of terror, in which media technologies become the site of political communication and struggle, and violence is a strategy for media attention. From the moment of the publication of his "manifesto," and intensifying with his arrest in April 1996, the Unabomber/Kaczynski himself became a focus of intense fascination and debate with websites, Internet discussion lists, and various print and broadcast media debating his ideas and actions. Becoming something of a cult figure,[47] the Unabomber shows how the contemporary moment is careening toward a form of identity construction where individuals constitute their selves through engaging in actions geared to attract media attention.[48]

Strangely, Kaczynski and McVeigh found themselves in the same federal prison, the so-called Supermax in Florence, Colorado, at the same time in 2000–2001. Whereas Kaczynski initially avoided McVeigh because he disagreed with McVeigh's bombing of innocents in favor of his own, more targeted approach, eventually they got to know each other and by the time of McVeigh's execution in 2001, Kaczynski gave the authors of a biography of McVeigh an 11-page document in which he shared his thoughts on McVeigh and the Oklahoma City bombing.[49]

Obviously, there are significant differences between McVeigh and right-wing militia and the loner anarchist Unabomber, although both represent a crisis of masculinity and use guns and weapons culture to express male rage and to create ultramasculinist celebrity identities through media spectacle. Contemporary youth, as well, fell prey to creating media identities and gaining revenge against defuse enemies in the school shootings in Littleton (Colorado), Blacksburg (Virginia), and elsewhere, as we'll see next in discussion of the Columbine High School shootings, and will then return to reflect on Seung-Hui Cho and the Virginia Tech massacre.

Middle-Class White Male
Columbine High School Shootings

"I hate the fucking world."

—*Eric Harris*

On April 20 1999, Eric Harris and Dylan Klebold left home for Columbine High School in a suburb of Denver, Colorado, with the intention of murdering as many of their teachers and fellow students as they could. Armed with high-powered assault rifles and an arsenal of bombs, they went on a rampage that left 13 dead, including themselves. The event was labeled the deadliest school shooting in American history and became the subject of a dramatic media spectacle and raging debate over the role of guns in American life and problems of youth and high schools.[50]

The Columbine Media Spectacle and Its Exploitation

> "You made me what I am. You added to the rage.... I hope we kill 250 of you."
>
> —*Dylan Klebold*

While in some parts of the country there are frequent school shootings, the Columbine massacre won attention because of the intense media focus on the event from the first report of gunfire in the school. The event occurred early in the 24/7 cable era, it was the first live "you are there" school-shooting drama, and the story took over TV news. A standoff provided intense live drama, as did cell phone calls from students stuck in the school and dramatic pictures of police leading students out with the reports of a number of students and teachers murdered and the shooters committing suicide.

When it was revealed that the assassins were middle-class white teenagers, the nation was shocked, and there was endless replay of the footage of the police evacuating the students and carrying out dead and wounded, with day after day of interviews with survivors, friends, and relatives of the dead, punctuated with discussion by pundits about what went wrong and how could two middle-class [white] boys do such a thing?

Initial media focus on the two shooters labeled them as members of a "Trench Coat Mafia" who were influenced by goth culture and rock music like Marilyn Manson, leading to a vilification of youth culture. Harris and Klebold were also avid Internet surfers and computer game players, and early reports claimed they were influenced by Nazi and neo-Nazi websites and chose April 20 as their murder spectacle date to celebrate Hitler's birthday.[51] Like Cho, Harris and Klebold left behind videos, photos, and writings expressing their rage, but authorities chose not to release this material, until some was leaked in later trials, or eventually partially released by the police, leaving ideologues of all sorts to target the alleged cause of their violent rampage.[52]

Early media reports were rampant with distortions and myths. It was claimed that the shooters were bullied by jocks and targeted them, while in fact most of the jocks had left school for lunch in town or went to the gym, and a wide array of students were apparently indiscriminately shot. Since one of the few African American boys at the school was shot, it was believed that there was racist targeting and motivation. There were rumors that Harris and Klebold both were gay and bullied for their sexuality, making the murder a Leopold-and-Loeb homosexual revenge drama. However, many of their friends insisted they were straight, and Klebold had an 18-year-old girlfriend who bought some of the guns for them.[53] There was a story that one victim, Cassie Bernall, was asked if she believed in God and, when answering in the affirmative, was shot. The young woman was made into a martyr by the Christian community when her mother published a book that became a best-seller, despite reports that the killers had made the comment to another young woman after shooting her and not to Bernall.[54]

A former friend of Harris and Klebold, Brooks Brown, was accused by a sheriff, live on MSNBC, of being part of the plot, whereas it turned out that Brown's parents had a year previously reported to the police Harris's threats against their son and showed that he was named on a "hit list" on Harris's website. The local police and the school did little to monitor Harris and Klebold, despite previous police records of the two and reports of numerous threats and threatening behavior by the two Columbine shooters.[55] Later, an article by Dave Cullen, based on an interview with chief investigator Kate Battan and other sources, concluded:

> The biggest myths about the tragedy have to do with the question of who Harris and Klebold were really targeting in their rampage. Jocks, African Americans and Christians have been widely described as their chief targets. Not a scrap of evidence supports that conclusion. In addition to voluminous evidence from the scene, Harris left behind a wealth of detailed plans and commentary making their targets plain.
>
> "It's pretty clear now that the initial plan was to have the two propane bombs they put in the cafeteria go off," a top investigator said. "And that's as indiscriminate as you can get. Every kid killed was a target of opportunity," not singled out to settle a score, he said.
>
> Battan called their behavior random: "Sticking a gun underneath a table and firing—they didn't even know who was under that table."...
>
> Five months after the massacre, investigators also refute other key allegations about the pair: that they were members of the Trench Coat Mafia, raised by negligent parents, practicing Goths or frustrated gays.[56]

While youth culture and the culture of bullying in Columbine High School were widely discussed,[57] there was little discussion of how male socialization and its imbrication with gun culture was involved in the shooting, nor was there discussion of male rage or violent male identity construction. While there was speculation about the two teen shooters' family lives, there was little initial discussion of how middle-class parents could allow their teenage boys to have such a deadly arsenal, apparently in plain view, in their homes.[58]

Indeed, whenever there have been school shootings over the past decade there is rarely a discussion of the role of the social construction of masculinity and gun culture in the shooting, and rarely do headlines describe the shooters as "boys" or "males," usually preferring gender-neutral descriptions, although there have been a few female school shooters.[59] My studies lead me to the conclusion that male rage is part of significant numbers of acts of domestic terrorism and school shootings. Further, in each case, the creation of violent male identities is part of the dynamics, as is the immersion in violent gun or weapons culture, a theme I return to in the concluding chapter.

Larkin points out how Harris and Klebold were bullied by hypermasculinist jocks (2007: 187ff., 196ff., 226ff.), thus putting in question their own masculinity. Harris reportedly had wanted to join the Marines but was unable to enlist because of his use of the drug Luvox, prescribed for psychiatric disorder (Larkin 2007, 170). Making up for their inability to play out the normative macho male role, the two compensated through excessive play of ultraviolent games of Doom and Quake (ibid.), and amassed an arsenal of guns and bombs, immersing themselves in paramilitary culture. The combination of their male rage, need to assert a masculine identity, and immersion in violent games, fantasies, and gun culture played the role described by Athens and Rhodes (1999) in desensitizing the two to others' suffering, creating the psychological preconditions for killing.[60] Preparing for their rampage, the two assembled their weapons, dressed in paramilitary regalia, and asserted their hypermasculinity in an orgy of violence.

The Columbine school shootings became a national media spectacle that dominated for weeks cable and television news and discussion shows and received intense Internet attention, leading various political groups and pundits to target their favorite ideological scapegoats. Just as in the Virginia Tech case, a variety of right-wing groups and pundits exploited the tragedy to push their own political agendas. As the People for the American Way's "Right-Wing Watch Online" noted in a July 20, 1999, report:

Focus on the Family's James Dobson blamed three things for the kind of school violence we saw at Columbine High School: the breakdown of the family (even though the two killers were from "intact, respectable homes"), the decline of a Judeo-Christian value system, and "today's media-saturated 'culture of death.'"

On *Meet the Press,* Bill Bennett alleged that the Colorado killers would have been hauled in for counseling if they had been walking the halls quoting the Bible instead of Nazi dogma.

The right-wing weekly paper *Human Events* ran a front-page editorial titled, "Forget God, get Littleton." They wrote that Littleton was "the latest example of what will become increasingly routine so long as our society expels God from the schools while allowing the raw sewage of Satanic rock and death-dealing videogames to flood the shopping malls and Internet."

Conservative radio host Dr. Laura Schlessinger blasted public schools in general and advocated school vouchers in a column about the shootings. "I gave up on the public school system a long time ago. Our son is in a private religious school. He starts every day thanking God for the gift of life and asking God to direct his thinking. I think school vouchers are a great idea. They would give all parents this opportunity. I know what I'm saying undermines the public school system. But I honestly think it's a lost cause, and I don't see any other way to protect our children from brain and soul pollution."[61]

The People for the American Way's report noted that in the weeks after the tragic shootings in Colorado, the religious right quickly renewed their call for a school prayer amendment and tried to make the issue a litmus test for Republican presidential candidates. Throughout the country, Christian right activists complained that God has been "thrown out of our schools" and militated for prayer in the school. Others attacked the system of public education and called for a voucher system and federal support of religious schools. Right-wing politicians pushed several bills that would permit posting the Ten Commandments in public schools and returning prayer and the teaching of religion to schools. Representative Tom DeLay (R-TX) "blamed the tragedy on daycare, divorce, the teaching of evolution and lack of religion," while Representative Bob Barr (R-GA) asserted that the shootings would not have happened had the Ten Commandments been posted in Columbine High School.[62]

Vice president Dan Quayle remarked in a speech delivered on the anniversary of his famed attack on the television character "Murphy Brown," that the shootings should help bring back prayer to public schools: "We have allowed our legal system to distort and deny the role of faith in American life," said Quayle. "In fulfilling its cultural agenda, the legal aristocracy has not worked alone. It was aided by a willing and compliant news media and an entertainment industry that transmits counterculture values." Christian activist and would-be politician Gary Bauer organized his presidential campaign around the Columbine shootings and used the issue to promote the return of prayer to schools. Many on the right also took the opportunity to blame liberals or liberalism for the shootings. In the People for the American Way's summary:

> Former House Speaker Newt Gingrich struck an accusatory tone in his first major speech since leaving Congress. "I want to say to the elite of this country—the elite news media, the liberal academic elite, the liberal political elite: I accuse you in Littleton, and I accuse you in Kosovo of being afraid to talk about the mess you have made, and being afraid to take responsibility for things you have done, and instead foisting upon the rest of us pathetic banalities because you don't have the courage to look at the world you have created." But Gingrich didn't stop there. He also cited the elimination of prayer and "the creator" from schools, an overtaxing government, violence in movies and video games, and a lack of teaching about the U.S. Constitution as negative influences on today's teenagers.
>
> American Family Association President Don Wildmon blamed liberals of all stripes, saying that Littleton has "been coming for 40 years." Among the culprits are "anti-Christian types like the ACLU," politicians, the "liberal" news media, and Hollywood "where pagans are in control." In rather conspiratorial tones, Wildmon also indicts the National Education Association for spending "hundreds of millions ... in seizing control of the schools and turning them into centers to promote their secular experiment."
>
> Samuel Blumenfeld, a right-wing critic of public schools, added a new twist to the right's recipe of blaming Littleton on liberalism and lack of religion. In his column on the right-wing WorldNetDaily website, Blumenfeld alleged that the real problem is prescription drugs, like Ritalin and Prozac, "most of which are prescribed and administered by the schools themselves." In addition to casting direct blame on such drugs, he blamed today's teachers for "using the most irrational teaching methods ever devised by so-called educators," saying that "there was no such thing as ADD [Attention Deficit Disorder] ... when I was going to school back in the 1930s and '40s."[63]

On MSNBC the day after the shooting, former Nixon advisor and Republican Party candidate for president Pat Buchanan blamed the tragedy on America's youth, calling them "godless" and "an immoral generation adrift." Senator Joseph Lieberman famously blamed the shootings on the music of Marilyn Manson. Others blamed it on a variety of factors like the "soullessness" of American small towns (Camile Paglia), video games like Quake and Doom, the Internet, or their favorite scapegoat.

Lead investigator Kate Battan, who had studied Harris's diary and video material made by Harris and Klebold, punctured some of the myths and one-sided explanations, as noted above. Another story by Dave Cullum, interviewing

Battan and others who had access to Harris's and Klebold's writings and artifacts, concluded that their desire for fame and celebrity was a key motivation
in the shooting and that the two Columbine shooters consciously produced a
media spectacle, as Cho was to do later, thus using media spectacle to create
violent male identities and celebrity.

> One thread running consistently through the texts is the desire for glory, the
> expectation of fame. "Like many of the school shooters, they seem to be expect-
> ing some sort of notoriety, in addition to wanting the vengeance," one source
> said. "Because they felt they have been mistreated by a number of people, they're
> going to strike back at the human race.
>
>   "But they also kind of expect notoriety." Harris' writings contain statements
> like "When you [the media] write about this … When you read about this …
> We were planning this before the kids in Jonesboro, and we're going to die in
> there," the source said.
>
>   Battan actually believes fame was the single biggest reason Harris and Klebold
> ultimately went through with the plan. "That's my personal opinion," she said.
> "And all the rest of the justifications are just smoke." Other key investigators
> backed that assessment.
>
>   The texts were littered with comments about their expected glory, Battan
> said. "They certainly wanted the media to write stories about them every day.
> And they wanted cult followings. They're going to become superstars by getting
> rid of bad people. And you know, it worked. They're famous."[64]

The media had obviously played into Harris's and Klebold's hands and inspired later generations of school shooters like Cho. Indeed, there were reports
that Harris and Klebold were influenced by McVeigh and the Oklahoma City
bombing. Their van had an arsenal of explosives and their plans indicated that
they intended to blow up the school as well as shoot teachers and students,
although the two bombs they took into the school did not explode so they
relied on their guns for their mayhem.[65]

Parents of the murdered students and others filed lawsuits against Harris's
and Klebold's parents, the police investigating the shootings, and Columbine
High. The first lawsuit featured lawyer Geoffrey Fieger, who had just defended
the infamous Dr. Jack Kevorkian, notorious for providing assisted suicides,
who had been featured in a Jenny Jones tabloid television trial. Fieger filed a
wrongful death lawsuit against the parents of the Columbine shooters Eric
Harris and Dylan Klebold, representing the family of Isaiah Shoels, the only
African American killed in the rampage, whose family had to leave Littleton,
Colorado, for Denver after racial attacks on them. In Dave Cullen's account:

"The suit charges each of the four parents with five counts of parental negligence, which involve their allowing their sons to amass a cache of semiautomatic weapons; stockpile bombs and explosives; continue to hang out together, since each was 'a co-conspirator and accomplice in a prior criminal act'; to 'author extremist writings of a hateful nature'; and to continue to grant their sons 'extraordinary privileges despite knowledge that [they] had been engaged in prior serious criminal activity.'"[66]

A lawsuit filed one year after the shootings by lawyers representing the family of slain Columbine High School teacher Dave Sanders, who allegedly bled to death because the police department waited hours after the shooters were dead to take control of the school, claimed that the police reports had serious cover-ups. In Dave Cullen's *Salon* account: "The Sanders lawsuit contained a host of major new allegations, including claims that a sharpshooter had Dylan Klebold in his sights in the library, but his supervisors wouldn't allow him to act. It also contends the sharpshooter saw Klebold and Eric Harris commit suicide, and thus officers were aware the pair were dead three hours before Sanders died, but failed to rescue him."[67]

Another lawsuit by families of the slain students takes to task the county sheriff's department for incompetence, claiming that there was evidence that the police had Harris and Klebold in their gun sights but did not fire, and that 911 operators told the students and teachers to stay in their classrooms while the police concentrated on "securing the perimeter." The suit claimed that the police waited hours to actually penetrate the building, during which time many of the shootings took place, and victims died who might have survived if they had received more timely medical treatment.[68]

The various lawsuits were either dismissed or settled out of court and, as indicated in Note 58, a judge ruled that all court documents, the basement tapes of Harris and Klebold, and other material pertinent to the case not be released to the public. Hence, there are still many mysteries and debates over what actually happened in the shooting and what the motivations and plans of the shooters entailed. Some material, to be sure, was released and evidently influenced later school shooters.

Republican groups and candidates continued to use the Columbine School shootings as a fund-raising device for the 2000 elections. Although there was much talk about reforming gun laws and efforts to get a reasonable Republican-Democratic consensus on controlling gun show sales, handgun access, and stricter criteria for gun purchasing, not much came of the discussion (see Chapter 4). After the stolen election of 2000 (Kellner 2001), the Bush-Cheney administration repealed the prohibition on sales of assault weapons passed by the Clinton administration and further deregulated gun laws, paying off the NRA and extremist groups for their support.

Shooting at Columbine with Michael Moore: Guns, U.S. History, and Violence in America

"Happiness is a warm gun."

—*The Beatles*

Agit-provocateur Michael Moore, however, took on the gun lobby and U.S. attitudes toward guns post-Columbine with his documentary film *Bowling for Columbine* (2002). The film won an Academy Award and became the highest-grossing documentary of all time, until Moore's next film, *Fahrenheit 9/11* (2004), and generated reams of controversy that made Michael Moore a major celebrity and bête noire for the right and conservatives.

Moore works in an exploratory documentary tradition that uses film as a medium to engage social problems. A standard mode of the left documentary tradition, exploratory films investigate social problems, such as in Emile de Antonio's exploration of McCarthyism in *Point of Order* (1960), his critique of the Warren Commission and investigation of the Kennedy assassination in *Rush to Judgment* (1964), or his look at nuclear weapons production and a Christian pacifist antinuclear movement in *In the King of Prussia* (1984). In *Bowling for Columbine*, Michael Moore explores connections between guns, militarism, and violence in American history and contemporary society, and investigates the question of why there has been so much violence in the United States.

Moore's previous and first documentary, *Roger and Me* (1998), was made for around $160,000 and turned a $7 million profit, making Michael Moore a hot item in the film and entertainment world. Moore turned next to television, using his populist "little guy against the system" persona to expose corporate and sociopolitical problems in a TV series broadcast by NBC and then the Fox network in 1994–1995 called *TV Nation*. Moore used his mode of personal witnessing, exploring of social problems, and good-natured humor to provide highly entertaining vignettes of corporate and political misconduct—a project he replicated in his later TV series *The Awful Truth* (1999–2000).

Moore's next major project, *Bowling for Columbine* (2002), takes his documentary aesthetic to new levels of complexity and controversy, eliciting both widespread praise and condemnation. By now, Moore was a genuine American celebrity and he used his strong persona to once again engage his audience in a quest narrative, this time to try to find out why there is so much violence by guns in the United States today. Moore's voice remains the narrative center of the film, and it is more confident, self-assured, and insistent than in his earlier work.

Moore's hook was the April 1999 Columbine shooting where two white middle-class small-town teenage boys took an arsenal of guns and home-made bombs to school and slaughtered their classmates. The film opens with a clip from an NRA promotional film and cuts to Moore narrating "April 20, 1999," another "morning in America," with footage of farmers, workers, milk deliveries, "the president bombing another country we couldn't pronounce," and the shootings at Columbine High School, with "The Battle Hymn of the Republic" playing on the soundtrack.

Moore's targets in *Bowling for Columbine* are much broader and more complex than in his previous work. Indeed, the real quest of the film is to understand America itself, in particular why the country has such an obsession with guns and so much violence. Once again, Moore opens the film by situating himself in relation to his topic with footage of receiving his first gun as a youth, accompanied by "I was born in Michigan" on the soundtrack. We learn that at 15, Moore won an NRA marksman award and has been a lifelong hunter and rifle owner.

Another montage introduces a fellow citizen who grew up in Michigan, Charlton Heston, who in movie images holds and shoots guns, and then emerges as NRA president. Moore has again developed a dialectical structure where he poses himself against a villain, and the Bad Guy in *Bowling* is Charlton Heston, Moses himself. In *Roger and Me*, Roger Smith incarnated corporate greed, insensitivity, and a privileged upper-class lifestyle immune to concern for the human suffering of General Motors employees and others in Flint devastated by the plant closings. Now, in *Bowling*, Heston represents the NRA, an organization that attacks all restrictions on gun ownership and use, and the film shows him appearing at an NRA annual meeting just after the Columbine shootings, despite requests from parents of the teenagers and the mayor of the city of Denver to stay home. Heston also represents a privileged white upper-class lifestyle, as he champions guns and conservative views while living in a gated mansion above Beverly Hills.

Whereas *Roger and Me* was in part a quest for Roger Smith, *Bowling for Columbine* is largely a quest to explore the question of guns and violence in the United States, in which the confrontation with Charlton Heston is a secondary theme. *Bowling for Columbine* has a much larger tapestry to weave, and it involves making connections among U.S. history, culture, guns, the military, violence, and racism. A section on the Michigan militia cuts to James Nichols, brother of Terry Nichols who, along with Timothy McVeigh, was responsible for the 1995 Oklahoma City bombing. While the opening on the Michigan militia was lighthearted and followed by a comedy routine of Chris Rock suggesting in a satirical riff that bullets should be much more expensive to restrain "bullet buyers," the Nichols section goes into a darker side of U.S. conspiracy mavens and gun fanatics. Nichols proves that he has a gun under his pillow by grabbing it out from his bedroom while off-screen, and startles Moore and the audience with the ferocity and weirdness of his behavior.

The film continues to make "six degrees of separation" connections by moving to Oscola, Michigan, home of the Strategic Air Command, where one of the Columbine killers grew up while his father worked for the military. Another scene focuses on Littleton, Colorado, and the Columbine murders, and notes that Lockheed Martin, one of the major military contractors in the United States, is located in the city and employed the father of one of the Columbine shooters. Further, by chance, one of the heaviest days of bombing took place in Kosovo on the day of the Columbine massacre and the film cuts from President Bill Clinton announcing the Kosovo events, and then shortly thereafter addressing the Columbine tragedy.

In addition to interviews and news footage that illustrate the connections, Moore uses a montage of images accompanied by the Beatles' song "Happiness Is a Warm Gun" that depict various incidents of violence in the United States. Another sequence uses "What a Wonderful World" as background in an ironical Brechtian fashion[69] against a panorama of U.S. military interventions ranging from U.S. complicity in the overthrow of democratically elected governments in Iran and Guatemala in the 1950s to support for Osama bin Laden's group that was fighting the Soviets in Afghanistan in the 1980s and support to the Taliban in the 1990s—followed by the horrendous spectacle of 9/11, a matrix he would explore in more depth in his following film, called *Fahrenheit 9/11*.

An animated cartoon, "History of the United States," in the style of *South Park* creators Trey Parker and Matt Stone, also provides a historical montage of violence in the U.S. against Native Americans, the horrors of slavery, bloodshed in the American Revolution and Civil War, and growing class division between the "haves" and the "have-nots" in U.S. society. Interviews with Stone reveal that the two creators of the popular *South Park* animation were from Littleton, went to Columbine, and modeled their highly acclaimed TV show after their oppressive experiences growing up in the Colorado suburb.

The sequence, and the film as a whole, suggests that—rather than just one or another isolated factor—the entirety of U.S. history and social organization is responsible for violence in the United States. Indeed, the history of the United States is a violent one with Indian wars against the native inhabitants, a long and bloody revolutionary war, continued westward expansion involving violence against natives, outlaws, and others, slavery in the South and a devastating civil war, colonial and world wars in foreign lands, and the emergence of a violent gun culture. Moore is thus correct that violence in the United States, and by extension school shootings, cannot be attributed to specific factors like race, guns, popular culture, or any single factor, but are part of a matrix of U.S. history and culture.

The film takes on the Columbine shootings in part to put in question one-sided or reductive explanations of Columbine, and more broadly violence in the United States. Moore goes through a litany of politicians and pundits who blame the Columbine terror spectacle primarily on heavy metal, the Internet, Hollywood and violent films, the break-up of the family, or Satan himself, including a rant by Senator Joseph Lieberman who blames the shootings on youth culture and attacks rock singer Marilyn Manson. In a long interview sequence, Manson intelligently defends himself, and makes the moralistic Lieberman come off a fool in comparison.

In one particularly strong sequence, Moore provides a montage of violence on local and network news that makes it appear that we are facing apocalyptic outbursts of violence on a local and national scale in the United States. Moore interviews University of Southern California sociologist Barry Glassner, author of *The Culture of Fear* (2000), in Los Angeles's fabled black neighborhood, South Central. The two discuss how the media greatly exaggerate the violence in the United States, especially by scapegoating African Americans.

Bowling also explores connections between the media and racism, while depicting in interview and montage footage how African Americans are in fact victims of poverty and inner-city violence. Moore devotes a long sequence to the story of the murder of a young girl, Kayla Owens, by a six-year-old boy student at Buell High School. It turns out that his mother was forced by welfare law to bus 60 miles from her Flint, Michigan, home to take two minimum-wage jobs in a mall; moreover, the young boy was left with a relative from whom the boy took the unattended gun and shot the young girl. In a tense sequence, Moore confronts *American Bandstand* and TV impresario Dick Clark on how he feels about the mother of the boy working at one of his restaurants and whether he supports the law that requires welfare mothers to work at minimum-wage jobs and leave their children unsupervised. Clark coldly turns away and another American icon is deflated with the cameras of the iconoclastic Moore.

Other sections show how youth are scapegoated in the media and subjected to humiliating surveillance and school discipline and suspension in an attempt to blame youth for the maladies of U.S. society. Moore is highly sympathetic to youth and has gained a large audience of adoring young fans, bringing documentary film and radical politics to a group not usually exposed to such fare. Indeed, there is a youthful and rebellious aura to Michael Moore's work that makes him a spokesman for alienated youth, as well as oppressed racial and class members.

In addressing the media and fear, Moore suggests in *Bowling for Columbine* that one of the major effects of the media is to generate fear that ruling politicians can exploit. While Moore is making connections among U.S. history and military actions, guns, the media, and violence, he is not attributing causal connections among these forces, but is suggesting that they interact in a complex social environment. Moore's film shows that it is not just one thing, but many, that caused the Columbine shootings and causes violence in the United States. *Bowling for Columbine* thus provides a multidimensional view of violence in the United States, gun culture, and teen shootings. It is open and nonreductive and does not provide simplistic answers to the question, as its critics claim.

This openness is apparent in one revealing sequence in which Moore interviews Tom Mauser, the father of one of the Columbine shooting victims, about what causes the United States to have more violence and gun victims than other industrialized countries. Mauser passionately asks, "What is it?!"—the shot then cuts rapidly back and forth with Moore and Mauser repeating the query multiple times, ending with Mauser saying, "I don't know." Neither is obviously able to answer the unanswerable question, and Moore's exploration of the issue does not offer simplistic or easy answers. His queries do, however, ferret out responses like Charlton Heston's, who in the film's penultimate sequence blames violence on American history and then the country's "mixed ethnicity," suggesting a racist response.

As we have seen, Moore has not really found the answer to the question concerning why there is so much gun violence in the United States. Yet *Bowling for Columbine* suggests connections among U.S. gun culture, history, the media, political organizations and policies, U.S. military interventions and the weapons industry, deteriorating families and living conditions as divisions increase between the rich and the poor, and the alienation of segments of youth are likely to produce violence and will require systematic social change and transformation.

Thus Moore deflates one-sided and reductive explanations of the Columbine shootings and violence in America and offers a more multiperspectivist vision. He fails, however, to address the issue of gender and violence in a country where over 90 percent of the violent crime is committed by males.[70] Moore's failure to address the gender issue is symptomatic of the failure of progressive males to more radically question gender, or it may express his own emotional attachment to guns that he connects, perhaps unconsciously, with his masculinity. He also does not make it clear that 25 times more black inner-city teens are murdered by gunfire and, at the time of making the movie, that "of 10,801 gun homicides in the U.S., 2,900 (a little more than one-fourth) involved whites; seven in 10 involved blacks and Latinos."[71] Further, Moore's critics insist that he exaggerates per capita gun violence and murder in the United States compared to other countries, and that his editing dramatizes certain points at the expense of accurately portraying historical sequences of events. Moreover, the standard conservative attack is that "Michael Moore hates America" and presents a wholly negative view of the United States.[72]

This latter conservative critique misses the point of who Michael Moore is and what he is doing. Moore presents his own special brand of political interventionist documentary that combines personal witness to wrongdoing and an exploratory quest for answers to social problems with satire and humor and the development of his own crusading character who exposes social wrongs and injustices. Moreover, he shows a vision of the United States rarely seen on film and television, which tends to idealize the United States as a beacon of affluence and prosperity, or as a highly functional system where (TV) cops get the bad guys and (TV) lawyers prosecute wrongdoers.

Bowling for Columbine won the 2002 Academy Award for documentary film, became the highest-grossing documentary of all time, and set up a debate on guns and violence in America that is still ongoing. But it appeared during the Bush-Cheney years where there was a rollback of gun control laws from the previous administration and an explosion of guns amok with a rash of school shootings, culminating in the Virginia Tech massacre.

Seung-Hui Cho in the Borderlands between the Korean and the American

> "You have vandalized my heart, raped my soul and torched my conscience."
>
> —*Seung-Hui Cho*

White male rage and violent constructions of male identity were shared in common with Timothy McVeigh and the right-wing militia movement, the Unabomber, and the Columbine shooters Eric Harris and Dylan Klebold. In the voluminous discussions of these individuals and their crimes, there has been little if any recognition of them as domestic terrorists constituting a threat to national security, nor have there been major media connections made between the Virginia Tech massacre and domestic terrorism.[73] Further, there has not been much description of how constructions of a violent masculinity through media spectacle are implicated in the terrorist actions described in this chapter.

Likewise, there were few connections of Cho and previous school shooters with a crisis in masculinity. *New York Times* columnist Bob Herbert was one of the few in the corporate media who noted the gender issue in the Virginia Tech murders and other school shooters when he wrote: "The killers have been shown to be young men riddled with shame and humiliation, often bitterly misogynistic and homophobic, who have decided that the way to assert their faltering sense of manhood and get the respect they have been denied is to go out and shoot somebody."[74] There was also little recognition that, although Cho was Korean American, most school shooters have been white. As Jonathan Zimmerman pointed out: "Black and Latino boys commit plenty of violence in school, of course, but they're more likely to assault an individual whom they know. White shooters [and Cho!] more often kill en masse and randomly."[75]

Seung-Hui Cho's construction of violent masculinity and identity seemed to have taken place within the conflicting pressures of Korean patriarchy and U.S. media, gun, and popular culture. His Korean American background apparently tore him between the strictures of a conservative Korean patriarchy and the pressures to succeed in American society. As noted, Bill O'Reilly explicitly denied Cho's American roots, trying to argue that Cho was not really an American, that America is not to blame, but rather Cho is Korean and it's the Korean in Cho that bears the weight of the pathology.[76] In fact, it could be, in part, the clash between excessive immigrant Korean demands to succeed and the hedonism and temptations of American culture that helped drive Cho over the edge.

Expectations that he succeed in school could have been met, as Cho had successfully negotiated high school and some years of college, but his trajectory was apparently mediated by American hedonistic "hook-up" culture, a violent media and gun culture, and his own personal demons. Cho's references to "debauchery" in the written text he left behind, combined with erratic efforts to make contact with women, suggest that on one hand he was attracted to a culture of easy "hooking up" sexually, but was devastated when he was continually shot down.

The notion that a successful college male identity involves success with women may have helped drive Cho to fantasize and ultimately to harass women, two of whom reported him to campus police but did not press charges. Reports that Cho took inappropriate pictures of women in class suggest his increasing need to see and experience the sexuality splashed throughout media and consumer culture, but that his behavior and desires were way over the boundaries of acceptable behavior. Suite mates recounted on an April 18, 2007, CNN report that Cho claimed he had a supermodel girlfriend from outer space named "Jelly" who called him "Spanky."[77] When classmate Andy Koch, who recounted the story, once knocked on Cho's door looking for a friend, Cho replied that he was making out with his girlfriend Jelly, a fantasy that calls attention to the extremity of Cho's need to assume a male identity and his utter failure to do so in the real world.[78]

This fantasy girlfriend and Cho's failures to find a real one reveal the pressures of "heteronormativity" on Cho, that proper male identity requires finding a female partner. To be sure, there were rumors that Cho was gay,[79] but at least in the Virginia Tech public sphere, he pursued a straight male identity, even if this was not possible due to his ineptness with women, and perhaps sexual confusion, exhibited in his bizarre behavior. And when it was impossible for him to create a normative male sexual identity, he went amok constructing an ultraviolent masculine identity, with tragic results.

As argued, Cho was stuck in a field of tension between the Korean and the American. Wishing to overcome the nerdy, asexual images of the Asian American male evident in the first picture released of him, he chose instead the ultraviolent macho male, another impossible choice that led to mayhem and self-destruction. Unfortunately, U.S. media culture does not offer many positive ideals for Asian American males who are typically represented in comedic characters like Long Duk Dong in *Sixteen Candles* (1984), or as innocuous and assimilated.

A report in the *Washington Post* on May 6, 2007, by Amy Gardiner and David Cho, "Isolation Defined Cho's Senior Year," indicates that Cho's mother was so desperate to help her alienated son that she sought help of her church's pastor to rid him of what she called "demonic power." The report indicated that Cho had evidently made an effort initially to fit into Virginia Tech, buying Virginia Tech baseball hats, jeans, and T-shirts that he wore to class, and evidently studied hard. But by his senior year, according to reports by fellow students, he seems to have been totally alienated and was rarely seen in class or studying.[80]

The *Washington Post* article also recounts growing isolation during his senior year and how, when one of his female classmates who shared a British literature class was "befriended" by Cho and invited to his Facebook page as a participant, another woman told her that Cho had bothered her and that she had gone to the police, thus leading the Facebook "friend" to delete herself from Cho's page.

Curiously, an episode on the April 29, 2007, week of the popular HBO TV series *The Sopranos,* titled "Remember When," featured a mentally disturbed Asian American male who looked like Cho incarcerated in a mental institution with Uncle Junior Soprano. In the episode, the young man, who has "anger management" problems, befriends Uncle Junior, whom he looks up to as a true man. But when his fashionable and attractive Asian American mother comes to visit him and criticizes the young man for his aberrant behavior in the institution, it is clear that family and social pressures to conform had unhinged the young man and he begins to explode with violence, an apt allegory, it seems, for Cho's situation.

Of course, ultimately it is still a mystery how Cho lived his ethnicity, family, and sexuality, and his desperate and violent attempt to construct an aggressive masculinity is obviously compensatory for failures in other areas of his life, as well as a sign of male rage that had evidently been building up since high school, when students made fun of his accent and way of speaking in class, or perhaps even earlier. Ultimately, while the extent of his alienation from school, community, and family appears extreme, we do not know precisely how he was influenced by his family and surroundings or how his ethnicity affected him.

Although Cho's play *Richard McBeef* has a character sexually molested in the family, we do not know if this was Cho's own experience or just another bizarre fantasy.[81] In another play written by Cho, *Mr. Brownstone,* three students sit in a casino expressing their deep hatred for their math teacher, Mr. Brownstone, who they claim tried to "ass-rape" them.[82] Whether or not Cho was sexually molested by a teacher or anyone else is unknown as of yet. No doubt the rejection of his writings and his clumsy failed attempts at making contact with women seriously unhinged him. But Cho was also of a generation of immigrants known as the "1.5 generation," between their first-generation parents who struggle hard to survive in the United States, but do not necessarily absorb its culture, and second-generation immigrants who grow up in the culture. Cho obviously had difficulties in mediating the space between the Korean and the American and could not produce a viable synthesis.

Although some blame the violent Korean films like *Oldboy* for influencing Cho, he might as easily have been influenced by nightly pictures in the news of the killing of Iraqis and Afghans in the name of a "war on terror," or by pictures of Iraqis tortured by U.S. soldiers in the Abu Ghraib scandal. Cho's twisted logic might be that if the Bush-Cheney administration could go outside the law and torture, imprison, violate habeas corpus against, and even murder individuals in the name of a higher good, it was his duty as well to serve as an avenging angel of his perceived wrongs. Cho is thus less aberrant than he might be perceived at first and fits into the absolutist and terrorist ethos of both a Bush or Cheney and a bin Laden. Every age generates its own monsters and Cho appears as a twisted symbol of George W. Bush's America.

As of October 2007, Cho's precise motives for undertaking the shootings are still a mystery. An article in the *Washington Post* on May 6, 2007, by Brigid Schulte and Chris L. Jenkins, "Cho Didn't Get Court-Ordered Treatment," suggests that Cho never received the treatment ordered by the judge and that neither the court, the police, the university, nor community services ever followed up on the order, showing the gaps and holes in the mental health and legal situation that left Cho ever more isolated and blocking himself off from receiving any treatment—with fatal results.[83]

A report released by agents from the Bureau of Alcohol, Tobacco, Firearms and Explosives (ATF) suggested that Cho displayed behavioral characteristics of a "collector of injustice," of "someone who considers any misfortune against him the fault or responsibility of others." The group also thinks "Cho mentally and physically tried to transform himself into an alter ego he called 'Ax Ishmael' before his rampage," transforming his personality in the weeks leading up to the shooting from "passive to active."[84]

For two months, an enormous law enforcement operation led by the ATF and FBI, called "Operation Prevail," examined a vast amount of records and actions connected with Cho. They have preliminarily concluded that Cho did not target anyone specific, but methodically assembled the weapons and uniform he used the day of his rampage. Investigators cite three pictures that depict his progression of self-image, moving from a smiling picture of himself to an image of himself with arms outstretched like Jesus on a cross to a third picture with his arms crossed, as if he were dead in a coffin.

But it was the *Report of the Review Panel* (2007: 31ff.) that contains the most detailed account of Cho's life, mental health problems, and challenges. Most significantly, it details how, during his middle school years, the Chos took their son in July 1997 to the Center for Multicultural Human Services for evaluation. He was prescribed art therapy, and one of the psychiatrists working with him diagnosed a severe "social anxiety disorder." Another psychiatrist in 1999 diagnosed Cho with "selective mutism" and "major depression: single episode," prescribing the antidepressant Paroxetine, which Cho took from June 1999 to July 2000 (2007: 35).

In fall 1999 Cho centered Centreville High School, and his barely audible communication brought him to the school screening committee, where he was tested and assigned an individualized education plan (IEP). Cho was encouraged to participate in extracurricular activities, and he seemed to be doing well in high school, receiving high grades in advanced placement and honors classes. In the 11th grade, Cho's weekly sessions at the mental health center came to an end. The report also revealed that "when his guidance counselor talked to Cho and his family about college, she strongly recommended they send him to a small school close to home where he could more easily make the transition to college life. She cautioned that Virginia Tech was too large" (2007: 37).

The advice appears to be on target in retrospect, but Cho was set on going to Virginia Tech and the rest is history. The *Report of the Review Panel* (2007: 38ff.) documents Cho's mental health history at Virginia Tech and sets out in detail how the system let him down, with disastrous consequences for the community. The various Virginia Tech school counseling and disciplinary programs did not seem to talk to each other, disregarded the admonitions from the English department that Cho required scrutiny and care, seemed not to know about his legal and mental health records, some of which appear to have been lost, and made no effort to contact Cho's parents, who evidently had successfully sought mental health care and counseling for him in middle and high school (2007: 40ff.).

As I have argued, Cho fell prey to a multiplicity and intersectionality of influences and fell through multiple social systems ranging from the family, church, school, healthcare, and legal systems, falling through the cracks in each and failing to get adequate mental health care treatment and help. Absorbing some of the worst features in U.S. gun and media culture, with some strong Asian influences in the latter, Cho constructed a violent masculine identity in the Virginia Tech massacre, which provided a macabre answer to the question mark that he used as a tag.

Hence, like Timothy McVeigh, the Unabomber Ted Kaczynski, and Dylan Klebold, Eric Harris, and other school shooters, Seung-Hui Cho ran amok and went on a fierce killing spree.[85] All of these murderers were suffering from excessive male rage and a crisis of masculinity, most were fanatics of gun culture and used guns and weapons in violent acts that made them media celebrities, and they all produced hypermasculine violent identities in their spectacles of terror.

I have attempted throughout to advance a multicausal and multiperspectivist analysis that attributes a multiplicity of causes to the Virginia Tech and other school shootings and to domestic terrorism from the Oklahoma City bombings to the present. If there is a multiplicity of causes for violent behavior, there is necessarily a complex multiplicity of solutions. Let us, then, in the concluding chapter, draw some lessons of our studies of crises of masculinity, male rage, gun culture, and a variety of cases of domestic terrorism examined so far and look at what sorts of things need to be done to help prevent or mitigate future acts of domestic terrorism or school and workplace shootings.

Chapter Four

What Is to Be Done?

In this book, I have argued that there is a constellation of specific factors responsible for the rise of domestic terrorism and events like the Columbine and Virginia Tech school shootings. Complex historical events like the Iraq invasion or the Virginia Tech and Columbine shootings require multiperspectivist interpretations of key factors so that such events can be better understood and interpreted. Thus addressing the causes of problems like societal violence and school shootings involves a range of apparently disparate things such as critique of male socialization and construction of ultramasculine male identities; the prevalence of gun culture and militarism; and a media culture that promotes violence and retribution, while sensationalizing media spectacle and a culture of celebrity. Such constellations contribute to driving individuals to use violence to resolve their crises in masculinity through creation of an ultramasculine identity and media spectacle, producing guys and guns amok.

Accordingly, solutions that I suggest range from more robust and rational gun laws to better school and workplace security with stronger mental health institutions and better communication among legal, medical, and school administrations, to the reconstruction of masculinity and the reconstruction of education for democracy. In addition, we must consider examining better ways of addressing crime and violence than prisons and capital punishment, draconian measures aimed increasingly today at youth and people of color. Today our schools are like prisons. In a better society schools would become centers of learning and self-development, and prisons could also be centers of learning, rehabilitation, and job training and not punitive and dangerous schools for crime and violence.

Guns amok today in the United States is a national scandal and serious social problem. Deaths in the United States caused by firearms run to about 30,000 per year, in which around 12,000 are murders and 17,000 are suicides, with the rest accidents.[1] Of the 105,000 gun shops in the United States, only about 1 percent are the origins of 60 percent of the guns that are seized in crimes.[2] As David Olinger notes: "Collectively, U.S. citizens are the most heavily armed in the world. Americans own about 250 million rifles, shotguns and handguns, nearly one per person and at least one-third of the guns in the world.... From 1999 through 2004, according to the U.S. Centers for Disease Control and Prevention, guns killed an average of 80 people a day. Gun homicides averaged 31 a day."[3]

The massacre at Virginia Tech was the twentieth-fifth school shooting on an American campus since Columbine in 1999. That figure represents more than half the number of shootings at schools across in the world in the same time span.[4] Deadly school shootings at a wide range of schools have claimed scores of student and faculty lives since Columbine.[5] As the back cover for a new edition of Lieberman's *The Shooting Game* (2006) indicates: "In March and April of 2006, 16 deadly Columbine-style plots were hatched by over 25 students arrested across the U.S.A. from the heartland up to North Pole, Alaska. As the fall semester began, there were more deadly shootings in Montreal, Colorado, Wisconsin and even a tiny Amish school in Pennsylvania."

Although school shootings dropped between 1994 and 2002, they have been edging up since then.[6] But killings of youth are not restricted to schools: On May 31, 2007, Brian Williams reported from Chicago on the *NBC Nightly News* that more than 28 youngsters had been killed in the Windy City, mostly by gunshot wounds, already in 2007. On July 21, 2007, there was a report that 11 people were wounded in 6 shootings during a two-hour period in Washington, D.C.[7] In early June 2007, the FBI reported that: "More murders and robberies in 2006 sent U.S. violent crimes higher for the second straight year, ... with the increase blamed on gangs, youth violence, gun crimes and fewer police on beats."[8] During the same time, the "Police Executive Research Forum, a U.S. law enforcement association, report[ed] that, among the American cities surveyed, homicides increased 71%, robberies increased 80% and aggravated assaults with guns increased 67% between 2004 and 2006."[9] Furthermore, as a recent FBI report indicates:

> The FBI's Uniform Crime Reporting Program shows that robberies surged by 7.2 percent and murders rose 1.8 percent from 2005 to 2006. Violent crime overall rose 1.9 percent, notably more than an increase of 1.3 percent estimated in a preliminary FBI report in June.
>
> The increase was the second in two years, following a 2.3 percent jump in 2005. Taken together, the two years comprise the first steady increase in violent crimes since 1993.[10]

After 1999, in the years following the Columbine shootings, there were attempts by lawmakers to introduce scores of bills to require child-safety locks on new handguns, increase the minimum age for gun purchases, require stricter background checks on weapons purchased, and close the gun show loophole through which guns can be purchased without background checks. As a *New York Times* editorial noted: "Many had expected that the shootings at Columbine High School in Colorado in 1999 would transform the politics of gun control. In May 2000, the Million Mom March rallied in the nation's capital with a message of 'enough is enough,' But after the 2000 election, in which Vice President Al Gore's support for new gun regulations was widely thought to have hurt his candidacy, many Democrats showed little appetite for challenging the gun lobby."[11]

Since then, the Bush-Cheney administration and Republican-led Congress have pushed through policies that restrict gun controls, letting the Clinton administration's groundbreaking assault-weapons ban expire in 2004. The Bush-Cheney administration and Republicans also pushed through in 2003 a measure preventing local enforcement agencies from consulting police in other states on firearms traces, and passed in 2005 legislation shielding gun makers from lawsuits, all in all a bonanza for criminals, terrorists, and would-be mass murderers.

Indeed, Cho was able to increase his body count with the help of an assault rifle with high-capacity ammunition clips that had been banned, which allowed him to fire more rounds without reloading. Moreover, both of the Columbine shooters got their guns illegally, with Klebold and Harris procuring guns through a friend, who purchased them at a gun show, and Klebold's 18-year-old girlfriend, who bought the 17-year-old killers other guns used in the slaughter. And Cho bought a gun from a pawnshop and Internet sites even though he had been involuntarily committed to a mental institution.

In 2006, New York mayor Michael Bloomberg organized a group of mayors committed to fighting illegal firearms in the United States, arguing: "It is time for national leadership in the war on gun violence. And if that leadership won't come from Congress or come from the White House, then it has to come from us."[12] Since then more than 200 mayors from cities in 46 states have signed on. When Bloomberg began sending undercover officials to Virginia to expose their lax gun sales controls and to demonstrate how easy it was for criminals to purchase guns,[13] the Virginia state legislature passed laws making it a felony to impersonate a gun buyer with the intention of exposing sales practices and failure to comply with the law—and this was just after the Virginia Tech shootings!

After a series of violent crimes culminating in a massacre of 35 people at a tourist site in Port Arthur, Tasmania, in 1996, Australia passed laws restricting the kinds of guns that could be sold and owned, and deaths from firearms declined. Within weeks of the shootings, the Australian government banned the manufacture and sale of all automatic and semiautomatic weapons and pump-action shotguns and also introduced an extensive gun registration system; a 28-day waiting period between attaining a gun permit and buying a gun; a provision that first-time gun purchasers undergo firearms training; and requirements that weapons and ammunition be stored separately. There was also a buy-back provision for certain automatic weapons. Ten years later there appeared to be general consensus that the gun laws had worked and that even stronger handgun restrictions are needed.[14]

In Scotland in 1996, after a former scoutmaster, Thomas Hamilton, took 4 guns and shot and killed 16 children and 1 teacher at Dunblane Primary School, wounding 10 others and killing himself, there was a campaign to restrict gun hand sales and ownership and eventual imposition of a strict ban on handguns. The results a decade later: "According to government statistics, the number of people killed by guns has essentially stayed the same, with dips and spikes, as before the 1997 gun control laws went into effect: There were 55 shooting deaths in 1995 and 50 last year in England and Wales. By comparison, there were 137 fatal shootings in the District of Columbia last year."[15]

Let us, then, examine the immediate aftermath to the Virginia Tech massacre and see what, if anything, came out of it in terms of informed national debate and solutions to escalating gun violence in the United States.

Aftermath

In the days following the Virginia Tech massacre, the *Chronicle of Higher Education* traced the fallout, with frequent reports of school closures because of threats of violence and arrests of students for making specific threats against faculty and fellow students and various ways that the incident had generated debate.[16] Virginia governor Tim Kaine signed an executive order on April 30 banning the sale of guns to people involuntarily committed to inpatient and outpatient mental health treatment, thus closing a loophole that allowed Seung-Hui Cho to purchase firearms and ammunition, even though he had been declared dangerously mentally ill. The Virginia State Police and the state Mental Health, Mental Retardation, and Substance Abuse Services Department were directed "to consider any involuntary treatment order ...

whether inpatient or outpatient" when determining who should be barred from purchasing a gun.[17]

Kaine's order intends to put people involuntarily committed to mental health institutions on a list that prohibits them from buying a gun until a court rules that they are no longer a threat to themselves or others. However, the Virginia legislature, hostile to restrictions on gun laws, needs to ratify and clarify the order. Moreover, the order does not apply to those who choose to voluntarily submit to mental health treatment, and shockingly, there are no restrictions on unlicensed dealers selling guns on a one-to-one basis at gun shows and the Republican-controlled legislature has repeatedly rejected efforts to close the gun show loophole.

Indeed, the Brady Campaign to Prevent Gun Violence has assigned Virginia a "C-minus" on legislation preventing gun violence (New York State gets a "B-plus," while Mississippi receives an "F").[18] There are no gun registration laws in Virginia, no permit is required to purchase a handgun, and there is no waiting period on gun sales. There have been complaints that guns sold in Virginia find their way to the streets of Washington, New York, and other high-crime East Coast cities (see Note 13), but so far no high-profile Virginia politician has taken on the challenge of working to reform Virginia's disgraceful gun laws.

Initial reports of the work done by the panel appointed by Governor Kaine to investigate the Virginia Tech shootings suggested that a whitewash was coming. Tim Craig reported in a May 11, 2007, *Washington Post* story, "Va. Tech Panel Outlines Agenda," that several members of the panel "concluded that law enforcement and university officials probably handled the initial response to the shootings appropriately, given the information that authorities had at the time."[19] Further, during the initial meeting of the Virginia Tech Review Panel, "the chairman and other members said they do not want their review to second-guess the first responders to the April 16 shooting." Instead, the panel indicated that they "will probably focus more on Cho, his access to weapons and the state's mental health system than on the performances of Virginia Tech officials and campus and Blacksburg police."

While surely the questions of Cho's mental health, the response by Virginia's mental health system, and Cho's access to guns are crucial to addressing issues raised by the shootings, so, too, are Virginia Tech's response to Cho's problems and its response to the initial shootings. Initially, there were signs that the Virginia panel would be limited in its scope, as when relatives of the Virginia Tech victims were told that they had not been granted representation on the panel investigating the killings, leaving them "both angry and disappointed."[20] While the relatives had "requested very respectfully to be represented on the panel ... the panel said no." The relatives were also concerned about "the accountability of the Hokie Spirit Fund," in which the university was raising money using the images and names of the 32 victims for major fund-raising purposes, but had not consulted with the relatives of the deceased.[21]

Yet the publication of the *Report of the Review Panel: Mass Shootings at Virginia Tech* (2007) revealed a comprehensive and critical look at the entire incident, including sections on the "Mental Health History of Seung-Hui Cho," "Virginia Mental Health Issues," "Privacy Laws," "Gun Purchase and Campus Policies," detailed description of the double murder at West Ambler and "Mass Murder at Norris Hall," the "Emergency Medical Services Response," the role of the office of the chief medical examiner, and attempts at "The Long Road to Healing." To the surprise of many, the report was sharply critical of Virginia Tech and made many constructive suggestions to deal with similar crises in the future.

Although the episode constitutes a major tragedy for the Virginia Tech community, there are three positive outcomes of the event that can now be identified. First, there is a more intense and comprehensive focus on school security. The Virginia Tech shootings were academia's 9/11, and colleges and universities throughout the country began serious discussion of responses to school security issues, with most universities adopting emergency plans to communicate with students in the case of a terrorist incident or threat to the university community, establishing crisis groups to deal with it, and planning ways to interface with campus and local police. Already, such heightened awareness has been visible in the September 21, 2007, school shootings at Delaware State University, when officials alerted students within 15 minutes of the shootings and locked down most buildings, cancelling class for the next day.[22]

The second positive outcome of the Virginia Tech shootings was more intense focus and scrutiny of mental health issues. On the positive register, on June 13, 2007, the U.S. House of Representatives passed a bill that would make it more difficult for people with mental health problems to purchase guns. Crafted with help from bipartisan lawmakers and the NRA, the bill was seen as the first major gun control legislation since 1994 and was intended to "improve the national gun background check system by requiring states to report their list of mentally ill people who are prohibited from buying firearms to the National Instant Criminal Background Check System."[23]

The same day, the White House released a report indicating that there was confusion over sharing health information among law enforcement, the medical community, the judicial community, and the university that blocked people with mental illness from getting the services they need. The report recommended clarification concerning how information could be shared, and also recommended that schools develop procedures for quickly notifying students when emergencies occur, as Virginia Tech had failed to do.[24]

After two months of public hearings by the state panel investigating the Virginia Tech massacre, members of the panel revealed that the state's system of dealing with mental patients was deeply flawed. In particular, the system's dealings with Cho appeared chaotic, with many records missing, ineffective responses to his problems, and indications that there was no treatment plan to deal with Cho's problems. The article noted that the "state's system of dealing with the mentally ill is in almost desperate need of repair," and that "panel members said they still do not have a complete picture of how the system handled Cho. So much information was missing, incomplete or destroyed, they said."[25]

The third positive outcome of the shootings was renewed debate about gun control and the role of guns in U.S. society, although here it is not certain that there will be much forward progress on this issue in the foreseeable future. Different groups, including the progun advocates, continued to exploit the tragedy. It was reported that one of the measures under consideration by the Virginia panel studying the problems of the shootings was "a proposal to lift a ban on concealed-carry firearms on Virginia college and university campuses."[26] Moreover, the Virginia Tech student paper article just cited indicated that: "In South Carolina a bill has recently emerged from committee in the state legislature that would allow adult permit holders to carry concealed handguns on public school campuses, from elementary to collegiate level."[27] The president of the Brady Campaign to Prevent Gun Violence, Paul Helmke, indicated that his group thought more guns on campus would make things worse, and, "in reality, students carrying guns only makes it more likely that they will be stolen, misused, accidentally discharged or used to commit crimes or suicide" (ibid.). Virginia Tech students interviewed for the article were split on the proposal.

Most shockingly, the longtime Washington, D.C., ban on handguns was challenged by gun activists, and a three-judge panel of the U.S. Court of Appeals for the District of Columbia Circuit ruled two-to-one against the city. District of Columbia officials said that they will request that the Supreme Court preserve their 30-year ban on private ownership of handguns, setting the stage for a dramatic Supreme Court decision (or for the Court to refuse to hear the appeal).[28]

Gun Laws, School and Workplace Safety, and Mental Health Care: The Delicate Balance

As for solutions to the problems of guns amok, domestic terrorism, and the crisis of masculinity described in this book, it is unlikely that there will be much clarification or action from establishment politicians, the corporate media, or the government. After the Columbine shootings, as noted, there was much discussion about crafting more rational gun laws, but after some progress in the Clinton administration, there was regression during the Bush-Cheney years. There should, however, be serious efforts at developing

- stricter gun control laws;
- improved campus and workplace security, sharing of information and databases concerning potentially dangerous people, and serious attempts to balance security with rights to privacy;
- better guidance and mental health care on campus and in communities;
- more responsibility on the parts of schools and local communities to deal with alienated and disturbed members of their family or community;
- profiling of schools to see that they have proper counseling, policing, administrative, and other procedures to deal with school security and problem students;
- a reconstruction of education with programs producing new literacies, advocating peace and social justice, and projecting new images of masculinity;
- a broad-based and wide-ranging questioning of hegemonic concepts of masculinity and construction of alternative masculinities;
- and perceiving prisons as schools for violence and transforming them into institutions of education and rehabilitation.

I will be dealing with some of these issues in the following sections. As noted at the end of the last section, there have been some positive developments in the aftermath of the Virginia Tech shootings on issues of school security and mental health but not much positive movement on gun control. I agree completely with Mark Ames, author of *Going Postal: Rage, Murder, and Rebellion: From Reagan's Workplaces to Clinton's Columbine and Beyond* (2005), that it is a question of profiling schools, the police, the legal system, and the mental health system and not just profiling individuals to deal with problems like school shootings and security.[29] After Columbine, there was a boom in the school security business and high-tech surveillance devices,[30] but few well-publicized efforts at better guidance counseling, mental health facilities, and not enough efforts to create an atmosphere where bullying and violence are rejected and rectified.

To be sure, some schools had been addressing the problem of bullying that came dramatically to the fore in the Columbine shootings. An article by Maia Szalavitz, "A Better Response to Rejection," noted that: "Across the nation, school doors are closing on one of the bloodiest years in U.S. history, with scores of violent deaths on both school and college campuses. The end of classes also means the end, for this term, of uneven school efforts to prevent the social rejection that may lie behind some of the violence."[31] Szalavitz summarized recent findings regarding children's school social lives and how the Virginia Tech shootings dramatize once again the need for schools to provide a protective environment and deal with problems of youth rejection and bullying by peers.

Gun control should be seen as part of the solution to providing better workplace and school security and addressing the more general problem of excessive violence in U.S. society. At the end of his reflections on the relevance for understanding violence of sociologist-criminologist Lonnie Athens, Richard Rhodes provides some "strategies of prevention and control" (1999: 313ff.). Rhodes believes that Athens's sociological studies of violentization, the process through which individuals learn to become violent, provides "for the first time a solid scientific foundation on which to build programs of violence prevention, interruption and control" (313). While Athens and Rhodes see problems of family violence and child abuse, the "place to prevent or interrupt violentization, Athens believes, is the school. 'Although the community cannot guarantee a good family to every child,' he writes, 'it can guarantee them a good school,' and 'a good school can go a long way in making up for a bad family'" (ibid.).

The key is to develop school-based violence prevention programs that teach nonviolent conflict resolution, that have counseling for students with problems, and that provide values and models of nonviolent social relations and community. Rhodes claims, however, that Athens neglects to critique dominant conservative Christian models for their concepts and practices of authoritarian discipline and response to school violence by recommending draconian "discipline and punishment." Drawing on the work of historian Philip Greven and his 1991 book *Spare the Child,* Rhodes presents critique of the philosophy advocated by James Dobson and other so-called Christian authorities who teach how to "break the will" of children, "punishing them to the point of 'unconditional surrender,' unqualified obedience" (315). Citing shocking passages from major "Christian" disciplinary texts,

Rhodes argues that "'discipline' carried to the point of violent subjugation can lead to the creation of another violent individual" (316).

As noted in Chapters 1 and 3, conservatives often find scapegoat targets to blame for school shootings and youth killings, such as permissive liberalism, a hedonistic mass culture, godlessness in a secular society, or other favorites. DeMause, Rhodes, and others, however, criticize conservative child-rearing philosophies that involve harsh punishment as producing violentization and potential killers (Rhodes 1999: 237ff.), thus contributing to the problem rather than the solution.

Besides serving as "centers for crime prevention," Rhodes argues that Athens's work proposes that "schools should also direct belligerent students to community rehabilitation programs while rehabilitation is still possible" (316). Hence, Athens's work supports intervention efforts to curtail violentization, including "efforts to stop family violence, to reduce school violence, to offer nonviolent coaching such as training in negotiation, anger management and conflict resolution, to discourage bullying, to offer (nonviolent) mentoring of children at risk, to discourage violent coaching of school athletes, to improve child welfare, to counsel belligerent young people, to support gun control, to dissolve or pacify street gangs and many more such antiviolent initiatives" (317).

Societal violence in this view is a public health problem and requires serious prevention and rehabilitation programs. But fighting societal violence, Rhodes concludes, also requires "personal witness to civil values; it is by personal witness, after all, that civil communities maintain their civility and the civilizing process proceeds" (322).

In terms of school shootings and the problems of school safety, Spina (2000) suggests in the conclusion to her reader *Smoke and Mirrors*, "When the Smoke Clears: Revisualizing Responses to Violence in Schools," ways that violence can be seriously engaged. Since violence is deeply rooted in self and society, it is difficult, but not impossible, to deal with it. Since violence is "about power" (229), it is rooted in institutions and dominant social relations, thus most reformist measures that reproduce the existing society do not seriously address the problem or provide real solutions.

Spina, like Rhodes, is sharply critical of harsh punitive disciplinary measures favored by conservatives, such as corporal punishment, and of dress codes, daily flag-raising ceremonies, school prayers, or high-tech surveillance systems (230ff.). Yet she is also critical of liberal conflict resolution programs if they are just about imposing middle-class American values on students, and is critical of school reform measures if they are just about imposing corporate models on schools. She also is skeptical of school reform programs such as providing school vouchers that help subsidize religious schools or charter and magnet schools that do not offer genuine alternatives.

Spina is also critical of "back to basics" and "higher standards" models that could be forms of imposing conservative modes of education and values on students and will not help ameliorate student alienation, inequalities, and social conditions that produce violence. Likewise, vocational training may just reproduce existing inequalities and track students into lower-paying jobs, while not giving them the tools of critical thinking needed to confront the novelties and transformations of the contemporary moment.

Ultimately Spina proposes a democratic reconstruction of education based on principles of progressive educators John Dewey and Brazilian Paulo Freire as the best hope for creating a meaningful education that will empower students, create good citizens, and prepare them for the challenges of a new millennium. While public health notions of education and public policy in transforming schools can help with the process of democratic reconstruction, it must be based on goals of social justice and fighting inequalities, racism, sexism, and homophobia—themes I take up in the next section.

Attempting to derive some lessons from their years of study of two rural communities that experienced school shootings, Newman and her associates in *Rampage* (2004) conclude their book with proposals on "Prevention, Intervention, and Coping with School Shootings" (271). Admitting a certain "humility," they note that there is no blueprint for prevention and that different measures should be a topic for discussion and debate among parents, teachers, schools, and mental health authorities.

Some practical proposals in dealing with the aftermath of school shootings involve lessons learned in dealing with the media and with community and student trauma, and in returning schools to a sense of normality and security (273ff.). On the latter topic, Newman and her colleagues are skeptical of fences that cut schools off from the community or surveillance systems (277, 286). Likewise, strategies for "adjusting the radar" in sharing information to target problem students involve questions of privacy and require cooperation among teachers, administrators, and mental health and legal authorities that is very difficult to produce (279ff.). The group did find that school resource officers (SROs), who specialize in helping maintain order, curtailing bullying, and working with schools to provide a safe learning environment, can help, but such measures require extra financing that many schools cannot afford (280ff.), and, as I note below, there may be better strategies.

Generally, Newman and her colleagues suggest moving from a law enforcement model to a mental health model (294ff.), and indicate that more resources are needed for counseling and mental health staffs, which are shamelessly underfunded and understaffed in most schools. Ultimately, the culture of schooling needs to be changed from disciplinary and standardizing environments that reproduce the status quo to genuine institutions of learning and development. In terms of changing school culture, Newman et al. see the virtues in hiring "hip" new teachers who give marginal kids new models and who may understand and engage teen culture in a way that older, more traditional teachers cannot. The authors also note that: "Schools could also explicitly challenge reductionist notions of masculinity that prevail in adolescence. Masculinity in adulthood can mean a range of things, but for adolescents it often signifies physical strength, athletic accomplishment, and sexual conquest. Exposing adolescents to a more expansive range and challenging them to confront their own parochialism is an important strategy in diversifying the range of viable options for manly behavior" (283).

While Newman and her associates argue for the need to address bullying and that bullying by privileged athletes should not be tolerated, they are skeptical of the draconian "zero tolerance policy" (285ff.) that would "require schools to follow formalized disciplinary procedures after any threat of violence and leave administrators with little discretion to separate serious offenders from casual jokers" (285). The punitive approach is counterproductive, because it "does little to change the underlying dynamics of peer relations and the flow of information in schools—factors that lie closer to the root of the problem" (ibid.). Yet there should be zero tolerance for systematic physical bullying and a "reign of terror" by violent groups or individuals (286), as there should not be tolerance for students bringing guns or weapons into school.

In regard to sports culture in the schools, Newman et al. (2004) observed the problems of the "great deal of damage done to the egos of boys who cannot compete" (284). While teams help produce positive school spirit and community, and "old-fashioned ideals of sportsmanship" can be important, there is danger that sports culture can be corrupted by money, celebrity, and privilege, leading to bullying and bad behavior by athletic elites. Underlining the importance of maintaining a healthy and safe school environment, Newman et al. (2004) argue that "adults who fail to discipline flagrant rule violators should be removed from positions of authority," and persistent "bullying should be grounds for forfeit of the privilege of representing one's school in athletic competition" (284). Moreover, they propose that the community should give some of the positive support given to sports teams to debate or art groups, and that "middle schools should try to develop more activities that will engage the interest of kids who are not involved in sports" (ibid.).

In a section titled "Encouraging Kids to Report Threats" (288ff), the authors recognize that whatever positive changes occur in schools there are likely to continue to be school shootings, as indeed there have been. Hence: "While the nation looks for ways to attack the root causes of adolescent rage, it must apply equal effort to increasing the likelihood that kids who hear threats come forward and tell someone who can make a difference. Intercepting threats is the most promising avenue for prevention of school shootings, but for that to happen, kids must feel comfortable coming forward with information that they typically conceal" (288). Having kids come forward with information requires that they can trust their information will be confidential, and so there should be hotlines for anonymous tips, as well as school officials who can mediate in threatening situations.

In a similar fashion, Lieberman concludes his *The Shooting Game* (2006) with the claim: "Above all, the common sense approach of fostering a willingness among students to report legitimate threats in the interests of their self-preservation is a tried and true solution. It has already resulted in the prevention of potential school shootings" (306–307). Lieberman notes that particularly after 9/11 a large number of students reported potentially deadly plots threatened by classmates and that many potential incidents were prevented, and the students who uncovered the dangers were seen as heroes.

Emphasizing dependence on students to inform on fellow students if there are dangers of violence shows the poverty of the liberal imagination that cannot see that more dramatic and thorough-going transformation is needed to deal with the problems of school shootings and societal violence. To be sure, schools should promote an atmosphere where students can talk to teachers and counselors about their own problems, those of other students, and general problems in the school and larger world. And, as Ralph Larkin spells out in the concluding chapter to his book *Comprehending Columbine* (2007), conflict resolution programs and peace education programs need to be instituted that make students participants in the process of creating nonviolent and positive learning environments.

In a concluding chapter on "Give Peace a Chance," Larkin discusses anti-violence and conflict resolution programs (217ff.). To engage school violence, one must, first, recognize the causes, and then take appropriate action. Major causes of the Columbine shootings involved, Larkin believes, bullying of marginal students by jock elites, and "the arrogance of evangelical students who established themselves as a moral elite in the high school" and saw themselves as superior and proselytized and criticized other students, generating retaliatory action (196ff.).[32] The solution, Larkin believes, involves changing the nature of school culture and instituting antiviolence programs in schools.

There is a "great deal of hidden physical and psychological violence," Larkin indicates, in both middle and high schools, that needs addressing (217). To be successful, an antiviolence program must be systemic, embracing middle school through high school, and it "must change the internal social climate of the school" (219). The program should reach beyond schools to local communities to work with parents, church groups, and other community organizations interested in education and the well-being of their community.

Larkin has mastered a wide range of literature on antiviolence programs and concludes by discussing a program developed by the International Center for Cooperation and Conflict Resolution at Teachers College, Columbia University, in which his wife Debra Larkin was trained as a conflict mediator; she then ran a program for more than 10 years in a high school in lower Manhattan. The success of the program, Larkin believes, lies in the creation of cadres of peer mediators who work with professionals to negotiate problems, working toward solutions. Such programs actively involve students and make them part of a problem-solving community, as well as educate them to become democratic citizens and take responsibility for their communities. Despite successful implementation of such programs all over the country in urban, suburban, and rural schools (226), Larkin notes that "sadly there is little political will to implement positive peace education policies in high schools" (227).

This is a shame, and such programs sound excellent and necessary, although as I will argue in the following sections, we need more thoroughgoing radical democratic reconstruction education of schools and society to deal with problems of school shootings and societal violence. Peace education should include courses in conflict resolution, nonviolence, and histories of war and peace. For the dominant culture of militarism, there should be alternative cultures of peace taught and cultivated. While Larkin titles a key section in his conclusion "Peace Education," the analysis focuses on conflict mediation programs in the schools. But in addition to this we need substantive peace programs that deal with war and peace, violence and nonviolence, conflict resolution and cooperation, democracy and community.

Addressing the culture of militarism needs to begin at home and school with critique of media, artifacts like toys, or ideologues and books that glorify war and the warrior. A warrior culture is inimical to a democratic society and should be countered by democratic values of dialogue, consensus, and nonviolent conflict resolution, as well as positive values like peace and community.

A critical media literacy should make students and citizens sensitive to the problems with hypermasculinized gender representations, as well as highly sexualized ones for women. The social construction of gender needs to be thoroughly discussed, and hypermasculinity, violence against women, and in general brutality and violence need to be addressed (see Katz 2006). Dialogical pedagogies should thematize war and violence as major social problems and discuss alternatives. Peace studies should address nonviolent philosophies like those of Jesus, Gandhi, and Martin Luther King.

Returning to the issue of guns in schools and society, it is obviously a big sociopolitical challenge for the United States to confront the problem of an out-of-control gun culture and escalating male rage. Given the power of the gun lobby and the cowardice of politicians, obviously only a minimal amount of gun control is foreseeable. Certainly, the attempts at reform after Columbine that were advanced during the Clinton-Gore years, and then repulsed during the Bush-Cheney years, are reasonable and in the national interest. Hence, for starters, reasonable gun control would involve 1) returning to earlier attempts to require child-safety locks on new handguns; 2) increasing the minimum age for gun purchases; 3) requiring stricter background checks on weapons purchased; 4) producing better data sharing among police, legal, and mental health institutions and universities; and 5) closing the gun show loophole through which guns can be purchased without background checks.

These are very minimal and extremely reasonable proposals that could mean significant differences between life and death for many people. No national politician has ever seriously challenged the rights of gun ownership in the United States and the paranoia of gun owners in the Clinton era was completely unfounded. Certain segments of the gun lobby virulently oppose any reasonable gun control as they argue that the beginning of gun reform will lead to guns being ripped out of their cold, fanatic hands, to paraphrase and spoof Charlton Heston.

As noted, Congress and even the Bush administration have recognized that better mental health care is needed with better communication between health authorities and university and legal communities. Mike Males, however, did not help the youth that he has so tirelessly championed in a May 27, 2007, *Los Angeles Times/Opinion* piece, "The Kids Are (Mostly) Alright" (M6). Males's response was critical of a University of California Student Mental Health Committee that reported that "students are presenting mental health issues with greater frequency and complexity." Males raises questions concerning the University of California system's response of devoting a significant amount of higher student fees to address the problem. He criticizes as well an American

Federation of Teachers report in their monthly *On Campus* magazine that college counselors are facing "an entirely new scale of difficulty" as "the number of students with depression has doubled, the number of suicidal students has tripled and sexual assaults have gone up fourfold." Males asserts that "claims of a 'campus mental health crisis' may be overblown" by referring to UCLA's Higher Education Research Institute and its annual survey of first-year college students that indicates that depression has dropped in the past two decades. And he claims further that his own study of eight UC campuses "and their surrounding communities were similar. Students 18 to 24 years old rarely died violently, and the rates of such deaths were declining dramatically."

It is unlikely that first-year college students are going to be open and forthcoming with UCLA researchers about their mental health problems, and it is not clear what Males's own research methods and agenda are that led him to push aside claims of mental health problems on campus. Those of us deeply concerned about higher education and the future of our country, however, should recognize the need for better mental health care for all our citizens, including young people and students, and support efforts at improving what many believe are seriously underfunded and understaffed programs to deal with serious mental health problems.

The state of Virginia, however, seemed to be ready to deal with the problems of mental health, as Virginia House of Delegates members called on June 17, 2007, for "a significant infusion of money into the state's mental health system to address shortcomings exposed after Seung-Hui Cho killed 32 people at Virginia Tech two months ago."[33] The article indicated that Virginia ranked near the bottom in funding of community-based mental health services and that the National Alliance for the Mentally Ill gave Virginia a "D" grade in 2006 for its overall performance in mental health services.[34]

Beyond the Culture of Male Violence and Rage

Dealing with problems of mental health and school and societal violence will also require reconstruction of male identities and critique of masculinist socialization and identities. Unfortunately, the media and some gang culture, gun cultures, sports, and military culture extol ultramacho men as an ideal, producing societal problems from violence against women to gang murder (see Katz 2006). As Jackson Katz urges, young men have to renounce these ideals and behavior and construct alternative notions of masculinity. Reconstructing masculinity and overcoming aggressive and violent macho behavior and values provides "a vision of manhood that does not depend on putting down others in order to lift itself up. When a man stands up for social justice, nonviolence, and basic human rights—for women as much as for men—he is acting in the best traditions of our civilization. That makes him not only a better man, but a better human being" (270).

Major sources of violence in U.S. society include cultures of violence caused by poverty; masculinist military, sports, and gun culture; ultramasculine behavior in the corporate and political world; high school bullying and fighting; general societal violence reproduced by media and in the family and everyday life , and in prisons, which are schools for violence. In any of these cases, an ultraviolent masculinity can explode and produce societal violence, and until we have new conceptions of what it means to be a man that include intelligence, independence, sensitivity, and the renunciation of bullying and violence, societal violence will no doubt increase.

As I was concluding this book in July 2007, a striking example of men and guns running amok circulated through the media in stories of how former Virginia Tech football player and NFL star Michael Vick was indicted on dog-fighting charges. It was alleged that Vick and three associates had been actively participating in the illegal sport of dog fighting for at least six years. The indictment states that Vick's associates executed eight dogs for performing poorly in the month of April, utilizing methods such as hanging, electrocution, shooting, and physical beatings. The outrage led 90-year-old senator Robert Byrd to denounce the practice from the Senate floor, declaring it "barbaric, barbaric, barbaric!"[35]

Throughout late July, network newscasts were showing dog-fighting culture all around the United States, with claims that there are at least 40,000 sites where dog fights regularly take place. A July 29, 2007, episode of *60 Minutes* indicated that a form of extreme fighting that combines boxing, wrestling, street fighting, and martial arts has become one of the most popular sports in the United States, and the accompanying montage showed groups of men cheering the most bloody fights and beatings.

Sports culture is thus also a major part of the construction of American masculinity that can take violent forms. In most of the high school shootings of the 1990s, jocks tormented young teenage boys, who took revenge in asserting a hyperviolent masculinity and went on shooting rampages. Larkin (2007: 205ff.) provides a detailed analysis of "football and toxic high school environments," focusing on Columbine. He describes how sports played a primary role in the school environment, how jocks were celebrities, and how they systematically abused outsiders and marginals like Harris and Klebold.

The "pattern of sports domination of high schools," Larkin suggests, "is apparently the norm in America" (206). Larkin notes how football "has become incorporated into a hypermasculinized subculture that emphasizes physical aggression, domination, sexism, and the celebration of victory." He notes that more "than in any other sport, defeat in football is associated with being physically dominated and humiliated" (208). Further, it is associated with militarism, as George Carlin, among others, has noted in his comedy routine:

> In football the object is for the quarterback, also known as the field general, to be on target with his aerial assault, riddling the defense by hitting his receivers with deadly accuracy in spite of the blitz, even if he has to use the shotgun. With short bullet passes and long bombs, he marches his troops into enemy territory, balancing this aerial assault with a sustained ground attack that punches holes in the forward wall of the enemy's defensive line.
>
> In baseball the object is to go home! And to be safe! (Carlin, cited in Larkin 2007: 208)

Larkin argues that football culture has "corrupted many high schools," including Columbine where "the culture of hypermasculinity reigned supreme" (209). Hence, Larkin concludes that: "If we wish to reduce violence in high schools, we have to deemphasize the power of sports and change the culture of hypermasculinity. Football players cannot be lords of the hallways, bullying their peers with impunity, sometimes encouraged by coaches with adolescent mentalities" (210).

Hypermasculinity in sports is often a cauldron of homophobia, and many of the school shooters were taunted about their sexuality and responded ultimately with a berserk affirmation of compensatory violence. Yet hypermasculinity is found throughout sports, military, gun, gang, and other male subcultures, as well as the corporate and political world, often starting in the family with male socialization by the father, and is reproduced and validated constantly in films, television programs, and other forms of media culture.

There have been educational interventions that address hypermasculinity, violence against women, and homophobia, and that provide alternatives to hegemonic violent masculinities. For example, since 1993 author and activist Jackson Katz and his colleagues have been implementing the Mentors in Violence Prevention (MVP) program, which trains high school, college, and professional athletes and other student leaders to speak out and oppose violence against women, gay-bashing, and other forms of domestic and sexual violence. Featuring interactive workshops and training sessions in single-sex and mixed-gender settings as well as public lectures, MVP has been expanded throughout North America to deal with men's violence in many arenas, from the corporation to politics, police and intelligence agencies, and other institutions where men's violence is a problem.[36]

This is not to say that masculinity per se or the traits associated with it are all bad. There are times when being strong, independent, self-reliant, and even aggressive can serve positive goals and resist oppression and injustice. A postgendered human being would share traits now associated with women and men, so that women could exhibit the traits listed above and men could be more loving, caring, emotional, vulnerable and other traits associated with women. Gender itself should be deconstructed, and although we should fight gender oppression and inequality, there are reasons to question gender itself in a more emancipated and democratic world in which individuals create their own personalities and lives out of the potential found traditionally in men and women.

Obviously, media culture is full of violence, and of the case studies in Chapter 3 of violent masculinity, Timothy McVeigh, the two Columbine shooters, and many other school shooters were allegedly deeply influenced by violent media culture. Yet, while media images of violence and specific books, films, TV shows, or artifacts of media culture may provide scripts for violent masculinity that young men act out, it is the broader culture of militarism, gun culture, extreme sports, ultraviolent video and computer games, subcultures of bullying and violence, and the rewarding of ultramasculinity in the corporate and political worlds that is a major factor in constructing hegemonic violent masculinities. Media culture itself obviously contributes to this ideal of macho masculinity but it is, however, a contested terrain between different conceptions of masculinity and femininity, and among liberal, conservative, and more radical representations and discourses (Kellner 1995).

After dramatic school shootings and incidents of youth violence, there are usually attempts to scapegoat media culture. After the Virginia Tech shootings, the Federal Communications Commission (FCC) issued a report in late April 2007 on "violent television programming and its impact on children" that called for expanding governmental oversight on broadcast television, but also extending content regulation to cable and satellite channels for the first time and banning some shows from time slots where children might be watching. FCC Commissioner Jonathan S. Adelstein, who is in favor of the measures, did not hesitate to evoke the Virginia Tech shootings, "particularly in sight of the spasm of unconscionable violence at Virginia Tech, but just as importantly in light of the excessive violent crime that daily affects our nation, there is a basis for appropriate federal action to curb violence in the media."[37]

In a *Los Angeles Times* op-ed piece, Nick Gillespie, editor of *Reason*, noted that the report itself indicated that there was no causal relationship between watching TV violence and committing violent acts. Further, Gillespie argued that given the steady drop in incidents of juvenile violence over the last 12 years, reaching a low not seen since at least the 1970s, it is inappropriate to demonize media culture for acts of societal violence. Yet, in my view, the proliferation of media culture and spectacle requires renewed calls for critical media literacy so that people can intelligently analyze and interpret the media and see how they are vehicles for representations of race, class, gender, sexuality, power, and violence.

In the wake of the Columbine shootings, fierce criticism and scapegoating of media and youth culture erupted. Oddly, there was less finger pointing at these targets after the Virginia Tech massacre—perhaps because the Korean and Asian films upon which Cho modeled his photos and videos were largely unknown in the United States, and perhaps because conservatives prefer to target jihadists or liberals as nefarious influences on Cho, as I point out in Chapter 1. I want to avoid, however, the extremes of demonizing media and youth culture contrasted to asserting that media are mere entertainment without serious social influence. There is no question but that the media nurture fantasies and influence behavior, sometimes sick and vile ones, and to survive in our culture requires that we are able to critically analyze and dissect media culture and not let it gain power over us. Critical media literacy empowers individuals over media so that they can produce critical and analytical distance from media messages and images. This provides protection from media manipulation and avoids letting the most destructive images of media gain power over one. It also enables more critical, healthy, and active relations with our culture. Media culture will not disappear and it is simply a question of how we will deal with it and if we can develop an adequate pedagogy of critical media literacy to empower our youth.

Unfortunately, there are few media literacy courses offered in schools in the United States from kindergarten through high school. Many other countries such as Canada, Australia, and England have such programs (see Kellner and Share 2007). In the next section, I will suggest that to design schools for the new millennium that meet the challenges posed by student alienation and violence and provide skills that students need for a high-tech economy requires a democratic reconstruction of education. But to address problems of societal violence raised in these chapters requires a reconstruction of education and society, and what philosopher and social critic Herbert Marcuse referred to as "a revolution in values" and a "new sensibility."[38] The revolution in values involves breaking with values of competition, aggression, greed, and self-interest and cultivating values of equality, peace, harmony, and community. Such a revolution of values "would also make for a new morality, for new relations between the sexes and generations, for a new relation between man and nature" (2001: 198). Harbingers of the revolution in values, Marcuse argued, are found in "a widespread rebellion against the domineering values, of virility, heroism and force, invoking the images of society which may bring about the end of violence" (ibid.).

The "new sensibility" in turn would cultivate needs for beauty, love, connections with nature and other people, and more democratic and egalitarian social relations. Marcuse believes that without a change in sensibility, there can be no real social change, and that education, art, and the humanities can help cultivate the conditions for a new sensibility. Underlying the theory of the new sensibility is a concept of the active role of the senses in the constitution of experience that rejects the Kantian and other philosophical devaluations of the senses as passive, merely receptive. For Marcuse, our senses are shaped and molded by society, yet constitute in turn our primary experience of the world and provide both imagination and reason with its material. He believes that the senses are currently socially constrained and mutilated and argues that only an emancipation of the senses and a new sensibility can produce liberating social change (1969: 24ff.).

Ultimately, addressing the problem of societal violence requires a democratic reconstruction of education and society, new pedagogical practices, new social relations, values, and forms of learning. In the following section, I sketch out aspects of a democratic reconstruction grounded in key ideas of John Dewey, Paulo Freire, Ivan Illich, and Herbert Marcuse.

New Literacies, Democratization, and the Reconstruction of Education

To begin, we need to recognize a systemic crisis of education in the United States in which there is a disconnect between youths' lives and what they are taught in school. Already in 1964, Marshall McLuhan recognized the discrepancy between kids raised on a fast-paced and multimodal media culture and the linear, book and test-oriented education of the time, where kids sit in a classroom all day. Since then there has been a proliferation of new media and technologies, but education has been retreating to ever more conservative and pedantic goals, most egregiously during the Bush-Cheney era and its phony

No Child Left Behind program, which is really a front for "teaching for testing." In this policy, strongly resisted by many states and local school districts, incredible amounts of time are wasted preparing students for tests, and teachers and schools are basically rated according to their test results.[39]

Reconstructing education will involve an expansion of print literacy to a multiplicity of literacies. An expanded multimedia literacy and pedagogy should teach how to read and critically dissect newspapers, film, TV, radio, popular music, the Internet, and other sources of news, information, and culture to enable students to become active and engaged democratic citizens. While 1960s cultural studies by the Birmingham School in England included a focus on critically reading newspapers, TV news and information programs, and the images of politics, many cultural studies of the past decades have focused on media entertainment, consumption, and audience response to specific media programs (see Kellner 1995). This enterprise is valuable and important, but it should not replace or marginalize taking on the system of media news and information as well. A comprehensive cultural studies program should interrogate news and entertainment, journalism, and information sourcing, and should include media studies as well as textual studies and audience reception studies in part of a reconstruction of education in which critical media literacy is taught from kindergarten through college (see Kellner 1995, 1998; Kellner and Share 2007).

Critical media literacy needs to engage the "politics of representation" that subjects images and discourses of race, gender, sexuality, class, and other features to scrutiny and analysis, involving critique of violent masculinities, sexism, racism, classism, homophobia, and other hurtful forms of representation. A critical media literacy also positively valorizes more progressive representations of gender, race, class, and sexuality, and notes how many cultural texts are ambiguous and contradictory in their representations.

The Internet and multimedia computer technologies and cultural forms are dramatically transforming the circulation of information, images, and various modes of culture, and the younger generation needs to gain multifaceted technological skills to survive in the high-tech information society. In this situation, students should learn how to use media and computer culture to do research and gather information, as well as to perceive it as a cultural terrain that contains texts, spectacles, games, and interactive media, which require a form of critical computer literacy. Youth subcultural forms range from 'zines or websites that feature an ever-expanding range of video, music, or multimedia texts to sites of political information and organization.[40]

Moreover, since the 1999 Seattle anti–corporate globalization demonstrations, youth have been using the Internet to inform and debate each other, organize oppositional movements, and generate alternative forms of politics and culture.[41] Consequently, at present, computer literacy involves not merely technical skills and knowledge, but also the ability to scan information, to interact with a variety of cultural forms and groups, and to intervene in a creative manner within the emergent computer and political culture.

Whereas youth are excluded for the most part from the dominant media culture, computer and new multimedia culture is a discursive and political location in which youth can intervene, producing their own websites and personal pages, engaging in discussion groups, linking with others who share their interests, generating multimedia for cultural dissemination and a diversity of cultural and political projects. Computer culture enables individuals to actively participate in the production of culture, ranging from discussion of public issues to creation of their own cultural forms, enabling those who had been previously excluded from cultural production and mainstream politics to participate in the creation of culture and sociopolitical activism.

After using the Internet to successfully organize a wide range of anti–corporate globalization demonstrations in Seattle, Washington, Prague, Toronto, and elsewhere, young people played an active role in organizing massive demonstrations against the Bush administration threats against Iraq, creating the basis for an oppositional antiwar and peace movement as the Bush administration threatens an era of perpetual war in the new millennium. Obviously, it is youth that fights and dies in wars that often primarily serve the interests of corrupt economic and political elites. Today's youth are becoming aware that their survival is at stake and that thus it is necessary to become informed and organized on the crucial issues of war, peace, and the future of democracy and the global economy.

Likewise, groups are organizing to save endangered species, to fight genetically engineered food, to debate cloning and stem cell research, to advance animal rights, to join struggles over environmental causes like climate change and global warming, and to work for creating a healthier diet and alternative medical systems. The Internet is a virtual treasury of alternative information and cultural forms with young people playing key roles in developing the technology and oppositional culture and using it for creative pedagogical and political purposes. Alternative sites of information and discussion on every conceivable topic can be found on the Internet, including important topics like human rights or environmental education that are often neglected in public schools.

Thus, a postmodern pedagogy requires developing critical forms of print, media, computer, and multiple forms of technoliteracy, all of which are of crucial importance in the technoculture of the present and fast-approaching future (Kahn and Kellner 2006; Kellner and Share 2007). Indeed, contemporary culture is marked by a proliferation of image machines that generate a panoply of print, sound, environmental, and diverse aesthetic artifacts within which we wander, trying to make our way through this forest of symbols. And so we need to begin learning how to read these images, these fascinating and seductive cultural forms whose massive impact on our lives we have only begun to understand. Surely, education should attend to the multimedia culture and teach how to read images and narratives as part of media/computer/techno-culture literacy.

Such an effort would be linked to a revitalized critical pedagogy that attempts to empower individuals so that they can analyze and criticize the emerging technoculture, as well as participate in producing its cultural and political forums and sites. More than ever, we need philosophical reflection on the ends and purposes of educational technology, and on what we are doing and trying to achieve with it in our educational practices and institutions. In this situation, it may be instructive to return to John Dewey and see the connections among education, technology, and democracy, the need for the reconstruction of education and society, and the value of experimental pedagogy to seek solutions to the problems of education in the present day.

A progressive reconstruction of education will be done in the interests of democratization, ensuring access to information and communication technologies for all, thereby helping to overcome the so-called digital divide and divisions of the haves and have-nots so that education is placed in the service of democracy and social justice as was advocated by Dewey (1997 [1916]), Freire (1972, 1998), and Illich (1970, 1971, 1973). Yet, we should be more aware than Dewey, Freire, and Illich of the obduracy of the divisions of class, gender, and race, and work self-consciously for multicultural democracy and education. This task suggests that we valorize difference and cultural specificity, as well as equality and shared universal Deweyean values such as freedom, equality, individualism, and participation.

Teachers and students, then, need to develop new pedagogies and modes of learning for new information and multimedia environments. This should involve a democratization and reconstruction of education such as was envisaged by Dewey, Freire, Illich, and Marcuse, in which education is seen as a dialogical, democraticizing, and experimental practice. New information technologies acting along the lines of Illich's conceptions of "webs of learning" and "tools for conviviality" (1971, 1973) encourage the sort of experimental and collaborative projects proposed by Dewey, and can also involve the more dialogical and nonauthoritarian relations between students and teachers that Freire envisaged. In this respect, the revisioning of education involves the recognition that teachers can learn from students and that often students are ahead of their teachers in a variety of technological literacies and technical abilities. Many of us have learned much of what we know of computers and new media and technologies from our students. We should also recognize the extent to which young people helped to invent the Internet and have grown up in a culture in which they may have readily cultivated technological skills from an early age.[42] Peer-to-peer communication among young people is thus often a highly sophisticated development and democratic pedagogies should build upon and enhance these resources and practices.

A democratic reconstruction of education will involve producing democratic citizens, and empowering the next generation for democracy should be a major goal of the reconstruction of education in the present age. Moreover, as Freire reminds us (1972, 1998), critical pedagogy comprises the skills of both reading the word and reading the world. Hence, multiple literacies include not only media and computer literacies, but also a diverse range of social and cultural literacies, ranging from ecoliteracy (e.g., understanding the body and environment), to economic and financial literacy, to a variety of other competencies that enable us to live well in our social worlds. Education, at its best, provides the symbolic and cultural capital that empowers people to survive and prosper in an increasingly complex and changing world and the resources to produce a more cooperative, democratic, egalitarian, and just society.[43]

In these chapters I have been trying to indicate interconnections among male socialization, a violent media culture, militarism, and lack of mental health care, and how these factors and other social conditions have produced a crisis of masculinity. In the next sections I want to discuss how men are especially brutalized in prisons and the military, and how we need to reconsider how to treat youth crime and, in general, our failed prison system, an institution even more scandalous than our failing educational system. Indeed, one of the major scandals of a scandalous society is that investment in prisons has skyrocketed in the United States in recent years, while there have been corresponding cuts in education. As Spina summarizes it:

Between 1980 and 1995, the U.S. federal education budget dropped from $27 to $16 billion (while the federal corrections budget increased from $8 to $20 billion.... California "now spends more for prisons than for public higher education," though the state once spent several times as much on universities as prisons. During the 1990s, New York State added more than $750 million to its prison budget while cutting the budgets for the City and State universities of New York by almost the same amount.... The United States ranks first in worldwide per capita income among eighteen industrialized countries, but fifteen of those countries spend a greater percentage of per capita income on public education than the United States.[44] (2000: 249–250)

In a concluding section we need to see how prisons are involved in the war on youth, violent masculinity, the culture of militarism, and systemic oppression in the United States today and how abolition of the current prison system is as necessary as the reconstruction of education.

Politics, Prisons, and the Abolition Democracy Project

> "In the contemporary era, the tendency toward more prisons and harsher punishment leads to gross violations of prisoners' human rights and, within the U.S. context, it summons up new perils of racism. The rising numbers of imprisoned black and Latino men and women tell a compelling story of an increasingly intimate link between race and criminalization. While academic and popular discourses assume a necessary conjunction between crime and punishment, it is the conjunction of race, class, and punishment that is most consistent."
> —*Angela Davis, "Racialized Punishment and Prison Abolition"*
> *(in Davis 2005: 104–105)*

Part of the result of the escalating war on youth is the rise of what Angela Davis and others call a "prison industrial complex." In dialogue with Eduardo Mendietta on "Politics and Prisons" and "Sexual Coercion, Prisons and Feminist Responses" in *Abolition Democracy* (2005), Davis provides aspects of a genealogy of prisons and the connections among prisons, the death penalty, torture, slavery, and the oppression of people of color. With the formal end of slavery after the Civil War, the state continued to incarcerate black people; prison was often a site of torture, as the plantation had been; the death penalty was legitimized as a means of executing rebellious people of color; and the practice of lynching served as an extralegal means for reproducing racial hierarchies and enforcing racial domination. Prisons have thus been constructed as a site of oppression and an instrument of enforcing race and class domination in capitalist societies.

Mendietta and Davis also discuss in detail the connections between the prison-industrial complex and the military-industrial complex and the continuities from the post–Civil War period (2005: 34ff.), with the rise of the prison-industrial complex as a new form of ghettoization, social control, and brutalization, as well as the connections between the Bush administration's use of torture, extraordinary rendition, and secret prisons, and the special case of Guantanamo.

Horrors of the Prison-Industrial-Military Complex

In a discussion of Abu Ghraib, Davis points out the continuity of the systematic sexual humiliation of prisoners in the U.S. prison-industrial complex with the humiliation of Arab prisoners in Abu Ghraib and other secret prisons in the new carceral regime of the Bush-Cheney gang. Davis notes that the techniques of punishment visible in the Abu Ghraib photographs emanate from practices "deeply embedded in the history of the institution of prison" and thus are not so much "exceptions" as illustration of the horrors of the entire prison-industrial-military system. Davis also notes the quasi-pornographic nature of the photos, which are parallel, Davis notes, to the pornographic dimension of lynching, and the "very revealing parallel between the sexual coercion and sexual violence within the Abu Ghraib context and the role sexual violence plays in lynching" (52ff.).

I would add that the hood in the Abu Ghraib photos indeed evokes Ku Klux Klan lynchings, but would also like to add two dimensions to this analysis, the first being that of *colonization,* as the kind of torture on display is a standard tool of colonial regimes to dominate native populations. The representation of the Iraqis in the infamous photos is part of a colonial gaze that sees the "Other" as less than human, and the pictures as a whole depict a brutal colonial mentality. Many of the quasi-pornographic images released of the Iraqi male prisoners depicted a feminization of them, naked or in women's undergarments, humiliated and emasculated. There is, of course, a long colonial tradition of taking photos of humiliated prisoners, as well as sexually objectifying and prostituting locals by colonial forces.

The second dimension I want to add concerning these photos is the *digital and viral dimension of the images.* The digital archive was not the work of professional photojournalists, but of young U.S. soldiers. It was as if a generation raised on the media and in possession of digital cameras and camcorders naturally documented its own life, as if it were participating in a reality television show or political documentary. Although there were reports that the images were intended for use to intimidate new Iraqi prisoners to "soften them up" for interrogation, the pictures also emerged from fascination with taking pictures and the digital documentation of everyday life.[45] They revealed as well how quickly such images could leave a foreign country under U.S. military control by way of the Internet and circulate around the world.

Whereas during the 1991 Gulf War the United States censored every image and word in the media pool system concocted for that intervention and had strict guidelines and control mechanisms for the embedded reporters in the 2003 Iraq intervention, the digital age has made it ultimately impossible to hide the dark sides of the current Iraq occupation, or, in general, imperialist crimes.[46] The widespread use of digital cameras and the ease with which images could be shot and disseminated, including direct transmission through wireless connections, demonstrated how media spectacle could trump U.S. military control. As Donald Rumsfeld exclaimed during the Iraq prisoner abuse hearings on May 7, 2004: "People are running around with digital cameras and taking these unbelievable photographs and then passing them off, against the law, to the media, to our surprise, when they had not even arrived in the Pentagon."[47] The Pentagon indicated during these Senate and House hearings that many, many more photos and videos existed, but in the light of the negative publicity already received, military leaders managed to prevent circulation of more scandalous material.[48]

There is a complex story of how the Abu Ghraib images circulated to which I can only briefly allude. Evidently, DVDs of the archive existed that different soldiers passed along and sent to others via e-mail, and one young soldier passed over a DVD to military police, while someone sent the images to CBS for *60 Minutes* and to Seymour Hersh for the *New Yorker*. Their circulation mushroomed globally, creating a great media spectacle and scandal, and Rumsfeld henceforth forbade digital cameras and sending images over the Internet. But a young Iraqi videotaped the Haditha massacres, leading to one of the most extensive prosecutions of crimes of U.S. soldiers in Iraq, and there is documentation of more atrocities, often from local photographers or videographers.

We have, therefore, new resistance to mainstream corporate global media from below and a threat to the monopoly power of traditional media, as anyone can be a photographer and send images throughout the globe, thus destabilizing imperial and military control of representations and images. This new opposition from below, as some were U.S. troops, creates a destabilization of journalism and new sources of information and opinion, creating the possibility for more democratic media and culture.

The Time of Abolitions

"The abolition of prisons is [linked to] the abolition of the instruments of war, the abolition of racism, and of course, the abolition of the social circumstances that lead poor men and women to look toward the military as the only avenue of escape from poverty, homelessness, and lack of opportunities."

—Angela Davis

One of the key goals of Angela Davis's political project over the years has been prison abolitionism, and she draws from W. E. B. Du Bois's notion of "abolition democracy" as the context for the project. This project historically involved "the abolition of slavery, the abolition of the death penalty, and the abolition of the prison" 2005: 95). Davis stresses that abolition "is not only, or not even primarily, about abolition as a negative process of tearing down, but it is also about building up, about creating new institutions" (73). Prison abolition itself will require a set of fundamental social changes and a new set of institutions and indeed process of democratic social reconstruction (as with Du Bois). The prison-industrial complex for Davis is a sign that abolitionism is far from completed and constitutes a key challenge of the present moment, compounded, as Davis notes, with the so-called war on terror and a horrific expansion of prisons and torture. More specifically, Davis sees abolition democracy as a "project that involves reimagining institutions, ideas, and strategies, and creating new institutions" (75).

Throughout the discussion, Davis and Mendietta connect the prison-industrial complex with the military-industrial complex, so obviously we need to rethink and reform together prisons with the military from the perspectives of democracy and social justice. We might also reflect here on the war on drugs, which—as Davis has long argued—is bound up with the current prison problem (half of those incarcerated are there on drug-related offenses). Like the "war on terror," a nebulous "war on drugs" cannot really be won, and we need realistic analyses of problems of, say, terrorism and drugs, and rational solutions (whereas both terrorism and drugs have been exploited by the last several U.S. administrations to promote their own quite problematic ideological agendas, Clinton as well as Reagan and two Bushes, as Davis notes in the interviews).

Prisons are also cauldrons of violent masculinity that teach certain kinds of survival skills or life lessons such as only the strong survive, it's a dog-eat-dog world, and it's every man for himself. Survival in prison often requires men to take on a tough, impenetrable shell, so prisons function essentially as institutions of hypermasculine socialization. Prisons are also bastions of racism and sexual abuse, greatly intensifying societal violence, as most inmates often return to their families and the streets more angry and fearful then when they went in. The U.S. prison system in the twenty-first century is a barbaric and backward institution few enlightened people would defend in its present state. Indeed, prisons in this country are a national embarrassment most citizens do not want to think about.

Daniel Lazare indicates how serious questions have emerged in the face of

America's homegrown gulag archipelago, a vast network of jails, prisons, and "supermax" tombs for the living dead that, without anyone quite noticing, has metastasized into the largest detention system in the advanced industrial world. The proportion of the U.S. population languishing in such facilities now stands at 737 per 100,000, the highest rate on earth and some 5 to 12 times that of Britain, France, and other Western European countries or Japan. With 5 percent of the world's population, the United States has close to a quarter of the world's prisoners.... With 2.2 million people behind bars and another 5 million on probation or parole, it has approximately 3.2 percent of the adult population under some form of criminal-justice supervision, which is to say 1 person in 32. For African Americans, the numbers are even more astonishing. By the mid-1990s, 7 percent of black males were behind bars, while the rate of imprisonment for black males between the ages of 25 and 29 now stands at 1 in 8.[49]

Here I would like to venture a suggestion for discussion and see how far we can practically envisage a world without prisons. I should note that I studied with Ernst Bloch, and have absorbed the work of Herbert Marcuse, so I am not allergic to utopian thought and imagination. In a genuinely democratic society with totally different priorities from those in today's United States, I can imagine taking all prisoners in jail for drug-related offenses out of jail and sending them to drug-rehabilitation centers that are also job-training centers where, while undergoing drug detoxification and counseling, persons could also get basic education.[50] In revisioning prison, I would agree with the quote from Davis above that we must reimagine "institutions, ideas, and strategies," while creating new institutions to solve the pressing problems of the contemporary moment.

Already about half of the previous prisons would be drug rehabilitation and job-training centers, and as for the other half, prisoners could begin rehabilitation, education, and job training programs, and those who could reasonably be released could be let out on parole if they had job skills and a support network to help them. Further, one could envision a thoroughly reconstructed military that might also provide opportunities for former prisoners (it's a dirty secret now that a lot of recent military personnel are people facing prison sentences who are given the option of joining up or going to the slammer).

Now, obviously, this is totally utopian in the present conditions, but as Bertolt Brecht used to delight in saying: "Ladies and Gentlemen, if you think this is utopian, then tell me please exactly why it is utopian." Angela Davis and others could obviously provide very precise analyses of the current role of the prison-industrial complex and the economic forces behind it, the ways it serves as means of social control and racial oppression, and how it benefits very specific social and political interests.

Accordingly, both the prison-industrial and military-industrial complexes should become targets of radical critique, and a process of social reconstruction is necessary that will attack poverty, a wide set of racial injustices, the oppressive force of incarceration, and the destructive force of war and militarism.

The scandal of prisons in the United States is stunning. In a recent review of Bruce Weston's *Crime and Punishment* and other books on U.S. prisons, Jason DeParle notes in the *New York Review of Books,* "The American Prison Nightmare," that with "more than two million Americans behind bars, the impact of mass incarceration is impossible to contain."[51] "Black men," he notes, "in their early thirties are imprisoned at seven times the rate of whites in the same age group. Whites with only a high school education get locked up twenty times as often as those with college degrees." Further, prison populations have been steadily rising since the 1970s and "there are now seven Americans in every thousand behind bars." Furthermore, "by 2000, high school dropouts of either race were being locked up three times as often as they had been two decades before. And racial disparities have become immense. By the time they reach their mid-thirties, a full 60 percent of black high school dropouts are now prisoners or ex-cons. This, Weston warns, has resulted in 'a collective experience for young black men that is wholly different from the rest of American society.'"

Hence, for Weston and other critics of the U.S. prison system, mass incarceration and the deeply unjust justice system are a major form of inequality and oppression in the United States. Davis warns that mere prison reform without more radical restructuring of society normalizes the notions of prisons and that the abolition of prisons needs to be conceived as part of a process of social reconstruction that addresses problems of education, poverty, housing, health care, job training, and other basic issues.

Here I would propose that the project of abolition democracy be put in a broad framework of the sort German social theorist and activist Karl Korsch was working on at the time of his death in 1961. In the words of his wife, Hedda Korsch: "His [Korsch's] uncompleted text, the 'Manuscript of Abolitions,' is an attempt to develop a Marxist theory of historical development in terms of the future abolition of the divisions that constitute our society—such as the divisions between different classes, between town and country, between mental and physical labor."[52]

Korsch also described his project "The Time of Abolitions" to his friend Paul Mattick, who writes:

> It is not clear whether the fragmentary state of Korsch's various endeavours to deal with the present world situation and its revolutionary, or counter-revolutionary, potentialities was due to difficulties inherent in the subject matter itself, or was related to the progressive loss of his own abilities—the result of an illness which was slowly destroying him. His last coherent attempt to formulate his new ideas has the significant title, *The Time of Abolitions.* This investigates the possibilities and requirements of the expected abolition of the capitalist mode of production, of capital, of labour itself, and of the state.[53]

A project aimed at abolition of key injustices and problems in U.S. society needs to see war and militarism as a major cause of societal violence and injustice in the contemporary moment. During the 1960s, the Vietnam War created tremendous destruction and death, killing millions of Vietnamese and over 50,000 Americans (see Gibson 2000). It produced tremendous social conflict and polarization in the United States, as the country was deeply divided over the war. It alienated a generation of young people who were subject to the draft for a war they deeply opposed, or were drafted or volunteered for the war and had their lives destroyed in the process. The Vietnam War raised international protest and alienated and isolated the United States from some of its strongest allies. It cost billions of dollars and forced the Johnson administration to cut back on its war on poverty.

The Bush-Cheney administration's militarism, and especially its Iraq War, is likewise dividing the country, isolating the United States from its allies, brutalizing U.S. soldiers and Iraqis, destroying countless lives, and wasting the treasure of American wealth and lives. As insidious and often unperceived, war disseminates a culture of militarism and creates an ethos of brutality and violence. I have noted in these chapters how crises of masculinity have intersected with a violent media culture and society to produce out-of-control hypermasculine men who can become school shooters, domestic terrorists, or other sorts of men run amok.

Communities and social movements as well as schools need to address key issues of war and peace in our times. We need to support a renewed antiwar movement that opposes military aggression wherever it occurs and produce a robust peace movement. In the United States during the post-9/11 context, combating militarism also requires fighting fear and rethinking our global solidarities. We must envisage the victims of U.S. imperial policy as human beings and strongly oppose dehumanizing and barbaric practices such as torture and the subversion of the Geneva Convention and international law by the Bush-Cheney administration and the Pentagon. Recognizing the lawlessness of the Bush-Cheney gang in a wide range of domestic and global spheres suggests that achieving any meaningful social changes will require the abolition of the Bush-Cheney regime so that we can start addressing the fundamental problems of this perilous era.

Hence, and to conclude, the only realistic way to envisage dramatically minimizing school shootings and violence in society is to dramatically reform and reconstruct schools into institutions of genuine learning; to provide robust mental health facilities; to create more rational gun laws and intersection among the legal, police, mental health and school systems; to reconstruct the ideals of masculinity; to confront the scandals of our prison and capital punishment systems; and to fight war and militarism. Such a transformation would require a revolution in consciousness and values, but without taking on the full magnitude and multidimensionality of the crisis, we will be doomed to a spiral of increasing violence and deteriorating social conditions in a frightening Spiral of the Worst. We should be able to do better.

Notes

Notes to Introduction

1. I am using the term "Terror War" to describe the Bush-Cheney administration's "war against terrorism" and its use of aggressive military force and terror as the privileged vehicles of what now appears as its failed foreign policy. The Bush-Cheney administration expanded its combat against Islamic terrorism following the 9/11 attacks into a policy of Terror War, in which it has declared the right of the United States to strike any enemy state or organization presumed to harbor or support terrorism and to eliminate "weapons of mass destruction" that could be used against the United States. The right wing of the Bush-Cheney administration seeks to promote Terror War as the defining struggle of the era, coded as an apocalyptic battle between good and evil. For my earlier studies of Terror War, see Kellner 2003b and 2005.

2. See my study "The Katrina hurricane spectacle and the crisis of the Bush presidency" (Kellner 2007) and Henry Giroux's *Stormy Weather: Katrina and the Politics of Disposability* (2006a).

3. Thanks to Christine Kelly for e-mailing me (April 23, 2007) that "what also has to be challenged is the media's assertion that the VTech tragedy is the 'deadliest mass shooting in U.S. history.' This isn't true. According to Peter Hart on FAIR's (Fairness and Accuracy in Reporting) *CounterSpin* radio program this week, 'The 1873 massacre of black militia soldiers during Reconstruction left an estimated 105 dead, the Sand Creek Massacre of Cheyenne left a comparable death toll, Wounded Knee was a massacre of around 300, the 1921 killings in Tulsa, OK, ... killings of African Americans in what is often referred to as "The Black Wall Street" left dozens dead.' I would add to that the 1871 killing of 19 Chinese men and boys in Los Angeles and the 1885 massacre in which 28 Chinese were killed and 15 wounded, some of whom later died, in Rock Springs, Wyoming. This is not to diminish what happened at VTech but if the media wants to make statements regarding an incident's historical context they should take the time to make sure they do the research. Or, perhaps, the killings of Native Americans, Asians, and African Americans by white mobs don't really matter." Roxanne Dunbar-Ortiz contributes an article, "Colonization and massacres: Virginia Tech and Jamestown," on the Jamestown, Virginia, massacres of native inhabitants at http://www.uta.edu/huma/agger/fastcapitalism/home.html.

4. Following Korean conventions of listing the family name first, the Virginia Tech shooter was first referred to as Cho Seung-Hui in the U.S. media, but the family intervened

and requested the more Americanized designation Seung-Hui Cho, and I will follow this convention in these studies.

5. Debord's *The Society of the Spectacle* (1967) was published in translation in a pirated edition by Black and Red (Detroit) in 1970 and reprinted many times; another edition appeared in 1983 and a new translation in 1994. Thus, in the following discussion, I cite references to the numbered paragraphs of Debord's text to make it easier for those with different editions to follow my reading. The key texts of the Situationists and many interesting commentaries are found on various websites, producing a curious afterlife for Situationist ideas and practices. For further discussion of the Situationists, see Best and Kellner 1997, Chapter 3; see also the discussions of spectacle culture in Best and Kellner (2001) and Kellner (2003a).

6. See Elihu Katz and Tamar Liebes, "'No more peace!' How disaster, terror, and war have upstaged media events," *International Journal of Communication* 1 (2007), http://ijoc.org/ojs/index.php/ijoc/article/view/44/23.

7. I use the term "Bush-Cheney administration" to call attention to the extraordinary role of Dick Cheney and his associates during the Bush Junior years. A recent series in the *Washington Post* under the rubric "Angler" documents the unprecedented role Dick Cheney has played in the Bush presidency that justifies speaking, as I do here, of the "Bush-Cheney administration." See http://blog.washingtonpost.com/cheney.

8. On diagnostic critique, see Kellner and Ryan (1988) and Kellner (1995: 116–117).

9. Morgan Spurlock's successful documentary film *Super Size Me* (2004) created a popular anti-McDonald's counterspectacle, in which the filmmaker went on a diet exclusively of McDonald's high-calorie food for a month and seriously endangered his health as well as shockingly expanded his body size!

10. For a balanced and informed account of the controversy, see Wiener (2005).

11. See Adam Liptak, "A liberal case for the individual right to own guns helps sway the federal judiciary," *New York Times,* May 7, 2007, A18. Liptak notes: "There used to be an almost complete scholarly and judicial consensus that the Second Amendment protects only a collective right of the states to maintain militias. That consensus no longer exists—thanks largely to the work over the last 20 years of several leading liberal law professors, who have come to embrace the view that the Second Amendment protects an individual right to own guns." Liptak suggests that opinions over the last two decades by liberal law professors helped produce a decision whereby a federal appeals court struck down in March 2007 a gun control law on Second Amendment grounds. Yet there is still contestation of the Second Amendment by legal scholars and courts, with many criticizing Liptak's article, such as Don T. Kates, who has long argued that the Second Amendment upholds an individual's right to own guns. See "Don Kates responds to NY Times" at http://armsandthelaw.com/archives/2007/05/don_kates_on_th.php.

12. Steven Pinker, *How the Mind Works* (New York: Norton, 1997), 364. While I agree with Pinker that the "amok syndrome" appears "quintessentially irrational" and that the killers' minds are "tightly interwoven with abstract thought and have a cold logic of their own," I am not sure this is a cultural universal, but rather it takes specific societal forms with different influences, as I will attempt to show.

13. In his classic *Manhood in America* (1996) and other texts, Michael Kimmel argues

that throughout history men have been impelled to prove their masculinity through so-cially approved means, and he discusses a crisis of masculinity in the modern era when, with the decline of industrial labor, many men lost their jobs and status as home providers, and then in the 1960s felt themselves under attack by feminism and other movements. See also my discussion of Faludi's *Stiffed* (1999) and the discussion of how conditions in the Reagan era contributed to the masculinity crisis in Chapter 3. For a wide range of views on masculinity, see *The Masculinity Studies Reader* (Adams and Savran 2002). The latter text makes clear that there is no one fixed hegemonic masculinity, but hegemonic masculini-ties, as the notion is intrinsically historical, socially constructed, malleable, and subject to contestation. Likewise, there is no one ideal alternative masculinity, but rather a plurality of alternative masculinities that individuals and groups must assess and respond to.

14. Fincher's 2007 film *Zodiac* tells the story of how a former cartoonist for the *San Francisco Chronicle*, Robert Graysmith, became obsessed with the hunt for the killer and published a 1986 book, *Zodiac*, which assembled documents and knowledge about the murder up to that point, followed by another book, *Zodiac Unmasked*, that purported to present the identity of the Zodiac killer, now diseased. The Fincher film combines the two stories; on its making, see "A supplemental report to the reader on David Fincher's *Zodiac*" in the paperback reprint of Graysmith's book *Zodiac* (2007: 338ff.).

15. Dave Grossman, Lt. Col., U.S. Army (ret.), also deals with this literature in his book *On Killing* (1996) and has done a foreword for Lieberman's *The Shooting Game* (2006: vii–viii), which I discuss below.

16. This study is dealing with male rage; for a compelling study of female rage in the contemporary moment, see Angela McRobbie, *Gender Culture and Social Change: The Postfeminist Masquerade* (2007). As Zillah Eisenstein argues (2007: 93ff.), gender in the contemporary era is highly contested and unstable, with women able to play traditionally men's roles as leaders and as highly assertive and competitive, while men can become more feminized. Likewise, both men and women can experience rage and experience crises in their gendered identities, although one should not forget that men are still largely dominant. Nonetheless, hegemonic gender constructions can be oppressive for men and women and individuals should try to overcome the restrictions of gender.

17. It is depressing to note that following Columbine and the other late-1990s school shootings, as Klein and Chancer (2000) note, there were serious efforts at gun control re-form, whereas in the present political climate there is both less discussion of the problems of guns in U.S. society in the aftermath of Virginia Tech and no visible efforts to undertake meaningful reform, a problem I take up later in this book.

18. Actually, the quote is from an article on Columbine by Katz and Sut Jhally (see Newman et al. 2004: 359n15). I will make use of Katz's book *The Macho Paradox* (2006) and will, like Newman et al. (2004: 384n6), point to the usefulness of Katz's videotape *Tough Guise* and efforts to create alternative masculinities. I will also discuss the many still relevant and important proposals by Newman and her team for prevention of school shootings in Chapter 4 of this book, which seeks solutions to the problem.

19. Curiously, Lieberman (2006) does not cite or seem to be familiar with *Rampage* (2004), a book that dealt with major school shootings prior to the one he wrote about and is perhaps the most discussed and cited book on the topic. Further, despite their involvement

in sociological research and explanation, the authors of *Rampage* do not cite either Athens or Rhodes (1999). I am trying to bring a diversity of research and perspectives to bear on the issues of societal violence and thus am drawing on a range of major sources.

20. On family violence, see Hammer (2002).

21. I should note that I have never systematically studied or lived in situations of inner-city poverty, so I do not have the experience or expertise to engage this sort of violence. I will instead focus on violence largely from white men in contexts that I am experientially familiar with, as well as having engaged the literature on the topics addressed. In particular, I will critically interrogate whiteness and masculinity, thus putting in question defining features of my own subject-position, though I have positioned myself theoretically and politically against dominant class, race, and gender oppression for decades. In any case, I am aware of some of the limitations of my studies.

22. See the critique of the post-Columbine installation of surveillance systems in schools in Lewis (2006). Newman et al. note that the effectiveness of surveillance systems is "debatable" (2004: 286).

23. I might note that I strongly agree with Faludi that feminism and women certainly are not the origins of the crisis in masculinity, but instead the problem began with changing socioeconomic conditions that threw men into crisis and engendered false images of masculinity. Importantly, feminists have called attention to gender construction, highlighted themes of gender relations, and helped illuminate many of the issues explored in my book. Faludi (1999) documents ways in which feminism was scapegoated for men's crises. She is highly sympathetic to men and critically engages the socioeconomic and cultural forces that have helped produce a contemporary crisis in masculinity. In Faludi's analysis, the media and consumer society created new false ideals for men in terms of images, performance, style, celebrity, wealth, and looks (37ff). In a "culture of ornament," she writes, "manhood is defined by appearance, by youth and attractiveness, by money and aggression, by posture and swagger," and by competitive success. Although Faludi is strongly critical of a problematic ideal of masculinity, she fails to note the emergence of a more virulent notion of violent masculinity that is apparent in the film and television superheroes, computer and video games, sports extravaganzas, and the rise of a gun and military culture. To be sure, she notes how violent masculinity has mutated into media images of superheroes, or star athletes like Mike Tyson, but claims that by and large men are relegated to spectatorship or cosmetic masculinity. Furthermore, Faludi does not substantively engage class and race, as ideals of masculinity differ in various classes, races, and ethnic groups, and new ideals of masculinity are much more accessible to middle- and upper-class men than working-class men who are more susceptible (at least on the surface) to the appeal of the hypermasculine ideal. Faludi also does not ground the changes in analyses of corporate and global capitalism or the policies of specific political regimes like the Reagan and George H. W. Bush administrations whose policies had major impact on men's lives in the period just preceding her research.

24. See also the articles in the Internet journal *Fast Capitalism* compiled by Ben Agger at http://www.uta.edu/huma/agger/fastcapitalism/home.html. I will periodically be reviewing books that appear on the Virginia Tech shootings and will continue to monitor its aftermath.

25. For the report, see http://www.washingtonpost.com/wp-srv/metro/documents/vatechreport.pdf?hpid=topnews.

26. See Karin Fischer and Robin Wilson, "Review panel's report could reverberate beyond Virginia Tech and Virginia," *The Chronicle of Higher Education,* August 31, 2007, http://chronicle.com/free/2007/08/2007083101n.htm (accessed on September 19, 2007).

Notes to Chapter One

1. Hank Kurz Jr., "Questions raised on Va. Tech security," Associated Press, April 16, 2007, http://abcnews.go.com/U.S./wireStory?id=3046864 (accessed on July 16, 2007). See also Michael D. Shear, "Campus shutdown never considered," *Washington Post,* April 22, 2007, A01, which indicates that when Virginia Tech president Charles W. Steger and his top advisors gathered to assess the first shooting, they were called from the dormitory by campus police chief Wendell Flinchum, who informed them that the police were on top of the case and were on the trail of the dead student's boyfriend, the suspect in the killing. Obviously, this assumption was wrong and a debate has unfolded concerning what the proper response should have been after the initial shooting. The *Report of the Review Panel* (2007) criticized campus police for their initial assumption about the first shooting and failure to immediately alert the university community of the dangers on campus, but generally it was favorable concerning police response to the second shooting.

2. Gilmore was quoted in Bobbie Johnson and Conor Clarke, "America's first user-generated confession: The U.S. college shooting marked a watershed moment for old and new media," *Guardian,* April 23, 2007, http://media.guardian.co.uk/site/story/0,,2063112,00.html (accessed on June 16, 2007).

3. Michael Bush, "Virginia Tech creates comms team in wake of tragedy," *PRWeek,* April 23, 2007, http://www.prweek.com/us/sectors/crisiscommunications/article/651936/Virginia-Tech-creates-comms-team-wake-tragedy (accessed May 16, 2007).

4. This story was first reported by Michael Steed in the *Chicago Sun-Times,* who claimed that the suspect was "a Chinese national who arrived in the United States last year on a student visa [who] reportedly arrived in San Francisco on a United Airlines flight on Aug. 7, 2006, on a visa issued in Shanghai," found at www.SunTimes.com (no longer accessible). The story quickly disappeared from the paper's website but not before it circulated through corporate media broadcasting networks and the Internet.

5. For instance, see the posting by Peter Brimlow, "Virginia Tech massacre: Gun control—or immigration control?" April 18, 2007, at the right-wing website VDARE, http://www.vdare.com/pb/070418_vt.htm (accessed May 16, 2007).

6. On the fringes, there was speculation by Mae Brussell on whether Cho had CIA or Moonie connections, given South Korea's close connections with the CIA, and on whether Cho was a Manchurian candidate whose programming ran amok or was intended to divert attention from Bush administration scandals; see Brussells, *The Conspiracy Theory Blog,* http://theconspiratorsnest.blogspot.com/search/label/VaTech%20Massacre (accessed May 13, 2007). See also Paul Joseph Watson, "Seung-Hui Cho was a mind-controlled assassin,"

Prison Planet, April 19, 2007, http://www.prisonplanet.com/print.php (accessed June 2, 2007).

7. See Sandy Banks, "Ethnicity brings an unwelcome focus," *Los Angeles Times,* April 19, 2007, A01.

8. Bill O'Reilly, "Politics and mass murder," April 18, 2007, posted on the *Fox News* website, *The O'Reilly Factor* link, http://www.foxnews.com/story/0,2933,266711,00.html (accessed May 16, 2007).

9. See Matt Apuzzo, "Former high school classmates say Va. Tech gunman was picked on in school," Associated Press, April 19, 2007, http://www.thetimesnews.com/onset?id=903&template=article.html (accessed May 16, 2007).

10. Evan Thomas, "Quiet and disturbed, Cho Seung-Hui seethed, then exploded: His odyssey," *Newsweek,* April 30, 2007, http://www.msnbc.msn.com/id/18248298/site/newsweek (accessed May 16, 2007).

11. Two of Cho's plays were available online on April 21, 2007, http://news.aol.com/virginia-tech-shootings/cho-seung-hui/_a/richard-mcbeef-cover-page/20070417134109990001. In its inimitable fashion, when these artifacts emerged on the Internet, a *New York Post* headline read "PSYCHO PENNED POISON PLAYS," April 18, 2007, http://www.nypost.com/seven/04182007/news/nationalnews/psycho_penned_poison_plays_nationalnews_leela_de_kretser_and_kate_sheehy.htm (accessed April 22, 2007). YouTube features a reading of Cho's play *Richard McBeef,* http://www.youtube.com/watch?v=2E1Z91QsZOs&mode=related&search=.

12. We still do not know exactly who participated in the Oklahoma City bombing (see Chapter 3 for discussion of various theories).

13. It was later revealed that Cho also sent a letter to the English Department at the University of Virginia, but officials did not release the details, claiming it was another rant; see Lauren K. O'Neill, "Review panel meets; learns of letter sent by Cho," July 17, 2007, http://www.collegiatetimes.com/news/1/ARTICLE/9177/2007-07-17.html (accessed July 31, 2007).

14. Cho's multimedia dossier was archived at http://boingboing.net/2007_04_01_archive.html (accessed May 8, 2007).

15. The phrase "Extreme Asia" was a marketing slogan used to highlight an extreme form of horror and violence film emerging in Asia over the last decade, and the Sundance Channel regularly features "Asian Extreme" films. *Oldboy* (2004) is one of the most praised of this genre; made by Korean director Chanwook Park, it is part of his "vengeance trilogy." Curiously, Park directed the second segment of *Three Extremes* (2005), an Asian Extreme horror fest by major Hong Kong, Korean, and Japanese directors. Park's segment features a successful director terrorized by one of the extras from his films, who kidnaps his family, cuts off fingers of his piano-playing wife, and induces the director to tell of his infidelity and to kill a young girl in the house to demonstrate that although the director is rich, successful, famous, and thinks he is "good," he is no better than the pathetic extra. Bizarrely, the extra who torments the director looks quite similar to Cho.

16. Stephen Hunter, "Cinematic clues to understand the slaughter: Did Asian thrillers like 'Oldboy' influence the Va. Tech shooter?" *Washington Post,* April 20, 2007, C01, http://www.washingtonpost.com/wp-dyn/content/article/2007/04/19/AR2007041901817.

html?hpid=topnews. A. O. Scott attacked Hunter's article, putting it in the context of attempts to blame media culture for shootings or acts of terror, but, in fact, Hunter does not overstep his claims on influence and was the first to call attention to the uncanny resemblance between Cho's dossier and images in Asian Extreme films. See A. O. Scott, "Drawing a line from movie to murder," *New York Times,* April 23, 2007, http://www.nytimes.com/2007/04/23/movies/23movi.html?ex=1180843200&en=9bb670a872403172&ei=5070. Throughout, I will argue for the mediated position that media culture may have significant impact on behavior but should not be stigmatized or demonized, as it is at most one factor among many in influencing violent behavior.

17. Jonah Goldberg, *National Review* blog, April 18, 2007, http://corner.nationalreview.com/post/?q=MWJlNDUxODE4NjQ5NGY3NjlmMGY4MWI0OGRkNjJhODE= (accessed May 14, 2007).

18. See "No answers," *Tampa Bay Times,* April 18, 2007, http://www.tbt.com/america/ataglance/article38944.ece (accessed May 14, 2007).

19. It was reported that Cho had taken courses in contemporary horror films and literature, a fact that enabled conservatives to attack the study of popular culture and literature. See Marc Santora and Christine Hauser, "Officials knew troubled state of killer in '05," *New York Times,* April 20, 2007, http://www.nytimes.com/2007/04/19/us/19gunman.html (accessed May 12, 2007).

20. Richard Engel, "Cho's 'religious' martyrdom video," *MSNBC World Blog,* April 19, 2007, http://worldblog.msnbc.msn.com/archive/2007/04/19/157577.aspx (accessed May 12, 2007). Another reading was offered by the *New York Post,* cited by the *New York Times*'s blog the *Lede,* http://thelede.blogs.nytimes.com/tag/virginia (accessed May 12, 2007): "The reference may be to the Islamic account of the Biblical sacrifice of Abraham, where God commands the patriarch to sacrifice his own son. Abraham begins to comply, but God intervenes at the last moment to save the boy.... Abraham uses a knife in most versions of the story, but some accounts have him wielding an ax." A more obscure reference may be to a passage in the Koran referring to Abraham's destruction of pagan idols; in some accounts, he uses an ax to do so. I should emphasize that these readings are all hermeneutical constructions and we will probably never know what meanings Cho had in mind.

21. On the role of pastiche in postmodern culture and its defining characteristics, see discussion in Jameson (1991) and Best and Kellner (1997).

22. Engel, "Cho's 'religious' martyrdom video."

23. Matt Apuzzo, "Va. Tech gunman writings raised concerns," Associated Press, April 17, 2007, http://news.yahoo.com/s/ap/20070417/ap_on_re_us/virginia_tech_shooting (accessed May 12, 2007).

24. Sacha Zimmerman, "The true roots of the Virginia Tech massacre: Generation Columbine," *TNR Online,* April 19, 2007, http://www.tnr.com/doc.mhtml?i=w070416&s=zimmerman041907 (accessed May 12, 2007).

25. Leslie Eaton and Michael Luo, "Shooting rekindles issues of gun rights and restrictions," *New York Times,* April 18, 2007, http://www.nytimes.com/2007/04/18/us/18pistols.html?ref=us (accessed May 12, 2007).

26. "Boortz, others blame VA Tech victims for not fighting back," *Media Matters,* April 18, 2007, http://mediamatters.org/items/200704180007 (accessed May 12, 2007). *Media Matters* further notes that: "In questioning the actions of Virginia Tech students involved in the April 16 incident, Boortz joined the ranks of various commentators, including *National Review Online* contributor John Derbyshire, *Chicago Sun-Times* columnist Mark Steyn, who also writes for the *National Review,* and right-wing pundit and Fox News analyst Michelle Malkin. In an April 17 weblog post on *National Review Online*'s *The Corner,* Derbyshire asked: 'Where was the spirit of self-defense here? Setting aside the ludicrous campus ban on licensed conceals, why didn't anyone rush the guy? It's not like this was Rambo, hosing the place down with automatic weapons. He had *two handguns* for goodness' sake—one of them reportedly a .22.'" Time.com Washington editor Ana Marie Cox criticized Derbyshire in an April 17 post on *Time* magazine's political weblog, *Swampland.* Steyn and Malkin have made similar statements, as the weblog *Think Progress* noted. In her April 18 syndicated column, Malkin wrote: "Instead of encouraging autonomy, our higher institutions of learning stoke passivity and conflict-avoidance. And as the erosion of intellectual self-defense goes, so goes the erosion of physical self-defense." In his April 18 *National Review* column, Steyn suggested that Virginia Tech students were guilty of an "awful corrosive passivity" that is "an existential threat to a functioning society" (quoted in *Media Matters*).

27. For a detailed account of the shooting, see David Maraniss, "'That was the desk I chose to die under," *Washington Post,* April 19, 2007, A01. See also Raymond Hernandez, "Inside room 207, students panicked at rampage and then held off gunman's return," *New York Times,* April 18, 2007.

28. See http://en.wikipedia.org/wiki/2007_Virginia_Tech_massacre#_note-61 (accessed April 22, 2007).

29. "Limbaugh said Virginia Tech shooter 'had to be a liberal,'" *Media Matters,* April 19, 2007, http://mediamatters.org/items/200704190008 (accessed May 12, 2007).

30. Thomas Sowell, "Are today's mass shootings a consequence of '60s collective guilt?" *Baltimore Sun,* April 26, 2007, 19A.

31. Glen Greenwald, "Charles Krauthammer takes rank hypocrisy to new lows," *Salon,* April 20, 2007, http://www.salon.com/opinion/greenwald/2007/04/20/krauthammer/print.html (accessed on July 21, 2007).

32. George Rush and Joanna Rush Molloy, "Critics: Scientologists' Va. trip a time to prey," *Daily News* (New York), April 18, 2007, 24. Unfortunately for the scientologists' crusade against prescriptive drugs, a toxicology report indicated that there was no evidence of prescriptive drugs or toxic substances in Cho's body. See "Cho's toxicology report released, Tech announces changes," *Collegiate Times,* June 21, 2007, http://collegiatetimes.com/news/1/ARTICLE/9130/2007-06-21.html (accessed June 23, 2007). While I think it is a mistake to blame school shootings fundamentally on prescriptive drugs, there are serious concerns about overprescription and misprescription of dangerous pharmaceuticals that I do not want to ignore.

33. See, for example, Michael Welner, "Cho likely Schizophrenic, evidence suggests," *ABC News,* April 17, 2007, http://abcnews.go.com/Health/VATech/story?id=3050483 (accessed May 12, 2007). For a detailed account of Cho's mental health history, see *Report of the Review Panel* (2007: 30ff.).

34. For discussion of the psychiatric debates concerning Cho's condition, which obviously no one can definitively resolve at this point, or probably ever, see the open-minded discussions on Robert Lindsay's blog at http://robertlindsay.blogspot.com/2007/04/did-cho-have-prodromal-paranoid.html (accessed May 12, 2007).

35. For an example, see John O'Sullivan, "Radical evil," *Chicago Sun-Times,* April 18, 2007, http://www.benadorassociates.com/article/20707 (accessed on September 27, 2007).

36. Anti–video game activist Jack Thompson appeared on *Fox News* the day of the shooting to point the finger of blame at video games, and Dr. Phil appeared on *Larry King Live* to attack video games; see Winda Benedetti, "Were video games to blame for massacre? Pundits rushed to judge industry, gamers in the wake of shooting," *MSNBC Commentary,* April 20, 2007, http://www.msnbc.msn.com/id/18220228/ (accessed May 12, 2007). The commentary notes that the *Washington Post* had just pulled a paragraph from a story that claimed Cho was an avid fan of the game "Counter-Strike," and then indicated that no video games were found in his room and that his suitemates had never seen him play video games. The lack of evidence concerning Cho's level of game involvement did not deter political extremist Lyndon LaRouche and his cult from blaming the Virginia Tech shootings on video games, while attacking the Bush administration for a cover-up in its initial report that Cho did not actively participate in games culture. The LaRouchite assault on video games, and in particular the Virginia Tech shooting, are followed on a webpage at "LaRouche camp cries foul at VA Tech Report," http://kotaku.com/gaming/they-know/larouche-camp-calls-foul-on-va-tech-report-272228.php (accessed July 19, 2007). Yet, as I indicated in Note 32, above, on prescription drugs, while it is a mistake to blame school shootings and other acts of violence on video games themselves, there are grounds for serious concerns about the effects of video games on people. Dave Grossman, for instance, whom I have cited for his book *On Killing,* which is critical of military socialization, is also concerned with the effects of video games.

37. Cited in Nancy Gibbs, "Darkness falls," *Time,* April 19, 2007, http://www.time.com/time/magazine/article/0,9171,1612715,00.html (accessed April 26, 2007).

38. Robert L. Depue, "A theoretical profile of Seung Hui Cho: From the perspective of a forensic behavioral scientist," *Report of the Review Panel,* 2007 (Appendix N-1-5). Depue also speculated that Cho was in a state of "fear and dread" in the face of his impending graduation, having few job skills or viable career plans.

39. Shaila Dewan and Marc Santora, "Officials knew troubled state of killer in '05," *New York Times,* April 19, 2007, http://www.nytimes.com/2007/04/19/us/19gunman.html (accessed April 26, 2007).

40. Ibid.

41. Santora and Hauser, "Anger of killer was on exhibit in his writing."

42. Bonnie Goldstein found and pasted on *Slate* "Cho Seung-Hui's commitment papers," which reference six different legal and mental health case filings relevant to his case, http://www.slate.com/id/2164842 (accessed April 29, 2007). Why were members of the Virginia Tech administration and others concerned about Cho not able to access these documents and connect the dots before Cho ran amok?

43. Dewan and Santora, "Officials knew troubled state of killer in '05."

44. Ibid.

45. Ibid.

46. Jan Greenberg, "Two bomb threats at Virginia Tech last week," *ABC News,* April 16, 2007, http://abcnews.go.com/print?id=3045900 (accessed May 12, 2007). The *Report of the Review Panel* (2007) concluded, however, that it was not certain who sent the earlier bomb threat notes.

47. See Tim Craig, "Cho had amassed enough ammo to kill many more," *Washington Post,* May 22, 2007, B01.

48. See Editorial, "Did minutes cost lives? Some say police took too long to enter building," *Grand Rapids Press,* April 26, 2007, A8; and Kristen Gelineau, "Examining Va. Tech police response," *Star-Ledger* (Newark, New Jersey), April 26, 2007, A22. Yet other security experts insisted that the police and medical response teams acted reasonably quickly and were praised for saving lives; see the account in Sari Horowitz, "8 Minutes after 911 call, a rescue from madness," *Washington Post,* June 22, 2007, A01, which describes the relatively rapid response, difficulties in breaking through the chained doors, and heroism of medical response personnel and police in saving lives, a point confirmed in the *Report of the Review Panel* (2007).

49. Tamar Lewin, "Unsettled day on campuses around U.S.," *New York Times,* April 18, 2007, http://www.nytimes.com/2007/04/18/us/18campus.html?ex=1334548800& en=ba70b5abb7da2f13&ei=5088&partner=rssnyt&emc=rss (accessed July 21, 2007).

50. Tami Abdollah and Seema Mehta, "School threats causing jitters," *Los Angeles Times,* April 21, 2007, B01.

51. A flier was passed out and sent through e-mail that read: "We are Hokie Nation and we need to mourn and heal. We need each other. The media has taken advantage of our situation and are exploiting us for their own sensationalism. We will not tolerate the abuse; we love our community far too much to stand for this any more. We, the students of Virginia Tech, are asserting ourselves. We are taking back our campus. All media, if they have any respect for Hokie Nation, will no longer attack our administration. They will no longer hound our students. Leave us to heal. Leave us to ourselves. Hokie Nation needs to be UNITED. Return our campus to us." *ABC News,* April 19, 2007, http://abcnews. go.com/U.S./VATech/story?id=3059025&page=1 (accessed May 12, 2007).

52. Michael Luo, "U.S. rules made killer ineligible to purchase gun," *New York Times,* April 21, 2007, http://www.nytimes.com/2007/04/21/us/21guns.html?hp=&pagewanted= print (accessed May 12, 2007). See also Michael Isikoff, "Did Cho buy the guns legally?" *Newsweek,* April 20, 2007, http://www.msnbc.msn.com/id/18217741/site/newsweek/ (accessed May 12, 2007).

53. Here is Gingrich's statement made after the 1999 shootings at Columbine High School in Littleton, Colorado: "I want to say to the elite of this country—the elite news media, the liberal academic elite, the liberal political elite: I accuse you in Littleton … of being afraid to talk about the mess you have made, and being afraid to take responsibility for things you have done, and instead foisting upon the rest of us pathetic banalities because you don't have the courage to look at the world you have created" (http://thinkprogress. org/2007/04/22/gingrich-liberalism-vatech). On ABC's *This Week* show on April 22, 2007, Gingrich defended and did not apologize for these remarks.

54. Rock musician Ted Nugent was one of Glen Beck's guests who blamed the massacre on the absence of guns on campus and heartily attacked all gun laws and restrictions. CNN rewarded him for his Wild West fantasizing by posting an article, "Gun-free zones are recipe for disaster," on April 19, 2007, on its website at http://www.cnn.com/2007/U.S./04/19/commentary.nugent/index.html (accessed April 20, 2007).

55. Unfortunately, it is true that the Democrats seem to have lost their will to do gun reform; see Derrick Z. Jackson, "Democrats still silent on gun control," *Boston Globe,* April 25, 2007, http://www.boston.com/news/globe/editorial_opinion/oped/articles/2007/04/25/democrats_still_silent_on_gun_controlhtml (accessed May 13, 2007).

56. See Anne Applebaum, "The world is watching: It takes a global village to cover a massacre," *Slate,* April 24, 2007, http://www.slate.com/id/2164828 (accessed on May 12, 2007). There was also a world press review collected in *Salon* and referenced in Note 58.

57. "America's tragedy: Its politicians are still running away from a debate about guns," *Economist,* April 19, 2007, http://www.economist.com/opinion/PrinterFriendly.cfm?story_id=9040170 (accessed on May 12, 2007).

58. Accessed from "The world press on Virginia Tech," *Salon,* April 18, 2007, http://www.salon.com/news/feature/2007/04/18/worldpress/index.html (accessed May 12, 2007).

59. John Brown, "The Cho in the White House," *Common Dreams,* April 25, 2007, http://www.commondreams.org/archive/2007/04/25/741 (accessed May 12, 2007).

60. On the similarity of the Manichean vision of Bush/Cheney and bin Laden, see Kellner (2003b).

61. Another alternative press article suggested a parallel with Republican presidential candidate and Arizona senator John McCain's lunatic singing before a conservative audience, shortly after the Virginia Tech shootings, of "bomb, bomb, bomb, bomb, bomb Iran" to the tune of "Barbara Ann." See Margaret Kimberley, "Seung-Hui Cho and John McCain," *Smirking Chimp,* April 26, 2007, http://www.smirkingchimp.com/thread/7073 (accessed May 3, 2007).

Notes to Chapter Two

1. On postmodern theory, see Best and Kellner (1991, 1997, and 2001). Initial studies of youth were undertaken by Best and Kellner for *The Postmodern Adventure* (2001), but space conditions prohibited including this material that was published as "Contemporary youth and the postmodern adventure" (Best and Kellner 2003). I draw on this essay here, but the analysis has been reconfigured and updated to engage the problematic of this book. I should also thank Richard Kahn for invaluable help in this chapter that drew on Kahn and Kellner (2003 and 2005) and other studies we have done on contemporary youth.

2. Howe and Strauss in their book *Generations* (1991) include in the Boomer category those conceived by soldiers on leave during the war, such as myself, and place the Boomer generation's birth years from 1943 to 1960. Gillon (2004) in *Boomer Nation* begins the Baby Boom in 1946, with its ending in 1964. Obviously, such definitions, as well as the

categories themselves, are generalizations subject to debate. In fact, as the situation of youth becomes more complex, differences between haves and have-nots increase; and as class, race, gender, and sexual oppression of groups of youth continues to intensify, the notion of a "generation" of youth as a unifying category becomes harder to sustain.

3. Coined by Howe and Strauss (1993), the term "13th Generation" refers to the thirteenth generation of American citizens born in the 1960s. As coincidence would have it, theirs is an unlucky number. "Generation X," popularized by Douglas Coupland (1991), signifies blankness and confusion and is taken from a British Boomer rock band. The term the "scapegoat generation" is used for those youth who are blamed for the social ills that were in large part produced by earlier generations.

4. See Howe and Strauss (1993), who later championed a new generation of "millennials" in 2000. Howe and Strauss delight in constructing ideal type categories for "generations," cycles, and "heroes" within the generations, and normative evaluations of different generations and types. So far their concept of "millennials" as an emergent "greatest generation" who would overcome the limitations of Boomers and the ill-defined GenX has hardly materialized. The task of defining today's youth is best left to the groups in question, so I am here just delineating some aspects of the situation of contemporary youth and some of the debates over how to best define and describe contemporary youth.

5. On postmodern culture, see Best and Kellner (1997 and 2001).

6. For a variety of studies of contemporary youth culture, see the works collected in Epstein (1998), and for a global range of forms of contemporary youth culture, see Dolby and Rizvi (2007).

7. A *Newsweek* cover story on "The Myth of Generation X" already by 1994 claimed that "a recent MTV poll found that only one in 10 young people would ever let the phrase 'Generation X' cross their lips" and cited several who rejected the label (June 6, 1994: 64).

8. See Coupland (1991: 181–183), who cites statistics indicating the growing amount of federal wealth and programs directed toward the elderly and the increasing tax burdens for younger generations. Third Millennium founder Jonathan Karl noted that in 1995 the federal government spent 11 times more on each senior citizen than it did on each child under 18 and warned of generational warfare if the budget deficit and high tax burdens on the young are not dealt with (*Swing*, September 1996: 53ff.). Obviously, as noted below, the Bush-Cheney administration has created staggering deficits that will present a daunting challenge to future generations.

9. In 2007, the media started following the scandal of mushrooming student debts, high-interest loans, and connections between college officials who advise students on loans and companies handing out the loans and pocketing the proceeds; see Carrie Sturrock, "Students resort to private loans, staggering debt," *San Francisco Gate*, October 25, 2006, http://www.sfgate.com/cgi-bin/article.cgi?file=/c/a/2006/10/25/MNGKKLVHCK1. DTL&type=printable (accessed September 23, 2007). The article indicates that: "The amount loaned to students nearly tripled between 2001 and 2006, from $6.1 billion to $17.3 billion, according to an annual student aid survey released Tuesday by the College Board."

10. Elizabeth Bumiller, "Bush's $2.2 trillion budget proposes record deficits,"

New York Times, February 4, 2003, http://query.nytimes.com/gst/fullpage.html?res=
9C02E1DB1138F937A35751C0A9659C8B63&n=Top%2FReference%2FTimes%
20Topics%2FPeople%2FD%2FDaschle%2C%20Tom (accessed September 23, 2007); and
Steve Inskeep, "Record $422 billion deficit projected," *National Public Radio*, September 8,
2004, http://www.npr.org/templates/story/story.php?storyId=3895515 (accessed September 23, 2007). See Giroux (2003), who traces out the growing impoverishment of youth
and expanding class divisions during the Bush-Cheney administrations.

11. See the statistics on these issues in Howe and Strauss (1993), Holtz (1995), Hammer
(2002), and Giroux (2003). On the pervasive moods of cynicism among contemporary
youth, what factors are producing it, and how a reconstructed democratic education can
fight it, see Van Heertum (2007).

12. By the age of five, Boomers had seen little or no TV, compared to the 5,000 hours
of viewing by their post-Boomer children (Howe and Strauss 1993). According to some
statistics in the 1990s, "the average 14-year-old watches on average three hours of television
a day, and does one hour of homework" (Howe and Strauss 1993). A July 2003 report on
TV and Internet use by young people indicated that: "On average, young people said they
spent nearly 17 hours online each week, not including time used to read and send electronic
mail, compared with almost 14 hours spent watching television and 12 hours listening to the
radio," Reuters, July 24, 2003, http://www.forbes.com/technology/newswire/2003/07/24/
rtr1037488.html. A December 2006 U.S. Census Bureau report indicated that: "Adults and
teens will spend nearly five months (3,518 hours) next year watching television, surfing the
Internet, reading daily newspapers and listening to personal music devices," http://www.
census.gov/ Press-Release/www/releases/archives/miscellaneous/007871.html (accessed
May 12, 2007).

13. Adam Nagourney and Megan Thee, "New poll finds that young Americans are
leaning left," *New York Times*, June 27, 2007, http://www.nytimes.com/2007/06/27/
washington/27poll.html?ex=1185249600&en=4157c47b57df85f8&ei=5070 (accessed
September 23, 2007).

14. See John DiIulio, "The coming of the superpredators," http://www.mcsm.org/
predator.html (accessed September 23, 2007).

15. Victor Rios, in Marable, Middlemass, and Steinberg (2007): 17.

16. Ibid, 17.

17. See Razzano, Skalli, and Quail (forthcoming).

18. Although it is true that youth have been stigmatized and demonized in U.S. society
since the 1950s, including the juvenile delinquency moral panic of the 1950s and the 1960s
counterculture where the excesses of the decade have been blamed on wayward youth,
specific attacks on youth have emerged from political administrations since the Reagan
era and in the judicial and legal system, attacks I'm engaging in this chapter.

19. See the statistics compiled by *Harper's Magazine*, http://home.earthlink.net/
~mmales/Harpers.txt (accessed September 23, 2007).

20. See Males's homepage for a wealth of information on the war against youth and
deflating of antiyouth myths at http://home.earthlink.net/~mmales (accessed September
23, 2007).

21. See Richard B. Du Boff and Edward S. Herman, "Review of *The Scapegoat*

Generation: America's War on Adolescents," December 1996, http://zena.secureforum. com/znet/ZMag/articles/dec96herman.htm (accessed September 23, 2007).

22. For my own analysis of the political attack on rap in the early 1990s, see Kellner (1995: Chap. 4). By 2007, however, in the wake of the Imus scandal, there were growing calls for hip-hop music to stop using the stereotyped and exhausted images of gangsta rap and words insulting to women, people of color, or gays and lesbians. Within the hip-hop movement, there were critiques that the excesses of the genre were due to commercial efforts by corporations that exploited the grossest stereotypes of women and gangstas to sell to their major audience—white, middle-class boys. See DaveyD, "Commerce is killing the true spirit of hip-hop," *San Jose Mercury News,* March 5, 2007, http://www.zmag. org/content/showarticle.cfm?ItemID=12258 (accessed September 23, 2007).

23. Jorge Mariscal Sojourners, "The making of an American soldier: Why young people join the military," *AlterNet,* June 27, 2007, http://www.alternet.org/waroniraq/57565 (accessed September 23, 2007).

24. See Grossberg (2001: 117).

25. Cited in "Sexual abuse by military recruiters," *CBS News,* April 20, 2006, http:// www.cbsnews.com/stories/2006/08/19/national/printable1913849.shtml (accessed September 23, 2007).

26. Henry Giroux, "Disabling democracy: The crisis of youth, education, and the politics of disposability," Canadian Teachers' Federation Conference (Ottawa), May 4–6, 2007. Thanks to Giroux for making this talk accessible to me and for indispensable help in this chapter.

Notes to Chapter Three

1. This section draws on unpublished work with Steven Best on *The Postmodern Adventure* (2001).

2. A *New York Times* reporter tells a revealing story of his visit to a white supremacy convention and how a guard at its entrance, a Mr. von Wolff, would not let in a Mr. McLean who was not "white" enough, although he insisted he was a member of the "white" race, creating a challenge to the group's system of racial identification. Other guards let him enter and as Mr. von Wolff escorted the reporters and Mr. McLean inside he muttered: "I wish we were marching you into the showers" (July 23, 1995: A8).

3. On the militia movements and right-wing extremism, see Coates (1987), Gibson (1994), and Dyer (1997).

4. Haya El Nasser and Paul Overberg, "Minorities majority in more areas," *USA Today,* September 30, 2004, http://www.usatoday.com/news/nation/2004-09-30-census_x.htm (accessed on June 24, 2007). The article opens: "From sprawling urban areas to rural counties, racial and ethnic minorities outnumber whites in more parts of the country, according to 2003 Census estimates out today." This tendency has been accelerating.

5. Soon after their arrest on charges of illegal weapons and munitions possession and alleged threats to destroy government buildings, the Viper militia members were described

by the *New York Times* as follows: "A mix of high school graduates and dropouts, all the Vipers are white, have no significant criminal records and are stuck in low-paying jobs. Largely a blue-collar mix, the Vipers include two janitors, a used-furniture salesman, an AT&T billing representative, an air conditioner repairman, a doughnut baker, an engineer and the doorman for Tiffany Cabaret, a Phoenix topless bar. Experts say they roughly reflect the demographics of the antigovernment paramilitary movement" (July 5, 1996: A1). See also the article in *Newsweek* (July 15, 1996: 20–23). It should be noted, however, that half of the Vipers were released on bail soon after their arrest and it was not clear how substantial government charges against them were, besides illegal gun possession and an active fantasy life; in any case, they serve as a marker of white male identity politics.

    6. Keith Olbermann's *Countdown!* TV show on MSNBC has regularly featured examples of Bush-Cheney administration dramatizations of alleged terror plots that in each case have diverted attention from scandals of the administration and have often turned out to be of slight consequence. The Fort Dix and JFK plots were numbers 12 and 13 in the series.

    7. See Best and Kellner (1997, Chap. 4), where we suggest that pastiche—the appropriation and combination of elements from past cultural forms—is one of the defining marks of postmodern culture. Modernist culture, by contrast, strove to break with the past, to create novel and up-to-date new cultural forms that expressed individual vision and an individual style.

    8. On the Ruby Ridge shootings, which I discuss below, see Walter (1995) and Spence (1995).

    9. An article in the *New York Times* (August 25, 1996: A1) stated that: "Across the nation, bombings and attempted bombings are soaring. They increased by more than 50 percent in the last five years, and have nearly tripled over the last decade. The number of criminal explosions and attempts went from 1,103 in 1985 to 3,163 in 1994.... Over the last six years, there has been a huge increase in the number of bombs aimed at local, state or federal governments. In 1990, there were 17 such blasts; by 1994, the last year for full numbers, the figure had grown to 51. This year may set a record, the anecdotal evidence indicates." Boggs writes that: "Throughout the 1990s more than 35,000 people in the United States were reportedly injured by acts of terrorism and physical violence waged by dozens of groups" (2000: 151). These acts of terrorism included assaults against women's health clinics, hate crimes against gays and minorities, and bombing of public facilities, including churches, mosques, and synagogues. Attacks, especially on black churches, have continued, and during 2006 nine black churches were bombed or burned in Alabama in one week; see "50 U.S. agents investigating church fires," *CBC News*, February 8, 2006, http://www.cbc.ca/world/story/2006/02/08/baptist-church-fires060208.html (accessed on June 21, 2007).

    10. Gibson notes that: "Reverend Robert Miles, a Christian Identity preacher, had been impressed by the Black Liberation Army and Weather Underground's holdup of a Brinks armored car in 1981. During a ceremony in which he blessed their guns, he told one of the assemblies: 'If we were half the men the leftists were, we'd be hitting armored cars, too'" (1994: 226).

    11. The aftermath of an apocalyptic war was graphically portrayed in *Left Behind 3:*

World at War, which depicts the destruction of the White House and bombing of a large building in New York that houses the supposed Antichrist. These fantasies of destruction lay bare some of the darker and destructive impulses of the Christian right, although the filmmakers who produced documentaries and commentaries for the DVDs of the *Left Behind* film series look and sound more like your typical Hollywood C-list wannabes, rather than agents of the Dark Apocalypse.

12. See Stephen Talty, "The methods of a neo-Nazi mogul," *New York Times Magazine,* February 25, 1996, 40–42.

13. On Waco, see Reavis (1995). Videotapes released by antigovernment groups such as "Waco: The Big Lie," "Waco: The Big Lie Two," and "70 Days" strongly blamed the government for the deaths, with footage showing government tanks invading the compound and shooting fire bombs into the building and thus starting the fire that killed so many of the inhabitants. The government claims that the video footage is phony and that the Branch Davidians started the fire and that many of them committed suicide or shot other members during the raid.

14. As I noted in Chapter 1, we still do not know exactly who participated in the Oklahoma City bombing. For two opposing accounts I draw upon, see Jones and Israel (2001) and Michel and Herbeck (2001); I also use Stickney (1996).

15. See also the analysis of "The Oklahoma City bombing: The jihad that wasn't" by Jim Naureckas in *Extra!* (July–August 1995): 6–8; and Terry Allen, "Professional Arab-bashing," *Covert Action Quarterly* (Summer 1995): 20–21. A computer database search for articles that linked the bombing with rightist militia groups reveals that on April 19, 1995, only the Inter Press Service published an article raising the question "U.S. terrorism: Mideast or U.S. militias behind Oklahoma bombing?" The article, with a byline of Yvette Collymore, suggested that there could have been right-wing militia groups involved. All other sources, as far as I can determine, stigmatized Middle Eastern groups as suspects during the first 24 hours after the explosion. Unfortunately, the media hysteria and targeting of Middle Eastern suspects led to a brief reign of terror against Arab Americans and those of Middle Eastern descent; many Arab Americans were arrested and questioned and there were dozens of terror incidents against the American Arab and Muslim communities, with attacks on mosques, assaults on Arab American homes, death threats, and dozens of acts of physical violence.

16. McVeigh had been stopped for speeding and driving without a license plate 90 minutes after the bombing on Interstate I-35, some 70 miles north of Oklahoma City. He was found to be in possession of an illegal weapon, so he was held in custody, and just hours before he was to be released on bond, there was communication between the FBI and the local Perry, Oklahoma, police station where McVeigh was being held and he was officially detained as a suspect. He was formally charged with the bombing shortly afterwards and was found guilty and sentenced to death for the crimes in June 1997. See Michel and Herbeck (2001, 234ff.).

17. On McVeigh and *The Turner Diaries,* see Stickney (1996: 138, 158, 196, passim); and Michel and Herbeck (2001, 38ff., passim).

18. On McVeigh, Nichols, and the intense and widespread right-wing paranoia about the Brady Bill, see Stickney (1996). As Stickney explains, opposition "to a gun-control

law dubbed the 'Brady Bill' mobilized the National Rifle Association and shortwave radio personalities. Named for James Brady, the White House press secretary who was shot during the March 30, 1981, assassination attempt on President Reagan, the Brady Bill was viewed as a knee-jerk response to one victim's wishes, and was approved by Congress in November of 1993. To powerful liberals in Washington, D.C., the Brady Bill would ban 'assault-type' weapons, impose a waiting period for gun permits, and enforce strict punishments on those who broke the law. To a growing undercurrent of right-wing leaders the Brady Bill was Attorney General Janet Reno's first step toward disarming America" (1996: 151). The Bush-Cheney administration eliminated the ban on assault weapons and blocked any restrictive gun laws, including creating a federal registry and databank of weapons ownership, a measure that was called for after 9/11 but was also checked by the Bush-Cheney administration.

19. See Stickney (1996: 74). On Milius's *Red Dawn* and *Rambo* and their many strange effects, see Kellner (1995). Curiously, although many saw the Iraqi insurgents as embodying the ideological position of the U.S. teen warriors who Milius valorizes in *Red Dawn* and the U.S. troops as the occupiers, the operation to capture Saddam Hussein was called by the U.S. military "Red Dawn" and the code names given to the two huts at Saddam's hideaway were Wolverine 1 and Wolverine 2, referring to the young resistance fighters in Milius's 1984 film. When questioned, Milius had no doubt that the references were influenced by his film and he claims that the soldiers who captured Saddam were "Wolverines who have grown up and gone to Iraq," thus making the U.S. troops liberators rather than occupiers, as most of the people of Iraq and the rest of the world see them. See Duncan Campbell, "Raid on hideout 'named after cold war film,'" *Guardian*, December 17, 2003. By contrast, Peter Hartlaub suggests that the Iraqi resistance fighters in the Iraq War represent the position of Milius's insurgents in *Red Dawn*. See Peter Hartlaub, "A mere 20 years ago, 'Red Dawn' depicted a nation invaded, overpowered: Only that nation was us," *San Francisco Gate*, June 30, 2004, http://sfgate.com/cgi-bin/article.cgi?f=/c/a/2004/06/30/DDGKO7DJ141. DTLe (accessed May 13, 2007).

20. A similar callousness toward innocent civilian victims of attacks on government installations is found in *The Turner Diaries*, in which Earl Turner, the right-wing extremist who bombs government installations, says that the victims of his political bombing are "pawns" and that "there is no way we can destroy the System without hurting many thousands of innocent people" (cited in Stickney 1996: 196).

21. Similarly, Nacos claims that Osama bin Laden was made a household name even before 9/11 with significant media coverage for his previous terror attacks. "In 2000, for example, CBS News and NBC News broadcast significantly more stories mentioning bin Laden than segments referring to Great Britain's prime minister, Tony Blair and Germany's chancellor, Gerhard Schroder. ABC News presented the same number of stories mentioning bin Laden and Blair, far fewer referring to Schroder" (100).

22. See the earlier studies of how media culture provided fantasy material for would-be Reagan assassin John Hinckley and other examples of how media culture provided resources for the construction of bizarre identities in Jewett and Lawrence (1988).

23. Curiously, in the weeks before McVeigh's and Nichols's notorious deed, there were two other violent crimes perpetrated by members of the Fort Riley military in Kansas,

where they had previously served. As Stickney explains (1996: 226): "Soldiers at Fort Riley, Kansas, found themselves the subject of the [FBI] probe because McVeigh had spent so much of his short life there. Charlie Company found its reputation tarnished by the bad press surrounding Public Enemy Number one. McVeigh's arrest and the media's biographical frenzy was the third major hit to the regiment in seven weeks. On March 2, Private First Class Maurice Wilford, a twenty-year-old Cleveland native, shot three officers before turning a shotgun on himself. In the end, three soldiers were dead and one wounded. Wilford had reportedly been angry with his supervisor. On April 6, tragedy struck again. Soldier Brian Stoutenburg, a twenty-four-year-old from Grand Blanc, Michigan, was found dead in his quarters after an apparent suicide."

24. I got information on the military background of some of these infamous assassins from *The CT Blogger,* http://theconspiratorsnest.blogspot.com/search/label/Manchurian%20Agents (accessed on June 27, 2007). I noted earlier that Boggs (2005) makes connections between military training and serial killers, as does Darrell Hamamoto, who also connects serial killers to racial targeting and motivations (in Boggs 2003: 277–292).

25. Bob Herbert provides a useful summary of Whitman's killing spree: "Charles Whitman, a former marine and Eagle Scout in Austin, Texas, stabbed his wife to death in their bed. The night before he had driven to his mother's apartment in another part of town and killed her. Later that Monday morning, Whitman gathered together food, water, a supply of ammunition, two rifles, a couple of pistols, a carbine and a shotgun and climbed and climbed the landmark 30-story tower on the campus of the University of Texas. Beneath a blazing sun, with temperatures headed toward the mid-90s, Whitman opened fire. His first target was a pregnant teenager. Over the next 80 or so minutes he killed 14 people and wounded more than 30 others before being shot to death by the police." See Herbert, "A volatile young man, humiliation and a gun," *New York Times,* April 19, 2007, http://select.nytimes.com/2007/04/19/opinion/19herbert.html?_r=1&n=Top/Opinion/Editorials%20and%20Op-Ed/Op-Ed/Columnists/Bob%20Herbert&oref=slogin (accessed September 24, 2007).

26. On Reagan's Manichean vision, see Rogin (1987), Kellner and Ryan (1988), Kellner (1990), and Kellner (1995).

27. Clinton was especially hated by the extremist right and rarely before has a president been so vilified as in the rightist anti-Clinton discourse found in extremist publications and the Internet. See Lyons and Conason (2001).

28. Just before federal agents arrived to serve them warrants for charges of threatening government officials and bank and mail frauds for which a grand jury had indicted them in April 1996, the Freemen invited a local minister to their compound to whom they expounded their racist views. According to Reverend Helen Young, the Freemen subscribe to the "two-seed theory," which holds that "God created white gentiles as a superior race, descended directly from Adam and Eve, but that Jews descended from a sexual union between Eve and Satan. Moreover, they told her, whites were the true 'Israelites,' a lost tribe who had migrated to America, the new promised land, but that the government was now corrupted by Jewish influences" (*New York Times,* April 12, 1996, A8). The Freemen and Christian Identity ideologues also denigrate people of color as "mud people."

29. Gustav Niebuhr, "Creed of hate called Christian identity is the heart of the Free-men's beliefs," *New York Times,* April 12, 1996, A8.

30. From the time of McVeigh's arrest when attention was focused on the extremism of the militia movement, its leaders and members regularly told the media that they believed that the Oklahoma bombing was a government plot. Michigan militia leader Mark Koernke, for instance, repeatedly suggested that "the Oklahoma bombing was actually the work of federal agents who made sure to be absent the day of the explosion." On *ABC News* (April 24, 1995), Koernke rhetorically asked: "Why weren't these people there? What is it that they were involved in? Even the secretaries have commented now at the site that it appeared it was almost like a morgue; that many people simply did not show up for work in the ATF and FBI offices." This conspiracy view continues to circulate in the militia movement and Internet to this day; see, for example, Steven Yates, "The Oklahoma City bombing: A morass of unanswered questions," http://www.lewrockwell.com/yates/yates33.html (accessed on June 27, 2007) and "The Oklahoma City bombing: What really happened?" http://www.whatreallyhappened.com/RANCHO/POLITICS/OK/ok.html (accessed on June 27, 2007).

31. In April 1995, Francisco Duran was arrested for firing a semiautomatic weapon at the White House; mainstream media reports dismissed him as a "paranoid schizophrenic," as an ex-GI out to avenge a drunk-driving conviction, but the Colorado weekly *Westword* indicated that "Duran belonged to groups like the Save America Militia in Calhan, Colo., and was an avid reader of militia literature. Duran's brother-in-law, Jose Guttierez, says Duran's assault on the White House was inspired in part by militia leader Linda Thomp-son's call for an armed march on Washington." See *Extra!* (July/August 1995): 9. During 1995–1996, there were 74 black churches burned across the South and the wave of burnings became a subject of national media attention (*New York Times,* July 21, 1996: A8) and *USA Today* (August 15, 1996: 3A).

32. A report by the Anti-Defamation League claimed that membership in paramilitary groups has grown since the Oklahoma bombing, that there are over 15,000 members in antigovernment groups active throughout the country (*New York Times,* June 18, 1995: A12). A year later, the Southern Poverty Law Center claimed that there are "441 paramilitary groups and that they can be found in all 50 states" (*New York Times,* June 23, 1996: 19A). The Southern Poverty Law Center has been for decades releasing a yearly Intelligence Report on right-wing extremist and paramilitary activity; see http://www.splcenter.org/intel/history.jsp (accessed on June 3, 2007). For current figures, see the discussion and notes below.

33. Interview with J. William Gibson, San Diego, March 1997.

34. See The Southern Poverty Law Center (SPLC), "The year in hate," *Intelligence Report,* Spring 2007 and the website at http://www.splcenter.org/intel/map/hate.jsp (accessed June 3, 2007).

35. Ibid., 49.

36. Ibid., 59ff.

37. Research indicates that the amount of violence in film culture was accelerating significantly; the number of episodes of violence in sequels to popular films like *Robocop* (1990), *Die Hard* (1990 and 1995), and *Young Guns* (1990) doubled or tripled in comparison to the originals, showing that a culture nurtured on violence needed ever heavier doses

to get its fix. For other documentation of the escalating violence in media culture, see Kellner and Ryan (1988), Gibson (1994), and Kellner (1995); on escalating violence in children's media in the 2000s, see the survey by the Benton Foundation at http://www.benton.org/?q=node/323 (accessed on June 13, 2007).

38. One of the few progressive national talk radio venues was that of Texas populist Jim Hightower, who had his syndicated program canceled when Disney took over the ABC network that broadcast his show; he was told it was low ratings and lack of adequate sponsorship that forced cancellation. Hightower retorted that major labor unions had volunteered to sponsor his show, but ABC refused this sponsorship on the grounds that labor was an "advocacy" group—as if the corporations that sponsor commercial media were not; see the report in the *Nation* (October 16, 1995: 410). Hightower moved to distribute his program independently on the RealAudio Internet site. For a critique of conservative talk radio, see the discussion in Boggs (2000) and Boggs and Dirmann (1999). In recent years, there has been an attempt to develop progressive talk radio on the Air America network, but it has had persistent financial problems and has not really yet provided a forum to compete with the right, which has its spokespeople on major networks like ABC, CNN, CBS, and NBC, as well as Fox News.

39. See the cover story on "Falling Down," in *Newsweek,* March 29, 1993.

40. References to the Unabomber "Manifesto" will cite paragraph numbers, since the text appears in so many different print editions and Internet sites. For the manifesto, see http://www.thecourier.com/manifest.htm (accessed in June 17, 2007) and its publication in both Gibbs, et al. (1996: 183ff.) and Douglas and Olshaker (1996: 191ff.).

41. The Unabomber/Kaczynski letter to the *New York Times* cited here is published in Douglas and Olshaker (1996: 182ff).

42. On the Unabomber, see Gibbs et al. (1996) and Douglas and Olshaker 1996).

43. Gibbs, et al. (1996: 100ff.) and Douglas and Olshaker (1996: 70ff.). The Unabomber/Kaczynski claimed he was a member of a group titled FC which was prepared to carry out more lethal bombings unless a major newspaper or national magazine would publish their manifesto and commit to publish three 3,000 word follow-up articles in succeeding years. The Unabomber had previously put the initials "FC" on several of his bombs and although his letters promoted the fantasy of an anarchist group, FC (standing apparently for "Freedom Club," while some analysts had earlier believed it signified "Fuck Computers"), there is no evidence that the Unabomber belonged to any group, so "FC" now appears to be the fantasy of an isolated loner, empowered by the notion of belonging to a conspiracy to overthrow the industrial system.

44. Ellul's *The Technological Society* (1964) was an influential antitechnology missive of its era.

45. See Gibbs, et al. (1996: 100ff.) and Douglas and Olshaker (1996).

46. See Serge F. Kovaleski, "Unabomber 'based his life on novel,'" *Washington Post,* July 9, 1996, http://www.ibiblio.org/eldritch/jc/sa/una.html.

47. In 1996, there was a neo-Dadaist "Unabomber for President" website and many other sites dedicated to information and debate. A Usenet newslist, alt.fan.unabomber (accessed September 24, 2007) debates the phenomenon, with a mélange of fans, critics, and analysts posting ideas and information, both before and after his capture. For the

current state of discussion of the Unabomber, see the entry in Wikipedia, which lists a large number of references to the Unabomber in contemporary popular culture at http://en.wikipedia.org/wiki/Unabomber (accessed May 6, 2007). A man was arrested in April 2007 for sending letters and two pipe bombs to investment companies, demanding a rise in the value of stocks he owned and citing the Unabomber as an influence; see Judy Keen, "Man accused of threatening companies with bombs," *USA Today*, April 26, 2007, 9a.

48. Carl Boggs and Eric Magnuson (1996), by contrast, see the Unabomber's antipolitics as symptomatic of the collapse of regular politics and a highly contradictory failed mediation between the drive toward total revolution and the destruction of the technological system, contrasted to "serial terrorist" bombings carried out by one lone "pathological hermit."

49. On the federal prison relations between McVeigh and Kaczynski, see Michel and Herbeck (2001: 359ff.), and for Kaczynski's thoughts on McVeigh and the Oklahoma City bombings, see ibid., 398–402.

50. On Columbine, see Larkin (2007), who has a solid sociological study of the Columbine shootings that is similar in many ways to my analysis, although we have different emphases and prescriptions. Curiously, though, Larkin downplays the factor of guns, and while he briefly mentions Harris's and Klebold's attraction to paramilitary culture, he does not discuss how they actually got the guns and how the guns functioned in their everyday lives, nor does he discuss problems of gun control. The *Salon* archives contain a treasure house of material with excellent reporting and commentary on the event that I closely followed during the shootings and their aftermath and found very strong in rereading; see http://archive.salon.com/news/special/littleton (accessed June 15, 2007). Dave Cullen's Columbine archive also includes a lot of valuable material at http://davecullen.com/columbine/all-in-1.html (accessed June 15, 2007). Otherwise, most of the books on the Columbine shootings were by participants in the event and represent specific and limited points of view.

51. Both Klebold and Harris told friends that they were planning shootings on Hitler's birthday, and the references appeared as well on their never-released "basement tapes." See M. E. Sprengelmeyer and Michele Ames, "Report's Columbine hindsight: Words of 2 were red flags," *Arkansas Democrat-Gazette*, November 23, 2000, A4. Larkin confirms the Hitler references and influence (2007: 156ff., passim).

52. Dave Cullen has archived on his website a vast amount of Columbine material, including Eric Harris's diary at http://www.davecullen.com/ (accessed June 15, 2007).

53. Dave Cullen punctures these myths in the article cited below. Ultimately, Klebold's and Harris' sexuality is a mystery, and the attempts to attribute gayness or straightness to them shows the obsession with labeling under the regime of heteronormativity.

54. On the growing skepticism toward the Cassie Bernall story, who was allegedly targeted for her belief in God, Dave Cullen writes: "Key investigators made it clear that an alternate scenario is far more likely: The killers asked another girl, Valeen Schnurr, a similar question, then shot her, and she lived to tell about it. Schnurr's story was then apparently misattributed to Cassie." See Dave Cullen, "Inside the Columbine High investigation," *Salon*, September 23, 1999, http://www.salon.com/news/feature/1999/09/23/columbine (accessed June 15, 2007). For a detailed demythologizing of the claim that the shooters

targeted Cassie Bernall, see Dave Cullen, "Who said 'Yes?' Local reporters have known for months that eyewitnesses disputed the account of Cassie Bernall's 'martyrdom.' So why did the truth take so long to see print?" *Salon,* September 30, 1999, http://www.salon. com/news/feature/1999/09/30/columbine. (accessed June 15, 2007). Larkin also refutes the claim that Bernall was martyred for her belief in God (2007: 43ff.) and has a detailed analysis of how Christian evangelicals exploited the shooting for recruitment and indoctrination (2007: 198ff., passim). Further, Lieberman (2006: 21) notes that claims by Christian fundamentalists that the Columbine shooters were targeting Christians produced a "slew of books—six on Rachel Scott, and two on Cassie Bernall that celebrated their martyrdom. One book title even called Rachel 'Columbine Joan of Arc.'"

55. For accounts of the stunning incompetence of the local Jefferson County police, who never investigated the Brown family's complaints, did not link the threatening website to Harris's and Klebold's van theft, and seemed to have lost files on the case, see the articles by Alan Prendergast, "The plot sickens: Another 'lost' Columbine report triggers new questions—and a long-overdue investigation of police ineptitude," *Westword,* November 6, 2003, http://www.westword.com/2003-11-06/news/the-plot-sickens/ (accessed June 15, 2007) and "Quagmire without end, amen," *Westword,* February 26, 2004, http://www.westword. com/2004-02-26/news/quagmire-without-end-amen (accessed June 15, 2007).

56. Cullen, "Inside the Columbine High investigation." The "Trench Coat Mafia" story was punctured when it was revealed the group had been at its peak the previous year and Harris and Klebold were never part of the clique. Newman et al. (2004: 246, passim) persist in referring to the shooters as part of a "Trench Coat Mafia."

57. Columbine High officials denied that there was bullying in the school, but a one-time friend of Harris and Klebold, Brooks Brown, wrote a book documenting intense bullying, and reporters also found significant evidence. On the culture of bullying at Columbine, see Larkin (2007: 187ff., 196ff., 226ff.), who makes bullying a major factor in triggering the Columbine shootings, a point I'll return to in Chapter 4.

58. Columbine officials have never released the "basement tapes" made by Harris and Klebold weeks before their rampage, which showed off their arsenal of bombs, guns, bullets and other weapons and contained obscenity-laced attacks on their school and their chilling farewells. A federal judge in Denver, Lewis Babcock, "ruled this month that the dispositions, the thousands of other records and the basement videos in which Harris and Klebold spelled out their sick plan must remain sealed for 20 years." See Marc Fischer, "Heed Columbine's lessons: Make information available, and speak out," *Washington Post,* April 19, 2007, A10. Larkin points out that later there were two books published which "blamed the Columbine shootings on lax and indulgent parenting within the middle class with absolutely no knowledge of how Dylan Klebold and Eric Harris were raised" (2007: 232).

59. See Katz (2006) who criticizes the gender-neutral description of school shooters and other crimes by youth that are overwhelmingly male.

60. Larkin (2007) rejects the theological explanations for the Columbine killers (i.e., that they were "evil"), as well as psychopathological categories, arguing that their life conditions and not just some hard-to-specify mental illness were responsible for their rampage. In addition, Larkin sharply criticizes evangelical students at Columbine as being major

harassers of marginal and outsider students who were seen as hypocrites by many (198ff.). Further, Larkin criticizes the rank distortion of the story of the Columbine students in a series of books by Christian evangelicals who falsely claimed that Harris and Klebold targeted evangelicals and killed them execution style and who systematically failed to address the issue of bullying and harassment.

61. People for the American Way, "Right-wing watch online," July 20, 1999, http://www.pfaw.org/pfaw/general/default.aspx?oid=3544 (accessed June 15, 2007). More recently, Dr. Laura's son, who was serving in Iraq, was caught up in a scandal when it was revealed that "his webpage, which has since been removed from MySpace.com, included cartoon depictions of rape, murder, torture and child molestation; photographs of soldiers with guns in their mouths; a photograph of a bound and blindfolded detainee captioned 'My Sweet Little Habib'; accounts of illicit drug use; and a blog entry headlined by a series of obscenities and racial epithets. The Army is investigating, but has currently issued no public findings" (cited on Dr. Laura's Wikipedia page, http://en.wikipedia.org/wiki/Dr._Laura).

62. People for the American Way, "Right-wing watch online."

63. Ibid.

64. Dave Cullen, "Kill mankind: No one should survive," *Salon,* September 23, 1999, http://www.salon.com/news/feature/1999/09/23/columbine (accessed June 15, 2007). Larkin (2007: 175ff.) agrees that the drive for celebrity was a major motivation for the Columbine shooters. Harris's diary has the shooters reflecting on whether Spielberg or Tarantino should make the movie on their exploits, but, in fact, so far all they've received are low-budget flicks like Ben Coccio's camcorder-shot video diaries *Zero Day* (2003), and Gus Van Sant's low-key *Elephant* (2005), which shows the students going through an ordinary school day, the shooters briefly preparing, taking a shower together, and then proceeding to the massacre in a form of naturalist banality.

65. In a later reflection on the plan to significantly blow up the high school and then shoot students and teachers fleeing from bomb explosions, see Dave Cullen, "The depressive and the psychopath," *Slate,* April 20, 2004, http://www.slate.com/id/2099203 (accessed June 15, 2007). Larkin criticizes Cullen for his use of these psychopathological categories for labeling the Columbine shooters and thereby psychologizing the tragedy (2007: 151, 191).

66. Dave Cullen, "Let the litigation begin," *Salon,* May 28, 1999, http://www.salon.com/news/feature/1999/05/28/families (accessed June 15, 2007). Later, lead investigators tended to exonerate the Harris and Klebold families, claiming that they did not have a clue of what their sons were up to, and they were never charged with any crime, although they continued to be criticized for not recognizing their children's problems and not speaking out on the issue. In 2005, they refused to participate in a state-mandated study of the Columbine shootings, angering some investigators, relatives of the victims, and others; see Kevin Vaughan, "Study of killings at standstill: Parents of killers decide not to take part in prof's effort," *Rocky Mountain News,* April 19, 2005, rockymountainnews.com/drmn/cda/article-print/o,1983,DRMN-15-3714175 (accessed June 15, 2007).

67. Dave Cullen, "Columbine 'coverup,'" *Salon,* April 21, 2000, http://www.salon.com/news/feature/2000/04/21/columbine (accessed June 21, 2007).

68. Ibid.

69. On Brecht, see Kellner (1997b). Moore effectively uses Brechtian "separation of elements," ironically playing off soundtrack and music with image and narrative. Like Brecht, he also makes strongly political works. I have, however, found no evidence in interviews with Moore or other material that would indicate that he was directly influenced by Brecht.

70. For sustained argumentation concerning the need to recognize gender violence, see Katz (2006).

71. See Mike Males, "*Bowling for Columbine* misframes gun quandary," November 6, 2002, http://home.earthlink.net/~mmales/bowling.htm.

72. See the anti-Moore films by Mike Wilson, *Michael Moore Hates America* (2004), and Larry Elder's *Michael and Me* (2004), or the attacks on Moore in Hardy and Clarke (2004).

73. A June 1, 2007, search of Nexis-Lexis indicated that no major newspapers, magazines, or journals made a connection between the Virginia Tech massacre and domestic terrorism.

74. Herbert, "A volatile young man, humiliation and a gun."

75. Jonathan Zimmerman, "In the wake of the Virginia Tech shootings, America needs a day of mourning and reflection," *Christian Science Monitor,* April 18, 2007, http://hnn.us/roundup/entries/37807.html.

76. Bill O'Reilly, "Politics and mass murder," April 18, 2007, on the *Fox News* website, *O'Reilly Factor* link, http://www.foxnews.com/story/0,2933,266711,00.html (accessed May 16, 2007).

77. See the interview clips on "Jelly" and "Spanky," http://www.liveleak.com/view?i=926_1176931737 (accessed May 16, 2007).

78. Allen G. Breed and Chris Kahn, "Those who knew Cho reflect on warning signs," Associated Press, April 23, 2007, http://www.decaturdaily.com/decaturdaily/news/070423/signs.shtml.

79. There was also a story that Cho was gay published in the *Globe* tabloid; see the critical summary by Robert Lindsay at http://robertlindsay.blogspot.com/2007/05/was-so-seung-hui-gay.html (accessed May 23, 2007), which questions the tabloid story. Possibly Cho was sexually ambiguous and confused, which could have contributed to his rage and construction of an ultraviolent masculinist identity.

80. Amy Gardiner and David Cho, "Isolation defined Cho's senior year," *Washington Post,* May 6, 2007, A01.

81. Cho's play *Richard McBeef,* posted on the Internet, has three characters—a 13-year-old boy, his father, and a stepfather whom he accuses of killing his real mother. The play also has the son accusing the stepfather of attempting to sexually molest him and has the stepfather striking "a deadly blow" at the son. This scenario could fit into the fantasy structure of having an imaginary father upon which he could project blame, while imagining a good father who would truly nurture him. Given the reports that Cho had a fantasy science fiction character girlfriend who visited him in his room and spent time with him, he could well have been living in parallel fantasy universes that propelled him to make the fantasy real in producing the media spectacle of the "Virginia Tech massacre." See Seung-Hui Cho,

Richard McBeef, http://www.thesmokinggun.com/archive/years/2007/0417071vtech1. html (accessed June 15, 2007).

82. Seung-Hui Cho, *Mr. Brownstone,* http://news.aol.com/virginia-tech-shootings/ cho-seung-hui/_a/mr-brownstone-title-page/20070417141309990001 (accessed June 15, 2007).

83. Brigid Schulte and Chris L. Jenkins, "Cho didn't get court-ordered treatment," *Washington Post,* May 6, 2007, A01. In addition, the *Report of the Panel Review* (2007) indicated that many of Cho's medical records were lost, showing a complete breakdown of the mental health system—or someone deliberately "losing" records to cover up incompetency.

84. Sari Horowitz, "Va. Tech shooter seen as 'collector of injustice,'" *Washington Post,* June 19, 2007, A01. The discussion of "Ax Ishmael" suggests broader semiotic ramifications than the right-wing readings of "Ismail" as an Islamic reference and Cho as a jihadist suicide bomber, motivations that appear to be of secondary or less importance in his material and behavior.

85. While copyediting this text, I ran across an article I had read earlier by Shankar Vedantam, "Cho's case similar to other mass killings by loners," *Washington Post,* April 22, 2007, A13. The article mentioned that Cho's shooting rampage at Virginia Tech reminded some scholars of the amok syndrome discussed in the Introduction, although "more conventional explanations have suggested he may have been suffering from a psychotic disorder or personality problems." In fact, Cho may have suffered from severe mental disorders and run amok. I am not using the "amok" concept as a privileged explanation, but as part of a complex scenario of school shootings and domestic terrorism that have taken place in the United States in the past years. As scholars noted in the article just cited, Cho's rampage had classical signs of amok behavior, as did that of some of the other school shooters and domestic terrorists. Technically, since McVeigh and Kaczynski did not commit suicide at the end of their rampages, they did not exhibit the full range of symptoms of classic amok behavior, and I am suggesting a different model to explain the actions of recent school shooters and domestic terrorists, in which the amok behavior sometimes occurs.

Notes to Chapter 4

1. For U.S. gun statistics, see the Centers for Disease Control's National Center for Health Statistics at http://www.cdc.gov/nchs/Default.htm (accessed September 26, 2007).

2. Ibid.

3. David Olinger, "U.S. gun culture back in spotlight," *Denver Post,* April 23, 2007, http://www.denverpost.com/portlet/article/html/fragments/print_article.jsp?articleId= 5728141&siteId=36 (accessed on June 4, 2007).

4. See "A time line of recent worldwide school shootings," Infoplease, http://www. infoplease.com/ipa/A0777958.html; see also "Number of children and adults killed and wounded in school shootings around the world since 1996," International Action Network

on Small Arms, http://www.iansa.org/women/documents/Schoolshootings1996-2006_000.doc (accessed June 2, 2007).

5. An excellent recent report by the Brady Center to Prevent Gun Violence, *No Guns Left Behind: The Gun Lobby's Campaign to Push Guns into Colleges and Schools,* documents the epidemic of school shootings and the gun lobby's efforts to push for more guns in schools after the Virginia Tech shootings; see http://www.bradycampaign.org/xshare/pdf/reports/no-gun-left-behind.pdf.

6. Ibid.

7. Allison Klein and Clarence Williams, "6 shootings in 2 hours stir worries about violence," *Washington Post,* July 21, 2007, B01.

8. See the CNN report "Murders, robberies drive up U.S. violent crime rate," June 4, 2007, http://www.cnn.com/2007/U.S./06/04/usa.crime.reut/index.html (accessed June 8, 2007).

9. Noises Naim, "The crime pandemic," *Los Angeles Times/Opinion,* June 17, 2007, M4.

10. Dan Eggen, "FBI report: Violent crime on the rise—First significant increase in homicides and robberies since 1993 continues." *Washington Post,* September 24, 2007, A07.

11. Robin Toner, "Renewed scrutiny for gun controls," *New York Times,* April 17, 2007, A25.

12. Sewell Chan, "Seeking a national voice, 15 mayors meet on gun violence," *Amherst Times,* April 26, 2006, http://www.amhersttimes.com/index.php?option=com_content&task=view&id=1333&Itemid=27 (accessed June 4, 2007).

13. Douglas Turner, "Virginia's gun laws are killing New Yorkers," *Buffalo News,* May 14, 2007, A06.

14. Janet Fife-Yeomans and Alison Rehn, "Gun debate triggered—Port Arthur laws place us apart from U.S.," *Daily Telegraph* (Australia), April 18, 2007, A7. In addition, Australian prime minister John Howard said after the Virginia Tech shootings that "tough Australian legislation introduced after a mass shooting in Tasmania in 1996 had prevented the U.S. gun culture emerging in his country." The Australians subsequently imposed laws banning almost all types of semiautomatic weapons. "We showed a national resolve that the gun culture that is such a negative in the United States would never become a negative in our country," said Howard, extending sympathies to the families of the victims at Virginia Tech university. Michael Perry, "Massacre sparks foreign criticism of U.S. gun culture," Reuters, April 17, 2007, http://news.monstersandcritics.com/usa/features/printer_1292565.php (accessed June 11, 2007).

15. See Mary Jordan, "Britain's gun laws seen as curbing attacks," *Washington Post,* April 24, 2007, A18.

16. During the first week in May, for instance, the *Chronicle for Higher Education* reported that Delaware County Community College reopened on May 1 after closing for six days following e-mail threats; a student was arrested at the University of Georgia after his comments worried a faculty member; Ohio University banned an armed student who had threatened others on campus; "Pulaski Technical College, in Arkansas, closed all of its locations this morning after the North Little Rock police said an unidentified caller

had reported overhearing two people talk about an incident that would be worse than the killings at Virginia Tech"; and "Campus security guards, jumpy in the aftermath of the Virginia Tech shootings, mistook an actor in a performance-art video for a gunman at the University of Hawaii–Manoa last week, evacuated a classroom building, and even detained someone who looked like the actor." See http://chronicle.com/news/?pg=8 (accessed May 8, 2007).

17. Tim Craig, "Ban on sale of guns to mentally ill is expanded," *Washington Post,* May 1, 2007, B01.

18. For information on gun control legislation, news, and statistics from the Brady Campaign, see http://www.bradycampaign.org (accessed June 4, 2007).

19. Tim Craig, "Va. tech panel outlines agenda," *Washington Post,* May 11, 2007, B01.

20. Martin Weil and Tim Craig, "Va. Tech relatives lambaste response," *Washington Post,* June 11, 2007, B01.

21. Ibid.

22. See Ian Urbina and Jon Hurdle, "2 Delaware students shot; campus is locked down," *New York Times,* September 22, 2007, http://www.nytimes.com/2007/09/22/us/22delaware. html (accessed September 23, 2007). During the same period, however, there was a negative example of excessive school security gone awry when a student protestor rambling on during a John Kerry speech was arrested and tasered at the University of Florida. See CNN, September 18, 2007, at http://politicalticker.blogs.cnn.com/2007/09/18/student-tasered-arrested-at-john-kerry-speech.

23. Chris L. Jenkins, "Confusion over laws impedes aid for mentally ill," *Washington Post,* June 14, 2007, A01.

24. Ibid. By June 2007, Virginia Tech announced a "VT Alert" system whereby "students, faculty, and staff may sign up for emergency alerts using their preferred methods of communication. Options include text messaging, AOL, Yahoo, and MSN Messenger." See "Cho's toxicology report released, Tech announces changes," *Collegiate Times,* June 21, 2007, http://collegiatetimes.com/news/1/ARTICLE/9130/2007-06-21.html (accessed June 23, 2007).

25. Brigid Schulte, "Va. Tech panel lacks full picture on Cho: Decisions were made without treatment plan," *Washington Post,* July 22, 2007, C01.

26. Gabriel McVey, "States look at gun policies, debate on-campus weapon carry," *Collegiate Times,* June 20, 2007, http://www.collegiatetimes.com/news/1/ARTICLE/9117/2007-06-20.html (accessed June 23, 2007).

27. Ibid.

28. Stephen Manning, "D.C. will ask Court to preserve gun ban," Associated Press, July 16, 2007, http://news.yahoo.com/s/ap/20070716/ap_on_re_us/gun_ban (accessed on July 18, 2007).

29. See Mark Ames, "Virginia Tech: Is the scene of the crime the cause of the crime?" *AlterNet,* April 20, 2007, http://www.AlterNet.org/story/50758 (accessed August 1, 2007).

30. For a critique of school high-tech security and surveillance equipment following Columbine, see Lewis (2006).

31. Maia Szalavitz, "A better response to rejection," *Washington Post*, June 19, 2007, HE01.

32. Although Larkin is highly critical of the bullying of jocks and the ultramasculine hegemony of sports culture at Columbine, recognizes that the "shooters' masculinity had been challenged" (191), and even recognizes that at Columbine "the culture of hyper-masculinity reigned supreme" (209), he does not emphasize the problems of male rage, the crisis of masculinity, and the need for alternative masculinities that I am stressing in this book.

33. See Chris L. Jenkins, "Panel targets funding gap in Va." *Washington Post*, June 19, 2007, B01.

34. Criticism of the Virginia mental health system and how it failed to function properly in Cho's case was highlighted in many newspaper articles and the *Report of the Review Panel* (2007: 52ff. and 60ff.).

35. See "Vick dog-fighting charges stir stinging reaction," *CNN News*, July 20, 2007, http://www.cnn.com/2007/U.S./07/20/vick.dogfighting/index.html?iref=mpstoryview (accessed on July 21, 2007).

36. While it would be illicit to prescribe a specific alternative masculinity, counter-hegemonic masculinities should be nonsexist, nonheterosexist, and non–male supremacist, and should be part of a process that seeks to establish egalitarian relations between men and women. They should also be multiple and flexible, recognizing that different men in differing historical, cultural, and institutional conditions will construct heterogeneous masculine identities. And counterhegemonic alternative masculinities should be subject to self-critique and reconstruction, as institutional structures, social practices, and individuals grow and develop. Information, publications, films, and other material on the Mentors in Violence Program can be found at http://www.jacksonkatz.com (accessed September 26, 2007). I refer to Katz's work elsewhere in these chapters and thank him for material and ideas that have been valuable for this book. There is also a book, *Violence Goes to College: The Authoritative Guide to Prevention and Intervention* (Nicoletti, Spencer-Thomas, and Bollinger 2001) assembled by a group that has yearly conferences on university violence in a multiplicity of forms and develops violence prevention strategies. See their website at http://www.violencegoestocollege.com (accessed September 27, 2007).

37. Cited in Nick Gillespie, "The FCC's not mommy and daddy," *Los Angeles Times*, May 2, 2007, A23.

38. See Herbert Marcuse, "A revolution in values," in Marcuse (2001), and on the new sensibility, see my introduction to the volume of collected papers of Marcuse on *Art and Liberation* (2006). On Marcuse's contributions to the critique and reconstruction of education, see Kellner, Cho, Lewis, and Pierce (forthcoming).

39. This misplaced pedagogy of teaching for testing did not just originate with the Bush administration, but has long been a feature of pedagogically challenged schools; see Janet Ewell, "Test-takers, not students," *Los Angeles Times*, May 26, 2007, A19. For some compelling criticism of the Bush administration's No Child Left Behind policies, see the dossier "Correcting schools," *Nation*, May 21, 2007, 11–21.

40. See Jones (2002) and Kahn and Kellner (2005). Some good sites that exhibit youth voices, participation, and politics include http://www.moveon.org; http://www.

raisethefist.com; http://www.tao.com; the youth blog site at http://www.Bloghop.com/ topics.htm?numblogs=14566&cacheid=1044419966.3569 (accessed May 14, 2007).

41. See Best and Kellner (2001) and Kahn and Kellner (2005).

42. For instance, Mosaic, Netscape, and the first browsers were invented by young computer users, as were many of the first websites, listservs, chat rooms, and so on. A hacker culture emerged that was initially conceptualized as a reconfiguring and improving of computer systems, related to design, system, and use, before the term became synonymous with theft and mischief, such as setting loose worms and viruses. On youth and Internet subcultures, see Kahn and Kellner (2003).

43. For my further perspectives on developing a critical theory of education and re-constructing education, see Kellner (2003c, 2004); Kahn and Kellner (2006); and Kellner and Share (2007).

44. The building of prisons and incarcerating of people in California has reached crisis point; see Jonathan Simon, "Addicted to prisons: California can't keep dealing with social problems by putting people behind bars," *Los Angeles Times*, August 1, 2007, A19.

45. See the discussion and documentation in Kellner (2005).

46. On the 1990–1991 Gulf War, see Kellner (1992), and on the 2003 U.S. and UK invasion and occupation of Iraq, see Kellner (2005).

47. Donald Rumsfeld, cited at http://www.pbs.org/newshour/bb/military/ jan-june04/rum_05-07.html (accessed September 25, 2007).

48. See the archive of images "The Abu Ghraib Files" in *Salon* at http://www.salon. com/news/abu_ghraib/2006/03/14/introduction (accessed June 21, 2007).

49. For an excellent article that summarizes five recent books on the disaster that is pris-ons in the United States, see Daniel Lazare, "Stars and bars," *Nation* (August 27–September 3, 2007): 29–36.

50. Jason DeParle notes (2007): "The 'war on drugs' led to the arrest of growing numbers of small-time users and dealers. By the late 1990s, 60 percent of federal inmates were in for drug offenses. The result is an ever-growing prison system, populated to a significant degree by people who need not be there. It was no liberal advocate but Supreme Court Justice Anthony M. Kennedy who offered a damning view of criminal justice in the United States: 'Our resources are misspent, our punishments too severe, our sentences too long.'"

51. See DeParle (2007).

52. Hedda Korsch, cited in Kellner (1977:102). On Karl Korsch's life and work, see Kellner (1977).

53. Paul Mattick, "The Marxism of Karl Korsch," http://www.marxists.org/archive/ mattick-paul/1964/korsch.htm (accessed June 17, 2007). Korsch was working on many ambitious projects when he died in 1961, involving the rethinking and updating of Marx-ism; see his letters to Mattick, Bertolt Brecht, and others in Kellner (1977: 283ff.).

References

Adams, Rachel and David Savran, eds., *The Masculinity Studies Reader*. Malden, MA: Blackwell, 2002.

Aries, Philippe. *Centuries of Childhood: A Social History of Family Life*. New York: Alfred A. Knopf, 1962.

Ames, Mark. *Going Postal: Rage, Murder, and Rebellion—From Reagan's Workplaces to Clinton's Columbine and Beyond*. New York: Soft Skull Press, 2005.

Aronowitz, Stanley. *Roll Over, Beethoven*. Hanover, NH: University Press of New England, 1993.

Baudrillard, Jean. "The Ecstasy of Communication." Pp. 126–134 in Hal Foster, ed., *The Anti-Aesthetic*. Port Townsend, WA: Bay Press, 1983.

Bellesiles, Michael A. *Arming America: The Origins of a National Gun Culture*. New York: Alfred A. Knopf, 2000.

Best, Steven, and Douglas Kellner. *Postmodern Theory: Critical Interrogations*. London and New York: Macmillan/Guilford Press, 1991.

———. *The Postmodern Turn*. New York: Guilford Press, 1997.

———. *The Postmodern Adventure: Science, Technology, and Cultural Studies at the Third Millennium*. New York: Guilford Press, 2001.

———. "Contemporary Youth and the Postmodern Adventure." *Review of Education/Pedagogy/Cultural Studies* 25, no. 2 (April–June 2003): 75–93.

Bloch, Ernst. *The Principle of Hope*. Cambridge: Massachusetts Institute of Technology Press, 1986.

Bloom, Allan. *The Closing of the American Mind*. New York: Simon and Schuster, 1987.

Bluestone, Barry, and Bennett Harrison. *Deindustrialization of America: Plant Closings, Community Abandonment, and the Dismantling of Basic Industry*. New York: Basic Books, 1982.

Boggs, Carl. *The End of Politics*. New York: Guilford Press, 2000.

———. *Imperial Delusions: American Militarism and Endless War*. Lanham, MD: Rowman and Littlefield, 2005.

Boggs, Carl, ed. *Masters of War: Militarism and Blowback in the Age of American Empire*. New York: Routledge, 2003.

Boggs, Carl, and Eric Magnuson. "Unabomber and the Flight from Politics." *L.A. Village View*, August 17, 1996.

Boggs, Carl, and Tina Dirmann. "The Myth of Electronic Populism: Talk Radio and the Decline of the Public Sphere." *Democracy and Nature* (March 1999): 65–94.

Boggs, Carl, and Tom Pollard. *The Hollywood War Machine: U.S. Militarism and Popular Culture.* Boulder, CO: Paradigm Publishers, 2006.

Brock, David. *The Republican Noise Machine: Right-Wing Media and How It Corrupts Democracy.* New York: Crown, 2004.

Coates, James. *Armed and Dangerous: The Rise of the Survivalist Right.* New York: HarperCollins, 1987.

Connell, R. W., and James W. Messerschmidt. "Hegemonic Masculinity: Rethinking the Concept," *Gender and Society* 19, no. 6 (2005): 829–859.

Coupland, Douglas. *Generation X: Tales for an Accelerated Culture.* New York: St. Martin's, 1991.

Cramer, Clinton E. *Armed America: The Story of How and Why Guns Became as American as Apple Pie.* Nashville, TN: Nelson, 2006.

Davis, Angela, with Eduardo Mendietta. *Abolition Democracy: Beyond Empire, Prisons, and Torture.* New York: Seven Stories Press, 2005.

Dayan, Daniel, and Elihu Katz. *Media Events: The Live Broadcasting of History.* Cambridge, MA: Harvard University Press, 1992.

de Beauvoir, Simone. *The Second Sex.* New York: Vintage, 1989 [1953].

Debord, Guy. *The Society of the Spectacle.* Detroit, MI: Black and Red, 1970 [1967].

DeParle, Jason. "The American Prison Nightmare." *New York Review of Books* 54, no. 6 (April 12, 2007), http://www.nybooks.com/articles/2007 (accessed July 21, 2007).

Dewey, John. *Democracy and Education.* New York: Free Press, 1997 [1916].

Diamond, Sara. *Roads to Dominion: Right-Wing Movements and Political Power in the United States.* New York: Guilford Press, 1995.

Dolby, Nadine, and Fazal Rizvi, eds. *Youth Moves.* New York: Taylor and Francis, 2007.

Dyer, Joel. *The Harvest of Rage.* Boulder, CO: Westview Press, 1999 [1997].

Eisenstein, Zillah. *Sexual Decoys: Gender, Race and War in Imperial Democracy.* London and New York: Zed Books, 2007.

Ellul, Jacques. *The Technological Society.* New York: Alfred A. Knopf, 1964.

Epstein, Jonathan S., ed. *Youth Culture: Identity in a Postmodern World.* Malden, MA: Blackwell, 1998.

Faludi, Susan. *Stiffed: The Betrayal of the American Man.* New York: William Morrow, 1999.

Feenberg, Andrew, and Jim Freedman. *When Poetry Ruled the Streets.* Albany: State University of New York Press, 2001.

Freire, Paulo. *Pedagogy of the Oppressed.* New York: Herder and Herder, 1972.

———. *A Paulo Freire Reader,* edited by Anna Maria Araujo Freire and Donaldo Macedo. New York: Herder and Herder, 1998.

Frymer, Benjamin. "Sacred Profanities: Youth Alienation, Popular Culture, and Spirituality—An Interview with Donna Gaines," *Interactions* 2, no. 1 (2006), http://repository.cdlib.org/gseis/interactions/vol2/iss1/art8.

Gaines, Donna. *Teenage Wasteland: Suburbia's Dead-End Kids.* Chicago: University of Chicago Press, 1998.

———. "America's Dead-End Kids," Pp. 107–128 in Stephanie Urso Spina, ed., *Smoke and*

Mirrors: The Hidden Context of Violence in Schools and Society. Lanham, MD: Rowman and Littlefield, 2000.

Gibson, J. William. *Warrior Dreams: Violence and Manhood in Post-Vietnam America.* New York: Hill and Wang, 1994.

———. *The Perfect War: Technowar in Vietnam.* 2d ed. New York: Atlantic Monthly Press, 2000.

Gillon, Steve. *Boomer Nation: The Largest and Richest Generation Ever, and How It Changed America.* New York: Free Press, 2004.

Giroux, Henry. *Border Crossing.* New York: Routledge, 1996a.

———. *Fugitive Cultures.* New York: Routledge, 1996b.

———. *Channel Surfing: Racism, the Media, and the Destruction of Today's Youth.* New York: St. Martin's, 1997.

———. *Stealing Innocence: Youth, Corporate Power, and the Politics of Culture.* New York: St. Martin's, 2000.

———. *The Abandoned Generation: Democracy beyond the Culture of Fear.* New York: Palgrave Macmillan, 2003.

———. *Stormy Weather: Katrina and the Politics of Disposability.* Boulder, CO: Paradigm Publishers, 2006a.

———. *Beyond the Spectacle of Terrorism: Global Uncertainty and the Challenge of the New Media.* Boulder, CO: Paradigm Publishers, 2006b.

———. *The University in Chains: Confronting the Military-Industrial-Academic Complex.* Boulder, CO: Paradigm Publishers, 2007.

Glassner, Barry. *The Culture of Fear: Why Americans Are Afraid of the Wrong Things.* New York: Basic Books, 2000.

Graysmith, Robert. *Zodiac.* New York: Berkeley Books, 2007.

Greenwald, Glenn. *How Would a Patriot Act? Defending American Values from a President Run Amok.* San Francisco: Working Assets, 2006.

Grossberg, Lawrence. *We Gotta Get Out of This Place.* New York and London: Routledge, 1992.

———. "Why Does Neo-Liberalism Hate Kids? The War on Youth and the Culture of Politics," *Review of Education/Pedagogy/Cultural Studies* 23 (2001): 2.

———. *Caught in the Crossfire.* Boulder: Paradigm Publishers, 2005.

Grossman, Dave. *On Killing: The Psychological Cost of Learning to Kill in War and Society.* Boston: Back Bay Books, 1996.

Hall, Stuart, and Martin Jacques, eds. *The Politics of Thatcherism.* London: Lawrence and Wishart, 1983.

Hamamoto, Darrell. "Empire of Death and the Plague of Civic Violence." Pp. 277–292 in Carl Boggs, *Masters of War: Militarism and Blowback in the Age of American Empire.* New York: Routledge, 2003.

Hammer, Rhonda. *Antifeminism and Family Terrorism.* Lanham, MD: Rowman and Littlefield, 2002.

———. "Globalization, Militarism, and Terrorism: Making Connections with Patriarchy and Colonization," *Resources for Feminist Research* 30, nos. 3 and 4 (2004): 90–98.

Hardy, David T., and Jason Clarke, *Michael Moore Is a Big Fat Stupid White Man*. New York: Regan, 2004.

Holtz, Geoffrey T. *Welcome to the Jungle: The Why behind "Generation X."* New York: St. Martin's, 1995.

Howe, Neil, and William Strauss. *Generations: The History of America's Future, 1584 to 2069*. New York: Quill, 1991.

———. *13th Generation: America's 13th Generation, Born 1961–1981*. New York: Vintage, 1993.

———. *Millennials Rising: America's Next Great Generation*. New York: Vintage, 2000.

Illich, Ivan. *Deschooling Society*. London: Marion Boyars, 1970.

———. *Celebration of Awareness*. London: Marion Boyars, 1971.

———. *Tools for Conviviality*. New York: Harper and Row, 1973.

Jameson, Fredric. *Postmodernism, or, the Cultural Logic of Late Capitalism*. Durham, NC: Duke University Press, 1991.

Jeffords, Susan. *The Remasculinization of America*. Bloomington: Indiana University Press, 1989.

Jewett, Robert, and John Lawrence. *The American Monomyth*, 2d ed. Lanham, MD: University Press of America, 1988.

Jones, Steven. *The Internet Goes to College: How Students Are Living in the Future with Today's Technology*. Washington, DC: Pew Internet and American Life Project, 2002.

Jones, Steven, and Peter Israel. *Others Unknown: Timothy McVeigh and the Oklahoma Bombing Conspiracy*. New York: Public Affairs, 2001.

Kahn, Richard, and Douglas Kellner. "Internet Subcultures and Oppositional Politics." Pp. 299–314 in David Muggleton, ed., *The Post-Subcultures Reader*. Oxford, UK: Berg, 2003.

———. "Oppositional Politics and the Internet: A Critical/Reconstructive Approach," *Cultural Politics* 1, no. 1 (2005): 75–100.

———. "Reconstructing Technoliteracy: A Multiple Literacies Approach." Pp. 253–274 in John R. Dakers, ed., *Defining Technological Literacy*. Hampshire, UK: Palgrave Macmillan, 2006.

Katz, Elihu, and Tamar Liebes. "'No More Peace!' How Disaster, Terror, and War Have Upstaged Media Events." *International Journal of Communication* 1 (2007): 157–166, http://ijoc.org/ojs/index.php/ijoc/article/view/44/23 (accessed September 26, 2007).

Katz, Jackson. *The Macho Paradox*. Naperville, IL: Sourcebook, 2006.

Katz, Jackson, and Jeremy Earp. *Tough Guise*. Directed by Sut Jhally. Northampton, MA: Media Education Foundation, 1999.

Kellner, Douglas. *Karl Korsch: Revolutionary Theory*. Austin: University of Texas Press, 1977.

———. *Television and the Crisis of Democracy*. Boulder, CO: Westview Press, 1990.

———. *The Persian Gulf TV War*. Boulder, CO: Westview Press, 1992.

———. *Media Culture*. London and New York: Routledge, 1995.

———. "Intellectuals, the New Public Spheres, and Technopolitics," *New Political Science* 41–42 (Fall 1997a): 169–188.

———. "Brecht's Marxist Aesthetic." Pp. 281–295 in Siegfried Mews, ed., *A Bertolt Brecht Reference Companion*. Westport, CT: Greenwood, 1997b.

———. "Multiple Literacies and Critical Pedagogy in a Multicultural Society." *Educational Theory* 48, no. 1 (1998): 103–122.

———. *Grand Theft 2000*. Lanham, MD: Rowman and Littlefield, 2001.

———. "Technological Revolution, Multiple Literacies, and the Restructuring of Education." Pp. 154–169 in Ilana Snyder, ed., *Silicon Literacies*. New York: Routledge, 2002.

———. *Media Spectacle*. London and New York: Routledge, 2003a.

———. *From 9/11 to Terror War: Dangers of the Bush Legacy*. Lanham, MD: Rowman and Littlefield, 2003b.

———. "Toward a Critical Theory of Education," *Democracy and Nature* 9, no. 1 (March 2003c): 51–64.

———. "Technological Transformation, Multiple Literacies, and the Re-Visioning of Education," *E-Learning* 1, no. 1 (2004): 9–37.

———. *Media Spectacle and the Crisis of Democracy*. Boulder, CO: Paradigm Publishers, 2005.

———. "The Katrina Hurricane Spectacle and the Crisis of the Bush Presidency," *Cultural Studies/Critical Methodologies* 7, no. 2 (May 2007): 222–234.

Kellner, Douglas, Daniel Cho, Tyson Lewis, and Clayton Pierce, eds., *Marcuse's Challenge to Education*. Lanham, MD: Rowman and Littlefield, forthcoming.

Kellner, Douglas, and Jeff Share. "Critical Media Literacy, Democracy, and the Reconstruction of Education." Pp. 3–23 in Donald Macedo and Shirley R. Steinberg, eds., *Media Literacy: A Reader*. New York: Peter Lang, 2007.

Kellner, Douglas, and Michael Ryan. *Camera Politicas: The Politics and Ideologies of Contemporary Hollywood Film*. Bloomington: Indiana University Press, 1988.

Kimmel, Michael. *Manhood in America*. New York: Free Press, 1996.

Klein, Jessie, and Lynn S. Chancer. "Masculinity Matters: The Omission of Gender from High-Profile School Violence Cases." Pp. 129–175 in Stephanie Urso Spina, ed., *Smoke and Mirrors: The Hidden Context of Violence in Schools and Society*. Lanham, MD: Rowman and Littlefield, 2000.

Larkin, Ralph W. *Comprehending Columbine*. Philadelphia: Temple University Press, 2007.

Larson, Ralph and S. Verma. "How Children and Adolescents Spend Time across Cultural Settings of the World: Work Play and Developmental Opportunities," *Psychological Bulletin* 125 (1999): 701–736.

Larson, Ralph, M. H. Richards, et al. "How Urban African American Young Adolescents Spend Their Time: Time Budgets for Locations, Activities, and Companionship," *American Journal of Community Psychology* 29, no. 4 (2001): 565–597.

Lewis, Tyson. *Discipline, Sovereignty, Education: A Genealogy of Bioschooling*. Ph.D. diss., UCLA, Graduate School of Education and Information Studies, 2006.

Lieberman, Joseph. *The Shooting Game: The Making of School Shooters*. Santa Ana, CA: Seven Locks Press, 2006.

Luke, Allan, and Carmen Luke. "Adolescence Lost/Childhood Regained: On Early

Intervention and the Emergence of the Techno-Subject." *Journal of Early Childhood Literacy* 1, no. 1 (2002): 91–120.

Lyons, Gene, and Joe Conason. *The Hunting of the President: The Ten-Year Campaign to Destroy Bill and Hillary Clinton.* New York: St. Martin's, 2001.

Males, Mike. *The Scapegoat Generation.* Boston: Common Courage Press, 1996.

———. Framing Youth: Ten Myths about the Next Generation. Boston: Common Courage Press, 1999.

Marcuse, Herbert. *One-Dimensional Man.* Boston: Beacon Press, 1964.

———. *An Essay on Liberation.* Boston: Beacon Press, 1969.

———. *Toward a Critical Theory of Society: Collected Papers of Herbert Marcuse,* vol. 2. Douglas Kellner, ed. New York: Routledge, 2001.

———. *Art and Liberation: Collected Papers of Herbert Marcuse,* vol. 4. Douglas Kellner, ed. New York: Routledge, 2006.

McLaren, Peter. *Critical Pedagogy and Predatory Culture.* London and New York: Routledge, 1995.

McLuhan, Marshall. *Understanding Media: The Extensions of Man.* New York: Signet Books, 1964.

McRobbie, Angela. *Gender, Culture, and Social Change: The Post-Feminist Masquerade.* London: Sage, 2007.

Messerschmidt, James W. *Masculinities and Crime.* Lanham, MD: Rowman and Littlefield, 1993.

Michel, Lou, and Dan Herbeck. *American Terrorist: Timothy McVeigh and the Oklahoma City Bombing.* New York: Regan Books, 2001.

Miller, Toby. "Children and the Media: Alternative Histories." In Rhonda Hammer and Douglas Kellner, eds., *The Media/Cultural Studies Reader.* New York: Peter Lang (forthcoming).

Nelson, Rob, and Jon Cowan. *Revolution X: A Survival Guide for Our Generation.* New York: Penguin Books, 1994.

Newman, Katherine S., Cybelle Fox, David J. Harding, Jal Mehta, and Wendy Roth. *Rampage: The Social Roots of School Shooting.* New York: Basic Books, 2004.

Nicoletti, John, Sally Spencer-Thomas, and Christopher Bollinger. *Violence Goes to College: The Authoritative Guide to Prevention and Intervention.* Springfield, IL: C. C. Thomas, 2001.

Phelps, Christopher. "The New SDS," *Nation,* April 16, 2007, http://www.thenation.com/doc/20070416/phelps.

Pierce, William. *The Turner Diaries.* Hillsboro, WV: National Vanguard Books, 1978.

Pinker, Steven. *How the Mind Works.* New York: Norton, 1997.

Pynchon, Thomas. *Gravity's Rainbow.* New York: Viking, 1973 [1967].

Razzano, Kathalene A., Loubna H. Skalli, and Christine M. Quail, "The Spectacle of Reform: Vulture Culture, Youth, and Television." In Rhonda Hammer and Douglas Kellner, eds., *The Media/Cultural Studies Reader.* New York: Peter Lang (forthcoming).

Reavis, Dick J. *The Ashes of Waco: An Investigation.* Syracuse, NY: Syracuse University Press, 1998.

Reich, Charles A. *The Greening of America.* New York: Random House, 1970.

Report of the Review Panel, *Mass Shootings at Virginia Tech,* http://www.washingtonpost.com/wp-srv/metro/documents/vatechreport.pdf?hpid=topnews (accessed April 16, 2007).

Rhodes, Richard. *Why They Kill: The Discoveries of a Maverick Criminologist.* New York: Vintage, 1999.

Rios, Victor. "The Hypercriminalization of Black and Latino Male Youth in the Era of Mass Incarceration." In Manning Marable, Keesha Middlemass, and Ian Steinberg, eds., *Racializing Justice, Disenfranchising Lives.* New York: Palgrave Macmillan, 2007, pp 17–32.

Ritzer, George. *The McDonaldization of Society.* Thousands Oaks, CA: Pine Forge Press, 1993, 1996.

Robinson, John P. "Television and Leisure Time: Yesterday, Today, and (Maybe) Tomorrow," *Public Opinion Quarterly* 33 (1992): 210–222.

Robinson, John P., Geoffrey Godbey, and Robert Putnam. *Time for Life: The Surprising Ways Americans Use Their Time.* University Park: Pennsylvania State University Press, 1997.

Robinson, John P., Meyer Kestnbaum, Alan Neustadtl, and Anthony Alvarez. *Information Technologies, the Internet, and Time Displacement,* http://www.stanford.edu/group/siqss/itandsociety/v01i02/v01i02a02.pdf (accessed September 26, 2007).

Rogin, Michael. *Ronald Reagan, the Movie.* Berkeley: University of California Press, 1987.

Roszak, Theodore. *The Making of a Counter Culture.* New York: Doubleday, 1968.

Sales, Kirkpatrick. *Rebels against the Future: The Luddites and Their War on the Industrial Revolution—Lessons for the Computer Age.* Boston: Addison Wesley, 1995.

Savage, Jon. *Teenage: The Creation of Youth Culture.* New York: Viking, 2007.

Spence, Gerry. *From Freedom to Slavery.* New York: St. Martin's, 1995.

Spina, Stephanie Urso, ed. *Smoke and Mirrors: The Hidden Context of Violence in Schools and Society.* Lanham, MD: Rowman and Littlefield, 2000.

Stickney, Brandon M. *"All-American Monster": The Unauthorized Biography of Timothy McVeigh.* Amherst, NY: Prometheus Books, 1996.

Turkle, Sherry. *Life on the Screen: Identity in the Age of the Internet.* New York: Simon and Schuster, 1995.

Van Heertum, Richard. *The Fate of Democracy in a Cynical Age: Education, Media, and the Evolving Public Sphere.* Unpublished Ph.D diss., University of California Los Angeles, 2007.

Walter, Jess. Ruby Ridge: *The Truth and Tragedy of the Randy Weaver Family.* New York: Regan Books, 1995.

Watson, James L., ed. *Golden Arches East: McDonald's in East Asia.* Palo Alto, CA: Stanford University Press, 1997.

Wiener, Jon. *Historians in Trouble: Plagiarism, Fraud, and Politics in the Ivory Tower.* New York: New Press, 2005.

Index

Abandoned Generation, The
  (Giroux), 80, 81
Abolition democracy, 164–165, 169
Abolitions, time of, 167–171
Abu Ghraib, 87, 135, 165, 166
Achilles in Vietnam (Shay), 17
Advertising, 3, 5, 10, 77;
  false, 9; youth in, 80
Affirmative action, 92, 93, 112
Afghanistan War: societal violence
  and, 15; trauma from, 17
African Americans: firearm homicides
  and, 77; media representation
  of, 77; in prison, 168, 169;
  spectacles featuring, 78
Age of Affluence, 68
Alcohol, 61, 76, 77
Alfred P. Murrah Federal Building,
  bombing of, 97, 98, 102, 103, 105
Al-Qaeda, terror events by, 37
American Airlines, bombing of, 114
American Federation of Teachers, 153–154
"American Prison Nightmare,
  The" (DeParle), 169
American Revolution, 128;
  gun culture and, 12
"America's Tragedy: Its Politicians Are
  Still Running Away from the Debate
  about Guns" (*Economist*), 53, 56
Amok, behavior/symptoms of, 13–14, 17
Amok (Zweig), 13
Anarchism, 96, 115
Anticommunism, 94, 95
Antiglobalization movement, 9, 65, 161

Antistatism, 95, 106, 107
Antiviolence programs, 151, 152
Antiwar movement, 65, 71,
  161, 171; spectacle of, 6
*Armed America: The Story of How and
  Why Guns Became as American
  as Apple Pie* (Cramer), 12
*Arming America: The Origins of a
  National Gun Culture* (Bellesiles), 11
Aryan Youth, 100
Asian Americans, stereotype about, 36
Asian extreme films, 40, 41
Asian Tsunami, as spectacle, 6
Assassins, 15, 105
Assault weapons, ban on, 105, 125, 141
Assimilation, 11, 133
ATF. *See* Bureau of Alcohol, Tobacco,
  Firearms, and Explosives
Athens, Lonnie, 15, 121, 148; rampages/
  mass murder and, 26; theories of,
  16, 18; violentization and, 147
Atlanta Olympic Games: disrupting,
  96, 109; as media event, 4
Atrocities, documentation of, 165, 166
Awful Truth, The (film), 126

Baby Boomers, 61, 64, 68, 76; government
  services and, 71; retirement of, 70
Background checks, 44, 141, 144, 153
Bad Guy, 127
Battan, Kate, 120, 123–124
Beatles, The, 126, 128
Bell Curve, The (Herrnstein and
  Murray): stigmatization in, 78

Bellesiles, Michael A.: gun
culture and, 11, 12–13
Bernall, Cassie: martyrdom of, 120
*Beyond the Spectacle of
Terrorism* (Giroux), 27
Bin Laden, Osama, 128; celebrity for, 103;
terrorist ethos of, 135; vision of, 57–58
BitTorrent, 72, 73
Blogs, 1, 42, 47, 125; conservative/
right-wing, 35
Boggs, Carl: on antipolitics, 95;
Hollywood films and, 27;
on militarism, 26, 27
Bombings, 110, 144; terrorist, 95–100,
113. *See also* Oklahoma City bombing
Bowling for Columbine (film), 29, 48;
Academy Award for, 126, 131; analysis
of, 90; controversy about, 126; gun
culture and, 130; guns/violence and,
127–128; media/racism and, 129
Boyz N the Hood (film), 78
Brady Campaign to Prevent Gun
Violence, 44, 50, 105, 143, 145
Branch Davidian Church, 97, 102;
obsessions of, 110; siege against, 101
Brecht, Bertolt, 74, 169
Bremer, Arthur, 15, 105
Brutalization, 16, 165, 170
Bullying, 20, 22, 28, 37, 119, 121, 151;
confronting, 147, 148, 150, 156;
culture of, 120, 157; violence and,
155; zero tolerance for, 150
Bundy, Ted, 15
Bureau of Alcohol, Tobacco,
Firearms, and Explosives (ATF),
95; Operation Prevail and, 135
Bush, George H. W., 92; conservative
reaction by, 68; external enemy
and, 106; federal deficit and, 70;
terrorism/drugs and, 167
Bush, George W., 1, 104; approval ratings
of, 2; Cho and, 57, 58; convocation
and, 38, 39; federal deficit and, 70;
gun laws and, 57; Iraq War and,
37, 38, 57, 69; mental health issues

and, 54, 58; right-wing extremists
and, 109; scandals for, 38; terrorism
and, 135, 167; vision of, 57–58
Bush-Cheney administration,
15, 30, 31, 51, 68, 70, 72, 73,
75, 172, 182, 183, 186, 188

Cable television, 1, 15, 89
California Forestry Association,
bombing of, 113, 114
Capitalism, 77; global, 8, 63, 93; techno-, 4
Capitalist restructuring, 67, 92, 107–108
Capital punishment, 55, 139, 171
Carneal, Michael, 20–21, 22
Caught in the Crossfire (Grossberg), 82
CBS, 58, 73, 166; Imus and, 112
Celebrity, 1, 15, 89, 103–104, 127, 137;
culture of, 139; desire for, 124; sports
and, 155; ultramasculinist, 118
Centreville High School, Cho at, 136
Centuries of Childhood (Aries), 63
Channel Surfing (Giroux), 79
Cheney, Dick, 104; Libby and,
2; terrorist ethos of, 135
Child abuse, 61, 147
Childhood: celebrated, 64; conception
of, 63; paradoxes of, 83–84
Children: disenfranchisement of, 84–85;
at risk, 148; violence against, 86
*Children's Report for the 2000
Campaign to Stamp Out Torture*
(Amnesty International), 86
Child-safety locks, 141, 153
Cho, David: on Seung-Hui Cho, 133
Cho, Seung-Hui: atypicalness of, 69;
bullying of, 37; Bush and, 57, 58, 135;
confronting, 45; domestic terrorism
and, 42, 59; guns/ammunition for,
50, 53–54, 142; harassment by, 133;
influences on, 158; isolation of, 133,
134; Korean/American borderline
and, 131–137; media culture and,
49, 87, 124; media spectacle and,
39–40, 42–43, 124; mental health
issues for, 31, 47–48, 51, 54, 135, 136,

143, 144, 145; multimedia dossier of, 38–43, 48, 53; profile of, 36, 39; quote of, 38, 131; rampage by, 29, 40, 53; representation of, 36–37; revenge fantasy of, 42; societal violence and, 30; testimony of, 42, 47; videography by, 43; violent masculinity and, 40, 132; writing of, 21, 37, 52, 55, 134

Christ, Jesus, 38, 41, 153

Christian right: Columbine shootings and, 122; *Left Behind* film series and; school prayer and, 122

Chronicle of Higher Education, 31, 142

Civil War, 13, 128

Class, 91, 160, 162; challenges to, 92; domination/enforcing, 164; representations of, 158; revenge, 42; social construction of, 18; terror and, 90; violence and, 19, 29; youth and, 63

Clinton, Bill: demonization of, 109; Kosovo and, 128; scandals of, 1, 6, 7, 38; terrorism/drugs and, 167

Clinton, Hillary Rodham, 109

Clockers (film), 78

CNN, 42, 54, 55, 133; Oklahoma City bombing and, 102; school shootings and, 19

Columbine shootings, 19, 20, 29, 31, 37, 42, 43, 71, 74, 87; aftermath of, 158; bullying and, 147; causes of, 46, 61, 151; Cho and, 39; culture of liberalism and, 54; as fund-raising device, 125; gun control and, 141; as media spectacle, 28, 104, 119–126; middle-class white male and, 118–119; multicausal/multiperspectivist interpretations of, 48, 90; reductive explanations for, 129, 131; scandals of, 53; violent masculinity and, 157; youth culture and, 129

Commission on the Virginia Tech Shooting, 56

Communication, 94, 111, 139

Comprehending Columbine (Larkin), 151

Computer literacy, 160, 161, 163

Computers, 75, 108; youth and, 62, 161

Conflict resolution, 30, 148, 151, 152

Conservatism, 71, 80

Consumer culture, 6, 65, 66, 68, 74, 77; sexuality and, 133

Copycats, 53–59

Corporal punishment, 147, 148

Countdown!, 58

Counterculture, 64, 71, 74, 92, 115; refuge in, 76; technologies and, 116

Covenant, the Sword, and the Arm of the Lord, raid against, 96

Crime, 76; addressing, 139; social construction of, 18; violent, 77, 80, 131, 140; youth and, 63

Crime and Punishment (Weston), 169

Critical theory, 8, 29, 62, 63; spectacle and, 9–14

Cullen, Dave, 120; Battan and, 123–124; on lawsuits, 124–125

Cultural studies, 29; as diagnostic critique, 8; spectacle and, 9–14

Culture, 74; alternative, 161; contemporary, 162

Culture of Fear, The (Glassner), 129

Culture wars, 6, 75, 113

Cyberspace, 61, 62, 72, 110

Davids, Chris: on Cho, 36–37

Davis, Angela, 83; on abolitions, 167; Mendietta and, 164, 165, 167; prison-industrial-complex and, 86–87, 164, 165, 169; war on youth and, 76

Death penalty, 164; abolition of, 167; youth and, 85, 86

Debord, Guy: spectacle and, 3, 4–5, 6, 7–9, 27

Deindustrialization, 107, 108

Delaware State University, shootings at, 144

DeLay, Tom, 2; Columbine shootings and, 122; on guns/juvenile violence, 43; Virginia Tech shootings and, 46

Democracy: abolition, 164–165, 169; challenging, 96; education and, 162;

future of, 161; multicultural, 162; revitalizing, 82; social justice and, 167
Democratization, 159–164
Dewey, John, 149, 159, 162, 163
Domestic terrorism, 38, 42, 46, 62, 75, 90, 112, 137, 146, 170; homegrown, 59, 100–106; key elements of, 28; male rage and, 19, 121; media and, 15, 24; military culture and, 30; multicausal/multifactor analysis of, 28; perpetrators of, 3; problem of, 31; rise of, 26, 139; school shootings and, 30; spectacle of, 28; Virginia Tech shootings and, 132
Doom (game), 121, 123
Dot-com boom/bust, 68, 69, 70, 71
Drug abuse, 61, 66, 76, 77, 167, 168
Duck Amuck (film), 13

Economic decline, 92, 93, 109
Economic growth, 64, 68
Education, 168; conservative modes of, 149; democratization of, 162, 163; environmental, 161; funding for, 163–164; mental health issues and, 154; public health and, 149; reconstructing, 82, 139, 146, 149, 152, 159–164, 169; test-oriented, 159, 160
End of Politics, The (Boggs), 95
Extreme fighting, 155
Extreme right, 95–100, 101, 103, 104, 109; capitalist restructuring and, 107–108; financing, 106; hatred by, 98; hysteria of, 107; iconography of, 102; ideologies of, 112; Internet and, 110; noise-machine of, 28; positions/ tactics of, 96; talk radio and, 111
Extremism, 91, 107; culture of, 113
Extremist movements, 92, 94, 100; affiliation of, 112; dangers of, 109; demonization of, 95; recruitment by, 110; rise of, 93

Facebook, 1, 4, 34, 43, 65, 66, 73, 89, 134
Fahrenheit 911 (film), 126, 128

Falling Down (film), 112
Farrakhan, Louis, 93
FBI, 51, 95, 98; Kaczynski and, 113, 114, 117; Operation Prevail and, 135; profiling and, 85; report by, 140; siege by, 96, 101
Fort Dix, plot against, 93
Fox News, 36, 46–47, 55, 126
Framing Youth: Ten Myths about the Next Generation (Males), 76
Frankfurt School, 5, 7–8
Freedom of speech, 2, 85, 97, 110
Freemen, 96, 106
Freire, Paulo, 149, 159, 162, 163
Fugitive Cultures (Giroux), 77
Fundamentalism, 82, 94, 100, 101

Games. *See* Video games
Gang culture, 154
Gender, 162; challenges to, 92; deconstruction of, 157; differences, 62; ideals, 62; reconstruction of, 83; representations of, 158; social construction of, 18, 153; violence and, 19; youth and, 63
Generation X, 65, 67, 68
G.I. generation, 69
Gingrich, Newt: culture of liberalism and, 54; liberal elite and, 123
Giroux, Henry, 83; on Dole, 78; images of youth and, 79; on Islamist radicals, 28; media culture and, 79; on militarism, 27; on minorities/military service, 81; pedagogies and, 80; on racist stereotyping, 78; right-wing moral panic and, 79; on scapegoating youth, 77; war on youth and, 76
Glen Beck Show, 54
Global capitalism, 8, 63, 93
Global economy, 68, 161
Globalization, 7, 10, 69, 95
Global warming, 69, 73, 161
Going Postal: Rage, Murder, Rebellion— From Reagan's Workplaces to Clinton's Columbine and Beyond (Ames), 146
Golden, Andrew, 21, 22

Golden Arches East (Watson), 9

Gonzalez, Alberto, 38, 39; spectacle of, 2

Gore, Al, 1, 141

Grand Theft 2000: Media Spectacle and a Stolen Election (Kellner), 1, 10

Gravity's Rainbow (Pynchon), 100

Grossberg, Lawrence, 10; on paradoxes of childhood, 83–84; on social order/ youth, 76; war on youth and, 76, 82

Guantánamo, 87, 165

Gulf War, 7, 35; censoring, 166; as media spectacle, 4; new world order and, 106

Gun control, 2; avoiding, 55, 56; Columbine shootings and, 141; debate over, 44, 54, 145; expiration of, 141; militias and, 12; reasonable, 153; support for, 20, 148; workplace/ school security and, 147

Gun control laws, 2, 25, 31, 39, 131, 142, 146–154; deregulation of, 126; opposition to, 56–57, 78, 103, 143; rational, 139, 171; reforming, 43, 125, 146

Gun culture, 11, 18, 49, 56, 57, 87, 104–105, 106, 110, 130, 132, 136, 137, 154; confronting, 82, 153, 157; focus on, 30, 58; history of, 12–13; hypermasculinity and, 75; male rage and, 118, 121; male socialization and, 120; manhood and, 97; out-of-control, 13, 14, 24; popular culture and, 129; prevalence of, 139; right-wing, 90; September 11th and, 30; social construction of, 121; ultramasculinist, 49; violence and, 26, 155

Gun deaths, number of, 53

Gun-free zones, 54, 55

Gun lobby, 54, 56, 153; challenging, 141

Gun ownership, 106, 110; federal government and, 13; mental health issues and, 144; stricter criteria for, 125, 141, 153

Gun Owners of America, 44, 50

Guns: access to, 125; ban on, 142, 145; illegal, 141; increase in, 140;

juvenile violence and, 43; male socialization and, 25; political scapegoating and, 43–50; proliferation of, 30; violence and, 12–13, 14–19, 126–131; youth and, 119

Gun show loophole, closing, 125, 141, 143, 153

Haditha massacres, videotape of, 166

"Happiness Is a Warm Gun" (Beatles), 126, 128

Harassment, 20, 133

Harlem Diary (film), 79

Harris, Eric: basement tapes of, 125; bullying of, 121; guns for, 141; Internet and, 119; marginalization of, 155; media and, 87, 124; psychiatric disorder of, 121; rampage by, 37, 118–119, 120; rumors about, 120; suicide by, 125; video by, 123–124; writing of, 123, 124

Hate.com: Extremists on the Internet, 110

Hate groups, 92, 93, 109, 110

Headliners and Legends (MSNBC), McVeigh and, 104

Health care issues, 73, 108, 136, 169. *See also* Mental health issues

Heath High School, shooting at, 20–21

Heston, Charlton, 127, 130, 153

Heteronormativity, 133

Hinckley, John, 105

Hip-hop culture, 77, 78

"History of the United States" (cartoon), 128

Hitler, Adolf, 111

Hollywood, 41, 129; Columbine shootings and, 123; militarism and, 27; people of color and, 78

Hollywood War Machine, The (Boggs and Pollard), 27

Holtz: on contemporary youth/ future, 70; on Free Generation, 67–68; post-Boomers and, 71

Homophobia, 72, 75, 112, 132, 160; confronting, 49, 156

How the Mind Works (Pinker), 13–14
How Would a Patriot Act? Defending American Values from a President Run Amok (Greenwald), 13
Human rights, 155, 161, 164
Hurricane Katrina, as spectacle, 6
Hussein, Saddam, 106
Hypermasculinity, 20, 58, 97, 105, 121, 137, 168, 170; confronting, 156; culture of, 156; gun culture and, 75; problems with, 153; promoting, 27; societal violence and, 24; sports culture and, 156; violence and, 91, 121
Hyperreality, 62, 63

Identities, 72, 74, 103; alternative, 89; celebrity, 118; collective, 71; constructing, 65, 89, 118, 120; empowering, 107; fantasy, 112; media, 90; national, 27, 95; newfound, 92; political, 93; secure, 91; shared, 91; social, 114; violent, 16; youth and, 63. *See also* Male identities
Identity politics, 92, 95, 107, 110, 117; media and, 114. *See also* White male identity politics
Ideological manipulation, 53–59
Illich, Ivan, 159, 162, 163
Immigration, 74, 108, 110; laws, 36; poll on, 73
Imperial Delusions (Boggs), 26
Imus, Don, 2, 111, 112
In the King of Prussia (film), 126
Industrial-technological civilization, 115
Information, 30, 72; sharing, 153, 144
Internet, 1, 3, 10, 30, 66, 67, 73, 123, 129; boom, 68; Cho on, 37; culture, 75; digital images on, 166; gun culture and, 49; influence of, 119; right-wing sites on, 43, 110; using, 160, 161; white male rage and, 112
Iran-Contra affair, 71
Iraq War, 38, 39, 55, 69, 170; digital age and, 166; orchestrating, 37; repoliticization of youth and, 73;

societal violence and, 15; spectacle of, 2, 4, 7, 9; trauma from, 17
Ismail Ax, 40–41, 47, 135

JFK airport, plot against, 93
Job-training centers, 168, 169
Johnson, Mitchell, 21, 22
Jordan, Michael, 10; spectacle of, 6, 8
Juice (film), 78
Juvenile delinquency, 75

Kaczynski, David, 117
Kaczynski, Theodore (Unabomber), 29, 42, 110, 132, 136; fascination with, 118; McVeigh and, 118; male rage and, 117; media culture and, 87, 117–118; media identity of, 90; Oklahoma City bombing and, 114, 118; politics of terror and, 113–118; spectacles of, 28, 114; technologies and, 115, 116, 117–118; white male identity politics and, 114, 116
Kaine, Timothy M.: convocation and, 39, 43; mental health issues and, 142, 143; Virginia Tech shootings and, 31, 49, 55, 143
Katz, Jackson, 83, 84, 154; on male socialization, 83; media event and, 4; MVP and, 156–157; on tough guise, 15; on violent masculinity, 19, 24
Kennedy, John F., 4, 56, 105
Kevorkian, Jack, 124
Kids (film), 80
Killer, The (film), 40
King, Martin Luther, Jr., 153
Kinkel, Kip, 14, 24, 25
Klebold, Dylan: basement tapes of, 125; bullying of, 121; guns for, 141; Internet and, 119; marginalization of, 155; media culture and, 87, 124; rampage by, 37, 118–119, 120; rumors about, 120; suicide by, 125; video by, 123–124; writings of, 124
Koresh, David, 97
Ku Klux Klan, 100, 110, 165

Larkin, Ralph: antiviolence programs and, 152; on conflict resolution, 151; on Harris/Klebold, 121; on school culture, 152; on sports culture, 155, 156

Left Behind (LaHaye and Jenkins), 98

Left Behind: The Movie (film), 98

Left Behind 2: Tribulation Force (film), 98, 99

Left Behind 3: World at War (film), 98, 99

Libby, Scooter, 2

Liberalism, 64, 82; youth killings and, 148

Lieberman, Joseph: on Columbine shootings, 123, 129; on Kinkel rampage, 24; on reporting threats, 151; on school shootings, 24, 25, 140

Limbaugh, Rush, 99, 111; on Virginia Tech shootings, 46

Literacy, 159–164; computer, 62, 160, 161, 163; economic/financial, 163; media, 10, 62, 153, 158, 160, 161, 163; print, 62, 160, 161, 163; techno-, 162, 163

Los Angeles Times, 53; males in, 153–154; on television/violence, 158

Lucas, Henry Lee, 15

Lynching, 164, 165

Macho Paradox, The (Katz), 19

Male identities, 154; asserting, 121; constructing, 89, 90, 132; normative, 132, 133; terror and, 90; ultraviolent, 133

Male rage, 17–18, 19, 33, 105, 110, 120, 137; domestic terrorism and, 121; expressing, 118, 153; gun culture and, 121; school shootings and, 121; Unabomber and, 117; white, 112. *See also* Rage

Male socialization, 154, 163; guns and, 25, 120; macho notion of, 83; problematic, 26

Male violence, culture of, 154–159

Males, Mike: images of youth and, 79; on mental health issues, 153–154; on violent crime, 77; war on youth and, 76

Manhood: gun culture and, 97; macho notion of, 83; violence and, 23; weapons and, 103

Manson, Charles, 15

Manson, Marilyn, 48, 119, 123, 129

Marcuse, Herbert, 115, 158, 159, 162, 168

Masculinities and Crime (Messerschmidt), 18

Masculinity, 131; aggressive, 134; alternative, 19, 146, 154; constructions of, 26; crisis of, 14, 19, 25, 59, 62, 87, 90, 97, 105, 118, 137, 146, 163, 170; femininity and, 157; hegemonic, 20, 83, 146; hyperviolent, 19; media and, 18; pressures of, 29; reconstruction of, 82, 139, 146, 154, 171; reductionist notions of, 150; social construction of, 3, 121; subordinate, 20; violent, 14, 18, 19, 23, 24, 26–27, 40, 124, 132, 136, 157, 160, 164

Mass culture, 64, 66, 148

Mass murders, 15, 19, 22, 26

McCarthy, Carolyn, 44, 54

McDonaldization of Society, The (Ritzer), 8–9

McDonald's, 10; anti-corporate globalization movement and, 9; consumption/consumer society and, 8; Greenpeace and, 9; spectacle of, 4, 6, 8–9

McLuhan, Marshall, 111, 159

McVeigh, Timothy, 29, 35, 42, 46, 89, 116, 128, 136; arrest of, 102; assault weapons ban and, 105; celebrity for, 103–104; Gulf War and, 103, 105; gun culture and, 102–103, 104–105; influence of, 124; influences on, 98; Kaczynski and, 118; media culture and, 87, 104; media event and, 37, 105–106; militia movement and, 132; obsession of, 25, 113; terrorism by, 100–106; violent masculinity of, 157; Waco and, 101

Media, 3, 26, 49; celebrity murderers and, 15; consumption, 72; corporate, 2, 56, 111, 146, 166; critical, 160;

demonization of, 53, 55, 158; digital, 1, 162, 166; domestic terrorism and, 15, 24; identity politics and, 114; inspiration from, 42; manipulation of, 158; masculinity and, 18; people of color and, 78; postmodern, 65; processing by, 1; proliferation of, 159; racism and, 129; ratings, 42; role of, 34–35; scapegoating of, 158; school shootings and, 24, 123; violence and, 24, 118, 132, 155, 157; youth and, 67, 81, 158

Media culture, 8, 18, 23, 26–27, 66, 67, 74, 75, 77, 80, 97, 136, 159; commercialized, 5; critique of, 79; demonizing, 158; fantasy world and, 104; as pedagogy, 79; people of color and, 78; proliferation of, 158; scapegoating, 157; sexuality and, 133; spectacles of, 4–5; stereotypes by, 34; violence and, 87, 110, 139, 157, 163; youth and, 62, 81, 161

Media Culture (Kellner), 10

Media events, 6; disrupting events and, 4; technologically constructed, 3

Media literacy, 10, 153, 163; expansion of, 160; youth and, 158

Media Spectacle and the Crisis of Democracy (Kellner), 8, 10

Menace II Society (film), 78

Mental health care, 146–154, 163; funding for, 154; improving, 82, 145, 146, 153, 171; profiling, 146

Mental health issues, 3, 18, 25, 31, 33, 39, 47–48, 50, 51, 54, 135, 136, 139, 143, 146–147, 149, 150; confronting, 153–154; gun purchases and, 144; higher education and, 154; scrutiny of, 144; Virginia Tech shootings and, 58

Mentors in Violence Prevention (MVP), 156–157

Militarism, 163; confronting, 82, 169, 171; domestic, 80; escalating, 15, 26, 77; Hollywood films and, 27; horrors of, 85; internal, 81; patriarchy and,

27; patriotism and, 26; prevalence of, 139; societal violence and, 27, 170; spectacle of, 27; sports culture and, 156; university and, 27

Military: intervention, 30; national identity and, 27; poverty and, 167; reconstructing, 168–169; socialization, 28; training, 17, 103, 105; values, 26; violence and, 155; working class/youth of color and, 81

Military culture, 26, 27, 152, 154, 157, 164, 170; domestic terrorism and, 30; school shootings and, 30

Military-industrial complex, 26, 27, 169; prison-industrial complex and, 165, 167

Militias, 26, 92, 95–100, 107; dangers of, 109; gun rights and, 12; joining, 93; McVeigh and, 132; right-wing extremist, 89, 94; rise of, 93, 95; well-regulated, 11, 12

Million Man March, 93

Million Mom March, 141

Minnesota bridge collapse, spectacle of, 6, 7

Minorities, 78, 90, 93, 116; hatred of, 98, 108; power of, 93

Minutemen, 110

Misogynist attitudes, 75, 132

Missing, Runaway, and Exploited Children's Act, 20

Moby Dick (Melville), 41, 47

Modernity, attacking, 94, 115

Moore, Michael, 29, 48; analysis of, 90; celebrity of, 127; Clark and, 129–130; Columbine shootings and, 126–131; criticism of, 131; films by, 126; Mauser and, 130; militarism and, 126

Mourning, 53–59

Mr. Brownstone (Cho), 134

MSNBC, 42, 43, 58, 103, 120, 123; Imus and, 112

MTV, 65, 71, 73

Multicausal/multiperspectival model, 28, 48, 82, 87, 90, 131, 137, 139

Multiculturalism, 62, 92, 93
Multimedia culture, 4, 62–63, 161, 162
Murder rates, historical, 16
Muslim male identity politics, 94
MVP. See Mentors in Violence Prevention
My Lai massacre, 17
MySpace, 1, 4, 30, 34, 43, 65, 72, 73, 87

National Center for Health Statistics,
    on firearm deaths, 77
National Instant Criminal
    Background Check, 144
National Rifle Association (NRA), 54,
    56, 78, 126, 127, 144; criticism of, 20
National School Safety Center, 24
NBC, 42, 126, 140; Cho dossier
    and, 39–40, 41
Neoliberalism, 73, 77, 79, 81, 82
Neo-Nazis, 93, 97, 100, 101, 112
Newman, Kathleen, 20, 149; mental
    health model and, 150; on school
    shootings/conditions, 22–23
News: tabloidization of, 30;
    violence on, 129
"New SDS, The" (Phelps), 73
New world order, 94, 106
New York Times, 114, 132; on Cho, 50,
    53–54; on gun control, 141; poll by,
    73; Unabomber letter to, 114; on
    Virginia Tech massacre, 29–30
Nichols, Terry, 128; arrest of, 102; assault
    weapons ban and, 105; Gulf War
    and, 103; gun culture and, 102–103,
    104–105; media culture and, 87, 104
Nickel Mines, Pennsylvania:
    shooting in, 53, 140
Nike, spectacle of, 4, 6, 8, 10
9/11 terror attacks, 2, 6, 7, 10, 30,
    42, 68, 71, 81, 172, 188, 189
9/11 to Terror War (Kellner), 10
No Child Left Behind act, 85, 159–160
Nonviolence, 152, 155
Norris Hall, 34, 42, 45, 52, 53, 144
Northwestern University, bombing of, 114
NRA. See National Rifle Association

Obama, Barack, 109
Oklahoma City bombing, 26, 59, 82, 89,
    100–106, 109, 128, 137; Clinton and, 38;
    influence of, 124; Kaczynski and, 114,
    118; media culture and, 87; spectacle
    of, 28, 37; speculation about, 35
Olberman, Keith, 186
Oldboy (film), 40, 135
One-Dimensional Man (Marcuse), 115
Operation Prevail, 135
Order (neo-Nazi movement), 97
Oswald, Lee Harvey, 15, 105
"Other," the, 74, 90, 106, 165;
    war on terrorism and, 58

Paramilitary culture, 97, 105, 121
Paranoia, 107, 110, 111, 112, 117
Patriarchy, 18, 26, 91, 93; ilitarism and, 27
Patriot Act, 10
Patriot groups, 26, 110
Peace education programs, 151, 152, 153
Peace movement, 65, 161, 171
Peer-to-peer (P2P) sharing,
    66, 73, 152, 163
People for the American
    Way, 121, 122, 123
People of color: Hollywood films and,
    78; media culture and, 78; oppression
    of, 164; representation of, 79
Persian Gulf TV War, The (Kellner), 10
Point of Order (film), 126
Political correctness, 115, 116
Political culture, 68, 72, 92; challenging,
    82, 96; youth and, 161
Politics, 74, 164–165; alternative, 161;
    antipolitical, 96; extremist, 99;
    hate, 92; as media spectacle, 5;
    postmodern, 96, 111; terror and, 90
Popular culture, 26, 132; gun culture and,
    128; Virginia Tech shootings and, 55
Port Arthur, Tasmania: massacre at, 142
Post-Boomers, 65, 68; computers
    and, 73; contemporary youth
    and, 69–74; pessimism of, 70,
    71; television watching by, 72

Postmodern culture, 66, 68;
    youth culture and, 65
Postmodernism, 8, 63, 66, 99, 162
Postmodern Turn, The (Best
    and Kellner), 94
Posttraumatic stress disorder, 17
Poverty: childhood, 70; confronting, 169,
    170; growth of, 79, 86; military and,
    81, 167; violence and, 28, 78, 79, 155
Power, 62, 158
"Prairie, The" (Cooper), 41
Presley, Elvis: spectacle of, 6
Prison-industrial complex, 81, 82,
    86–87; economic forces behind,
    169; military-industrial complex
    and, 165, 167; rise of, 164, 165
Prisoners, 169; emasculation of, 165;
    interrogating, 166; number of in
    United States, 168; photos of, 165–166
Prisons, 164–165; abolition of, 167; abuse
    in, 28, 165; African Americans in,
    168, 169; embarrassment of, 168, 169;
    funding for, 164; reforming, 82, 139,
    171; secret, 165; survival in, 167–168;
    violence in, 146, 155, 167–168
Privacy, 58, 144, 146, 149
Profiling, 85, 146
Promise Keepers, 93
Public Spaces, Private Lives (Giroux), 80
Pulp Fiction, 100

Quake (game), 121, 123

Race, 162; hierarchies, 164; politics of,
    33–38; representations of, 158; social
    construction of, 18; terror and, 90;
    violence and, 19, 29; youth and, 63
Racism, 36, 72, 91, 94, 112, 116, 124,
    128, 160, 168; abolition of, 167;
    confronting, 149, 169; embracing, 96;
    media and, 129; speculation and, 35
Rage: culture of, 154–159; harvest
    of, 107–113; root causes of, 151;
    violent, 17. *See also* Male rage
Rambo (film), 10

Rampage (Newman), 20, 22, 23, 24, 149
Rap music, 77, 78
Reagan, Ronald, 10, 92, 105; conservative
    reaction by, 68; external enemy and,
    106; terrorism/drugs and, 167
Reason, 158
Red Dawn (film), 103
*Report of the Review Panel: Mass Shootings
    at Virginia Tech,* 49, 51, 52, 144; on
    Cho mental health problems, 135, 136
Report on School Associated Violent Deaths
    (National School Safety Center), 24
Representation, politics of, 160
Resistance, 66–67, 74
Rhodes, Richard, 15, 17, 63, 64, 121;
    child-rearing philosophies and, 148;
    discipline and, 147, 148; on killers,
    30; rampages/mass murder and, 26;
    on societal violence, 148; theories
    of, 16, 18; violentization and, 147
Richard McBeef (Cho), 134
Roger and Me (film), 126, 127
Ruby Ridge, 96, 101
Rush to Judgment (film), 126

Sanders, Dave: death of, 125
Scapegoat Generation, 65
*Scapegoat Generation: America's War
    on Adolescents, The* (Males), 77
Scapegoating, 79, 80, 81–82, 121, 123,
    130, 148, 158; political, 43–50
School culture, 150, 152
School prayer, 122, 123, 148
School reform, 148–149, 171
School security, 2–3, 25, 29, 33, 139,
    144, 146–154; debate over, 50–53;
    gun control and, 147; improving,
    50, 146; problems with, 148
School shooters, 3, 25, 62, 75, 105,
    136–137; male rage and, 19;
    societal violence and, 23
School shootings, 15, 119, 129, 131, 139,
    144, 170; aftermath of, 149; blame
    for, 148; conditions for, 22–23;
    confronting, 22, 151, 152, 171; drop

in, 140; epidemic of, 19–26; as
gender issue, 25; male rage and, 121;
media and, 15, 24; military culture
and, 30; multiple causes of, 28, 87,
137; number of, 140; plots for, 140;
problems with, 31, 151; right-wing
exploitation of, 28; social processes
and, 30; violent masculinity and, 157

School violence, 132, 147; conditions
for, 149; societal violence and,
19; socioeconomic factors in,
19; stopping, 148, 171

School vouchers, 122, 149

Schwarzenegger, Arnold, 78, 112

Second Amendment, 11,
103; context of, 12

Secret Agent, The (Conrad), 117

Secularism, 94, 96

Security issues, 59, 132

Semiautomatic weapons, ban on, 142

Separatist politics, 96, 97

September 11th, 26, 39, 42, 51, 69,
71, 99; backlash following, 36;
Bush exploitation of, 10; gun
culture and, 30; spectacle of,
2, 6, 7; youth incarcerations/
executions following, 80

Serial killers, 19, 105; media
and, 15; military training for,
27; obsession with, 15

Sexism, 72, 112, 156, 160; fighting, 149

Sexual abuse, 84, 86, 134, 168

Shock entertainment, 111

Shoels, Isaiah, 124

Shooting Game, The (Lieberman),
24, 140, 151

Silent Generation, 64, 69

Simpson, O. J., 1, 7, 8, 93

Sirhan, Sirhan, 15, 105

Slavery, 86, 90, 164, 167

Smoke and Mirrors (Spina), 19, 148

Social change, 30, 71, 96, 130, 159, 167, 171

Social conditions, 18, 33, 69, 79, 152;
abolition of, 167; improving, 171

Social environment, 68, 72

Socialization, 28; processes, 62; terror
and, 90. *See also* Male socialization

Social justice, 149, 155, 162, 167

Social life, 5, 147

Social order, 76, 116

Social problems, 29, 38, 77, 153;
investigating, 126, 139

Social reconstruction, 83, 167

Social relations, 147, 159

Societal violence, 6, 113, 139, 168;
confronting, 148, 152, 154, 158, 159;
expansion of, 30; facets of, 29; guns
and, 14–19; hypermasculinity, 24;
increase in, 155; media and, 155;
militarism and, 27, 170; model of,
82; problems with, 15, 151; school
shooters and, 23; school violence and,
19; social factors producing, 18, 19

Society: one-dimensional,
5; reconstructing, 169; of
the spectacle, 7–9

Society of the Spectacle, The (Debord), 3, 7

Son of Sam, 15

Sopranos, The, 72, 134

Southern Poverty Law Center,
110; hate groups and, 109

South Park, 128

Spare the Child (Rhodes), 147

Spectacle, 15, 28, 37, 42, 49, 113, 119, 124,
139; analysis of, 30; celebrity identities
and, 118; commodity, 4, 6; concept of,
5, 7; construction of, 33; consumer,
27; consumption of, 5; manipulation
of, 29; mega, 6, 7, 8; multiple forms of,
3; notion of, 3, 4; political, 6; reading,
9–14; society of, 3, 7–9; tabloid, 1,
5, 30; time of, 3–7; totalitarian, 9;
U.S./global society and, 8; war as, 4

Spina, Stephanie Urso, 148; on education
cuts, 163–164; school reform and,
149; on school violence, 19

Sports culture, 28, 154; confronting, 157;
hypermasculinity and, 156; militarism
and, 156; violence and, 155–156

Stallone, Sylvester, 112

Stealing Innocence (Giroux), 79
Stereotypes, 34, 36, 78
Stern, Howard, 111
Students for a Democratic
    Society (SDS), 74
Subcultures: confronting, 157; cyberspace
    and, 72; hypermasculinized,
    156; Internet, 92; male, 156;
    resistance to, 66; youth, 66–67
Suicide, 71, 84, 125, 140, 145
Supermax, 118, 168
Surveillance, 86, 146, 148
Survivalists, 92, 94, 96, 97, 99

Taliban, 128
Talk radio, 1, 92, 99, 110; male rage
    and, 112; public discourse and,
    111; right-wing, 109, 111
Taxi Driver (film), 40
Technoliteracy, 162, 163
Technologies, 74, 108; communication,
    110; computer, 61, 163; countercultural
    attacks on, 116; development of, 115,
    159; educational, 162; information,
    72; media, 163; potential of,
    61; social, 73; Unabomber and,
    117–118; youth and, 62, 66
*Teenage Wasteland: Suburbia's Dead
    End Kids* (Gaines), 76, 84
Television: cable, 1, 15, 89; reality, 73;
    violence and, 158; watching, 72
Terror: male identity construction
    and, 90; politics of, 113–118;
    spectacles of, 6, 7, 27, 89, 90, 137
Terrorism, 39, 71, 135, 167; Islamic, 28,
    93, 94, 109; homegrown, 100–106;
    multiple causes of, 87; threat of,
    69; war and, 61; youth and, 63.
    See also Domestic terrorism
Terror War, 1, 5, 7, 71
Threats, reporting, 151
"Three strikes and you're out" law, 80
Thurston High School, rampage at, 24
"Time of Abolitions, The" (Korsch), 170
Torture, 86, 164, 165, 171

Trench Coat Mafia, 119, 120
Turner Diaries, The (Pierce), 95,
    106; impact of, 98, 102, 117
TV Nation (film), 126

Ultramasculinity, 20, 87, 89, 139;
    rewarding of, 157; violence and, 155
Unabomber. *See* Kaczynski, Theodore
Unabomber Manifesto, 113, 118;
    publishing, 114–115; racism in,
    116; technologies and, 115
United Nations, 86, 100, 108
*University in Chains: Confronting
    the Military-Industrial-Academic
    Complex, The* (Giroux), 27
Utah mine tragedy, spectacle of, 6, 7
U.S. history, violence in, 129, 130
U.S. Supreme Court, youth/
    death penalty and, 85

Video games, 18, 26, 49, 75, 123;
    confronting, 157; violence in, 121
Vietnam War, 6, 15, 97, 104, 170;
    protesting, 170; training for, 17
Violence, 16, 74–75; bullying and,
    155; conflict resolution and, 30;
    confronting, 139, 147, 157; culture
    of, 15, 22, 23, 28, 110, 113, 155;
    dangers of, 151; domestic, 84; ethos
    of, 170; family, 24, 28, 147, 148; gun,
    12–13, 14, 48, 49, 126–131, 141, 155;
    hypermasculinity and, 121; increase
    in, 70; juvenile, 158; male, 83,
    154–159; manhood and, 23; media
    and, 20, 24, 110, 118, 157; military
    and, 28, 155; multiple causes of,
    87; outbreaks of, 15; physical,
    152; poverty and, 28, 78, 79, 155;
    psychological, 152; racial coding of,
    77, 78; reducing, 156; representations
    of, 30, 158; school, 19; sexual, 76,
    165; sociological studies of, 18;
    sources, 28, 155; sports culture
    and, 155–156; television and,
    158; ultramasculinity and, 155;

urban, 46; U.S. history and, 129,
130; white male identity politics
and, 116; youth, 63, 79, 140, 158
Violent Crime Control and Law
Enforcement Act (1994), 80
Violentization, 64, 147, 148
Violent masculinity, 14, 18, 19, 23, 24,
26–27, 40, 124, 132, 136, 164; critique
of, 160; media culture and, 157
Virginia Tech: bomb threats at, 52;
convocation at, 38–43; criticism of,
52, 53, 144; Korean students at, 36;
memorial services at, 38–43, 53–54
Virginia Tech shootings, 2–3, 26, 71,
74, 82, 90; aftermath of, 59, 142–
145, 146, 157, 158; amok and, 13;
comprehending, 61; covering, 38;
debates over, 29, 31, 35, 46; domestic
terrorism and, 132; exploitation of,
46–47; impact of, 144; investigating,
143, 145; media culture and, 34, 49,
87; mental health issues and, 39, 54,
58; multiple causes of, 48, 137; Muslim
community and, 35; popular culture
and, 55; privacy laws and, 58; race and,
3, 33–38; review panel, 143; right-wing
response to, 45–46; spectacle of,
7, 13, 28, 29, 33, 37, 53, 56, 104

Waco, Texas, 37, 101
War: confronting, 169; societal
violence and, 170; threat of,
15, 69; youth and, 63
War on drugs, 167
War on poverty, 170
War on terror, 57, 69, 135, 167;
orchestrated events of, 4;
the "Other" and, 58
War on youth, 74–75, 164; culture wars
and, 75; struggle against, 76–83
Warrior culture, 26, 97, 107, 109, 152
Washington Post, 133; on Cho, 134,
135; *Unabomber Manifesto* and,
114; Virginia Tech shootings
and, 31, 46–47, 143

Weapons culture, 87, 90, 103, 121;
growth of, 26; male rage and, 118
Weaver, Randy, 97, 101
Welfare, 78, 92, 93; child, 148
West Ambler Hall, 33, 34, 144
Westside Middle School, shooting at, 21
We the Media (Gilmor), 34
White male identity politics, 89, 90–93,
95, 97, 105–106, 110, 113; examples of,
102; modernity and, 94; rise of, 95;
theories/politics of, 94; Unabomber
and, 116; violence and, 116
Whiteness, 78, 90, 100; challenging,
91; societal violence and, 29
Why They Kill (Rhodes), 15
Willis, Bruce, 78, 112
Women, violence against,
25, 85, 86, 154, 156
Working-class culture, assaults on, 10, 79
Workplace security, 29, 139, 146–154;
debate over, 50–53; gun control
and, 147; improving, 50, 146
Workplace shootings, 15, 137

Youth: alienation of, 29, 33, 74–75, 130,
147; challenges for, 62; characterizing,
68; commercialization of, 81;
conception of, 63; control complex, 75;
criticism of, 61, 67; death penalty and,
85, 86; demonization of, 77, 82, 85;
economic/political/social challenges
of, 83; future of, 70; government
services and, 71–72; guns and, 119;
identity of, 72; incarceration of, 80;
interrogation of, 90; media and, 67, 81,
158; perils of, 83–87; post-Boomers
and, 69–74; postmodernism
and, 66; repoliticization of, 73;
representations of, 67, 81; at risk,
79, 81, 83; scapegoating, 77, 79, 80,
81–82, 130; situation of, 61–62, 65;
as social construct, 63; technologies
and, 74; transitional period of, 64;
violence and, 79; working-class, 10
Youth culture, 64, 74, 100, 120; Columbine

shootings and, 129; demonization of, 29, 55, 59, 75, 77, 119, 158; postmodern culture and, 65; resistance by, 74; scapegoating, 158; technologies and, 66
Youth mentoring, 148

Youth of color: military service and, 81; representation of, 79, 80
YouTube, 1, 4, 30, 34, 43, 65, 66, 72, 73, 89

Zero tolerance, 79, 80, 85, 150
Zodiac (film), 15

THE RADICAL IMAGINATION SERIES
Edited by Henry A. Giroux and Stanley Aronowitz

Beyond the Spectacle of Terrorism: Global Uncertainty and the Challenge of the New Media, by Henry A. Giroux (2006)

Global Modernity, by Arif Dirlik (2006)

Left Turn: Forging a New Political Future, by Stanley Aronowitz (2006)

Stormy Weather: Katrina and the Politics of Disposability, by Henry A. Giroux (2006)

The Politics of Possibility: Encountering the Radical Imagination, edited by Gary A. Olson and Lynn Worsham (2007)

The University in Chains: Confronting the Military-Industrial-Academic Complex, by Henry A. Giroux (2007)

Guys and Guns Amok: Domestic Terrorism and School Shootings from the Oklahoma City Bombing to the Virginia Tech Massacre, by Douglas Kellner (2007)

Against Schooling: For an Education That Matters, by Stanley Aronowitz (2008)

Forthcoming

Afromodernity: How Europe Is Evolving toward Africa by Jean Comaroff and John L. Comaroff